Fame: Ain't It a Bitch

FAME

ain't it a bitch

Confessions of a
Reformed Gossip Columnist

A.J. BENZA

talk
miramax
books

HYPERION
NEW YORK

Library of Congress Cataloging-in-Publication Data

Benza, A.J.
    Fame, ain't it a bitch : confessions of a reformed gossip columist / A.J. Benza.
      p. cm
    "Talk Miramax books."
ISBN: 0-7868-6753-1
    1. Benza, A.J. 2. Gossip columnists—United States—Biography. I. Title.

PN4874.B45 A3 2001
070.4'44'092—dc21
[B]   00-066656

Book design by Casey Hampton

FIRST EDITION

10 9 8 7 6 5 4 3 2 1

FOR KARA RUTH YOUNG
Because after the fire, the fire still burns

Acknowledgments
and Apologies

I am lucky that I have had and continue to have an army of people around me who are keepers of my ego. No group is more responsible for keeping me grounded or allowing me to dream than my beautiful family. I am a mess without them. And I miss them so.

I am also blessed to have loved some wonderful women who, when truth be told, are a huge reason why awkward boys grow into good, strong men. They are my ex-wife, Jennifer Colletta, and the other four loves of my life, Karen Cito, Becky Soto, Vanessa Mastrangelo, and Kara Young. Lucky am I that they are all still in my life.

And I would be nowhere without the boys I made friends with in the schoolyards of my youth. My first Rat Pack consisted of Chico, Peppe Cavilieri, Marvin, Whitey, Ron, Ago, 'Zilla, Freddie, Ronnie, Johno and Jamie—our beautiful Shirley MacLaine. The Rat Pack that runs with me more often these days includes my boys Rocco, JohnnyBoy, Giant, Tico, Johnny Diaz, Mario, Vinny Argiro and Tony Finetti. And there is always a seat and drink waiting for my nephews and truest best friends, Jake and Joey. I hope I am the first to go. I don't want to see any of their funerals.

I will always take a bullet in the chest for Linda Stasi, anywhere or anytime, for having the balls to take me on and teach me. If she wanted the moon, somehow I'd rob it for her.

The columns and the years wouldn't have had nearly the same snap without the dry wit of my genius cowriter, Michael Lewittes. My love for Michael is hard to put down on paper. Ask Batman if he could even find his tights without Robin.

A big embrace goes out to Jimmy "The Kid" Ruttenberg, for asking the tough questions that needed to be asked when Linda, Michael, and I were too mortified to ask them.

I cannot ever repay Martin Dunn and Larry Hackett for turning me loose on New York City and allowing me to be me. And for Pete Hamill who put the brakes to it all upon his arrival. Pete did me a favor and I think he knew that all along. Long may his words move me.

To Hollywood's truest maverick, Bob Evans, who will be my hero forever. Whether I was on the lam, against the wall or in a jam . . . Evans always opened his home and his heart to me. I don't want to live in this town without him.

The rest of the lot have, indeed, meant a lot to me in some way, shape, or form. Whether it was helping me fly straight, keeping me anchored down, or just staying up and listening to the ravings of an insane friend whose heart was shot to pieces. You all know what you did for me and I might not have amounted to a damn thing without you. And some of you deserve an apology, too. The ones who come to mind, in no particular order of importance and in danger of forgetting a few hundred, are the following: John Gotti, Dan Rather, Kim Akhtar, Allie Boy, Brian Grazer, Ron Howard, Richard Wilen, Richie Palmer, Mort Zuckerman, Fred Drasner, Bo Dietl, Allie and Lauren Salerno, Lonnie Hanover, Gina Franano, Richie Valvo, Howard Stern, Robin Quivers, Gary Dell'Abate, Apollonia Kotero, Aunt Anna, Uncle Larry, Chaunce Hayden, Jack, Warren, Hef, Sly Stallone, Hail Mary, Arlene Benza, Frankie Mormando, Patti Davis, Mariah Carey, Liz Smith, Danny Madonna, Jon Penley, Kamal Ahmed, Tammy Tyson, Michael Danahy, Gary Socol, John Rieber, Betsy Rott, Ruben Malaret, Mickey Rourke, Mel Berger, Mark Itkin, Suzi Unger, Georgianna Robertson, Marc Roberts, Sunday Galiano, Traci Adell, Adolfo Galella, Andrea Radatoiu, Abel Ferrara, Ella Brown, Shane and Sia Barbi, Desiree Gruber, Joanna Molloy, George Rush, Richard Johnson, Jeannie Mac-

Intosh, Beth Landman, Louie Scoops, Jaid Barrymore, Louie Domes, Angela Pentinen, Nancy Sinatra, Lara Shriftman, Hayley Sumner, Christine Mangano, Joan Rivers, Jama Podell, Geraldo Rivera, Vivian Bernal, Marvet Brito, Lucy Goncalves, Marci Engleman, Lana Clarkson, Dominic Barbara, Fran Curtis, Christina Youri, Doug Vaughan, Tony Scaduto, Don Forst, Margaret Maldonado, Amy Lynn Baxter, Nicole Nassir, Ricky Phillips, John MacDonald, Ray Brown, Roy Leibenthal, Tim, Ro Terenzio, Nikki Cascone, Medhat, Anastasi, Peter Gatien, Jason Binn, BeBe Buell, Steve Lewis, Tony Theodore, Michael Ault, David Sarner, Ian Schrager, Chris Gambale, Richie Esposito, Kelly Cutrone, John Miller, Billy Stanton, Gary Zarr, Lee Soltors, Barbara Dare, George Gallo, Diane Collins, Michael Michele, Ronnie Madra, Natasha Esch, Dieter Esch, Johnny B., Raquel Brulee, Joey Morrissey, Lina Sivio, Flavia, Cesare Bruni, Michael Martucci, Radha Mitchell, John Capouya, Mark Baker, Geoffrey Murray, Lizzie Grubman, Frank Vincent, John Gallagher, Allen Bernstein, Rosalia Hayakawa, Ian Kessner, Sal Marchiano, Alex Lasky, Wass, King, Jeff Gossett, Joey Gossett, Carol Barton, Mel Gibson, Dan Cracchiola, Richard Donner, Jenny McShane, Lisa Izzo, Monique Pillard, Petey Collision, Malaak Compton-Rock, James von Veit, Nacho Arenas, Maria Elena, John Scotto, Shauna O'Brien, Richie Lefkowitz, Linda Beauchamp, Melanie Bonvicino, Debi Mazar, Clem Caserta, Karin Taylor, Lisa G., Anna David, Dyonne, Jason Weinberg, Nancy Kane, Tasha Mota e Cunha, Gypsy Impala, Andy Karp, Frankie Menna, Ron Rosa, Mark Roberts, Denene Milner, Andrew Kitching, Johnny Santiago, Malou Corrigan, Issa Giustebelli, Bev Camhe, T.K., Ernie Grunfeld, John Cirillo, Chris Weiler, Jules Asner, Stephanie Adams, Richard Price, Adam and Pascal, J. P. Parlevecchia, Darren Maddern, Stephanie Janes, Tina Hungerford, Sy Presten, Eric Handler, Billy Bob Thornton, High Voltage, Clicker, Wendy Williams, Dr. Michael Lavyne, Angela Wong, Donna Daniels, Debbie Halo, Gabriella Burlando, Prince, Dr. Small, Janice Dickinson, Oscar Blandi, Chuck Zito, Chris Paciello, Snoop, Jeannie Gianis, Nick Paumgarten, Frankie Pellegrino, Nicky Vests, Joey Hunter, Rob Weiss, Michael Musto, Jane Frieman, Eddie Faye, Mike Walker, Maureen Gallagher, Jon Enos, Inna DaSilva, Roger Friedman, E Factor, Tony Gerrato, Shari Headley, Tina Malave, Noel Ashman, Sandy Taylor, Unique and KiKi, Bill Maher, Sam Phillips, Cindy Rackowitz, Steve Randall,

Jennifer Sutter, Meryl Poster, Tatiana Castrillo, Donald Trump, Nancy Jo Sales, Sean Patterson, Dog the Cat, Alan Finkelstein, Jeff Fahey, Kara Sands, Michael Flutie, Mike Flemming, Lisa Gastineau, Cindy Clayman, Lisa DaCosta, Samantha Stein, Eric Goode, Serge Becker, Chrisena Coleman, Paul Fischer, Susan Crimp, Kelly Cole, Cygalle Dias, Peter Bill, Samantha Cole, Sante D'Orazio, Mia Tyler, Vanessa and Peter Daou, Yvette Savedra, Ingrid Casares, Mel Gorham, Liz Harrison, Karen Duffy, Eddie Clontz, Norah Lawlor, Ken Sunshine, and The Rolling Stones.

Huge gratitude for Harvey Weinstein, Jon Burnham and everyone at Talk/Miramax Books. And a little liquor on the ground for Ralphie Coppola, Mike McAlary, Bernie Bennett, Mike Hall, Pete Seligman, and Kevin MacMahon, Tupac Shakur, and John Kennedy Jr.—eight great men who passed away before this book was published.

And, lastly, for anyone else who ever rang me up with a story or a tip or a rumor. From my lips to God's ears—your secrets die with me.

I was hoping my book cover would contain a picture of me at a joint I made mine several years ago, Giambone's over on Mulberry Street, in Little Italy. It was John Gotti who first introduced me to the place back in 1990 and, ever since he was locked away, Johnny the bartender (pictured behind me) always made sure I got Gotti's table. Johnny was the best bartender in town because he listened to all your problems but he never burdened you with his. I wish he had. A few weeks after this shot was taken, Johnny killed himself. Nobody knows why. Thanks for the pours pal.

Fame: Ain't It a Bitch

One must harden himself, but without ever losing his tenderness.

—CHE GUEVARA

Whenever my phone rang at three A.M., somebody was either dead, drunk or wanted to get laid. But this time it was Mickey Rourke, shaking me from my own high, with a bone to pick with *New York Post* gossip columnist Richard Johnson.

"I need you to tell me where this motherfucka lives. And then I want to go there tonight and have a talk with him."

"Mickey, what time is it, man?"

"It's time for me to deal with him."

"Where you at?" I asked.

"Some bar for pussies," he told me. "Frederick's uptown."

"Who you with?"

"Tupac and Enos," he said, referring to the rapper Shakur and his acting pal Jon Enos. "Hey, man, where's Johnson live? I know you know."

"Don't do anything stupid," I said. "I'll be right there."

It had been going on like this for a while between me and Mickey, who I'm not ashamed to say was somewhat of an idol of mine. It had also been going on like this between Mickey and Johnson, because of the columnist's insistence on knocking Mickey's acting, his boxing career, his hygiene, and lately his high-profile separation from his supermodel wife, Carré Otis.

Anybody who would have taken the time to listen to Mickey would have learned that the actor was genuinely heartbroken over the split and was at his wit's end in terms of getting her back in his life. Back in the day, I don't think anybody listened more intently to his stories than I did. And it's only because I fell in love with his acting ever since *Diner*, and my obsession just grew from there. By the time I was a gossip columnist, I was thrilled to see that I could actually help him in any capacity.

By the time I got to Frederick's, I found Enos and Tupac at the bar and Mickey in the men's room looking over an early edition of the *New York Post*'s Page Six. Johnson had written a scathing attack on Mickey and the actor was raving mad.

"Look at what this motherfucka wrote," Mickey said, pushing the paper my way.

"Don't worry about it," I assured him. "I'll fix it tomorrow in my column. And I'll go on TV and punch holes in his whole fuckin' story."

No sooner had I finished the sentence, Mickey started pummeling the plumbing in the empty bathroom. During the course of his one-minute tirade, the sink was broken, a mirror shattered, some pipes were ruined and his reputation—as far as I was concerned—was intact: You didn't fuck with Mickey.

I whistled out to Tupac and Enos and the three of us dumped Mickey in his limo and headed downtown. As usual, Bob Dylan's "Knockin' on Heaven's Door" was blaring on the tape deck. Mickey would have his driver play that damn song all night long.

"You're all right, partner. Feel any better?" Tupac asked him.

"Why'd you go and do a thing like that?" Enos asked. "Now the guy has another story to write about you."

Nothing anyone said would've mattered to Mickey at that point. He wanted Johnson so bad, he could taste it.

"Come on, man," Mickey poked me. "Where's Johnson live? Just tell me and I'll go another night. I won't do it when I'm with you."

"I have no idea," I said, though I knew exactly where Johnson resided. "You can't hit a journalist, man. You're just gonna give him another story to write about you."

"Does that motherfucka want a story? I'll give him a story," Mickey said.

Mickey's driver, Kevin, always tear-assed down Manhattan streets and that night was even worse. We were doing at least 70 mph down Fifth Avenue when Mickey told Kevin to hit the brakes. We laid a long line of rubber right outside Cipriani's Bar, Mickey's favorite dinner spot at the time.

"What are you doing?" I asked.

"Giving him a story," he said.

Tupac and Enos, a bit more familiar with Mickey's dramatics, let out sighs. "Here we go . . ."

With no cars in sight for at least twenty blocks, Mickey stretched himself across the middle of the street, waiting for a car to run him over. He was in leather pants, a sleeveless tank top, and a hoody. He looked like a hip-hop Jesus.

"Motherfucka, you buggin'?" Tupac shouted.

"Come on, Mick, stop the shit," Enos said. "I just want to go home and sleep."

I just sat there amazed at what was going on.

"A.J., you think Johnson would like this story?" Mickey shouted up to the sky. "Either I kill myself or I kill him. What makes a better story? I ain't getting up until you tell me."

"So, it's in my hands now. You die or Johnson dies, is that it?" I said.

"Yeah."

"Well, it'd be nice not having any more competition," I said. "On the other hand, you have made a few bombs recently . . ."

"Yeah, the niggah was whack in *Bullet*," his costar, Tupac, laughed.

"Don't believe a word that motherfucka says," Mickey said. "I carried his ass."

"Can I decide?" Enos asked. "I say Mickey kills himself. Johnson ain't a bad guy."

"I got a better story," Tupac said. And with that, the rapper laid down beside Mickey. Seconds later Enos and I followed suit. And there we were—four assholes staring up at the heavens above Fifth Avenue.

"Now what?" I asked.

"Now we wait," Mickey said. "If a car don't come soon, I'll just have Kevin run us over."

And Richard Johnson's life, thanks to me, was spared.

This is only one moment in my story. A five-year span of my life that, at times, felt more like a runaway dream than an actual day-to-day existence. If my life were a movie, this was the part where the big, bold-type headlines spun at the screen. Where the pages on the calendar fly off the wall. It's a story that has an everyday Joe like me suddenly rubbing elbows with movie stars, models, murderers and millionaires before I nearly drowned in the deep end of a beautiful built-in pool called pre-tension.

There is a part of me that wants to tell you everything.

But, it's important you know that I am not just a reporter. Fuck that part of me. If you really want to know the truth, I never felt that was a part of me to begin with. I've always hated the word *reporter*. I never wanted to be a *reporter*. Jimmy Olsen was a *reporter*. I was a writer with strong convictions and wide opinions. Still am.

I ain't no reporter.

Anyhow, the part that wants to tell you everything is the storytelling man, the man who loved to walk into a room and face head-on the same inquiry for five years.

"Whattaya hear? Whattaya know?"

There are worse things a man can hear, so it ain't like I hated this question every time I heard it. But I'd be lying if I told you it never, ever bothered me or that I never bolted from a room at the first sight of someone moseying over with the same boring little ice-breaker. Any-how, I'd always follow that up with a promise to deliver the goods—no matter how ugly—so long as they didn't say my stories sounded untrue. The minute someone heard one of my stories and said, "Come on, I don't believe that," the game was over. I'd fold up and walk away. I did this because I didn't need to be considered a liar or unprofessional at how I made my living.

Think about it for a second: If you asked a doctor how he was going to save someone's life and he told you the procedure that he believed would prevail, would you look at him and turn the room cold by saying, "Come on, Doc, I don't think you can do that. I just can't see that happening." Damn right, you wouldn't. It was the same thing with me and my stories. I wasn't saving lives or anything, but I'd like to think—on my best days—I was, maybe, preserving careers. And to most showbiz types, a stalled career has some of them ready to take a hot bath with their toaster. Anyhow, I've got a lot of stories to tell. Let's just keep it at that. And the storytelling man in me wants to enlighten you. But if I told you everything I've come across, half of you would love it while the other half of you would disbelieve it. But, most important, the entire Hollywood community would ostracize me. I might as well be Roman Polanski at a Girl Scout meeting.

Instead, what I'll do is tell you just enough to let you in on the big little world I worked in. I'll give you enough stuff that you'll understand what made me stay out till four A.M. and rise again at nine A.M. just so I could be near that action every night and record it the following morning and afternoon for my columns and TV appearances. And maybe with each page turned you'll begin to understand why I wanted to get the hell out. I'll give you stories behind the stories, the hidden colors within the mosaic and the sidecar of calamity that made writing my columns both the wildest fuckin' ride of my life and a sobering hard pain in the ass when I least expected it. You don't know the half of it. But you will.

Yesterday's Papers

I'm bad with years. But I remember sometime in my high school days—let's just say the late seventies—I would pour out a couple of bowls of Cap'n Crunch in the mornings before class and watch my mother read the newspapers at the kitchen table. There she sat, with her cigarette and bad cup of coffee—which no other relative or family member could drink except her—licking her fingers through the *New York Post* and the *Daily News*. My family never bought a *New York Times* in their lives and—what can I say?—old habits die hard: I only bought that paper once, and that was on the day the *Times* Metro section ran a Page One story on my trouble with the *News* after four years of high-profile service. But more on that fuckin' story later.

Anyhow, I remember my mother, on any given morning, stopping at the gossip pages and sucking her teeth at some of the scandalous mentions the columns presented. You can imagine that noise did nothing to make me enjoy my cereal any better, but it did stop me in mid-chew to ask what she was reading.

"What, Ma? What are you reading?"

"Says here your friend Cher was turned away at the door at Studio 54 the other night."

Everybody was my "friend."

"Ma. Who says she was turned away? She's Cher, Ma. She can go anywhere."

"Liz Smith says so right here." Then she'd twist the paper my way and get up to pour herself another cup of bad coffee. Even she'd grimace at the first sip of the second cup.

And then I'd read the story, to see what old Liz had to say. Eventually I'd make my usual announcement, as I pushed away from the table and headed for the bus. "Ma. This ain't true. You're better off reading the horoscopes. Gossip is bullshit."

"Your ass," my mother would say, which was meant to convey that I was full of shit as much as it was meant for me to have a good day at school. Tough love, I was raised on.

This sort of thing went on well into my high school years and it wasn't long before the old lady got me hooked, despite my initial beliefs that all gossip—no matter from whose lips or pen or typewriter—was bullshit. I would read it and often disregard it. But I would *read* it. And that's the key, see. That's all a newspaper publisher ever dreams of when he buys his own newspaper—to have the kind of columnists that New York City's people *read*. They might hate the words, even hate like hell the columnist, but they make sure they *read* the damn column every day.

So little by little, I became a regular reader of the gossip pages. Mind you, I still hadn't graduated to the dreaded supermarket tabs yet—which are to housewives what Ecstasy is to rave kids. But I was happy with Liz Smith's sweeping niceties, Cindy Adams's wise-ass retorts, the snobbery of Page Six, Suzy's society shit and the blue-blooded blow jobs of Billy Norwich. Anyhow, there was no use sharing my habit with the pack of guys I hung with in high school because they only cared about acquiring the talents that would eventually help us acquire what we all really wanted to acquire—girls. Therefore, street fighting and sports were high on our Things To Learn list. Occasional forays into Manhattan's Hell's Kitchen to chat up the hookers was also a rite of passage in those days, too. But, trust me when I tell you, gossip had no place there. So I read that stuff on the side, only sharing it with my mom.

Paint It Black

I didn't know it then, but my very first week at college—Long Island's C. W. Post—would set the tone for the rest of my life. I had absolutely no idea what to major in. I mean *no* idea. So I did what everyone does. I signed up for a Liberal Arts curriculum until I knew what the hell I wanted. Meanwhile, all I wanted was to make the basketball team as a walk-on—be near all the stylin' black guys—and screw all the Jewish girls who couldn't wait to escape their million-dollar homes in Great Neck, Roslyn, Manhasset, Port Washington and Five Towns. Some of these girls were chauffeured to school in Jaguars. Some broke out their sable coats at the first sign of a green tomato dying on the vine.

But then something happened to me that shouldn't have. Or, I guess it should have, if you believe in Fate and things like that. I didn't believe in that stuff then. But I have ever since.

I wandered by the little theater on the edge of campus one night and I'll tell you why. When you enroll in a snobby, rich private school that you can't really afford, and are on every kind of financial aid and partial scholarship, you learn that the tough kids and the rough kids and the kids who don't quite fit in are always theater majors. It's easy for everyone to view them as slackers, but these kids—and me—all shared one thing in common: We were the ones who would not sit in a row. We wanted to stand out. We wanted to do something different. I mean, God bless the kids who were desperate to grow up and become accountants or teachers or cops or doctors or lawyers. That just wasn't our desire. And I have this thing about not wanting to see my giant retirement cake with whatever my profession was elegantly displayed on it with decorative cream. Know what I mean?

I had an uncle who was a locksmith for forty-five years before he dropped dead. At his retirement party, his wife and kids told the baker to paint a fuckin' skeleton key on the cake. And, of course, everyone gave him gifts that had something to do with keys. His grandson made him a key holder in the shape of a key. His daughter got him a special picture frame in the shape of a key. He got chocolate keys, key-shaped pillows, etc. And I just remember thinking, "Please, somebody put a key to my throat and slice it now because I can't bear it anymore." Anyhow, I decided right then and there—I would never pursue a career in which it could all be summed up on a fuckin' birthday cake sixty years later.

Anyhow, I walked by the theater and spotted a beautiful black girl— killer body, gorgeous long hair, fine features—silently practicing some ballet routine all by herself in one of those mirrored rooms. I kept looking at her until she could feel me watching her. And you have to understand why I was watching her. I came from a lily-white Long Island high school with one black kid in the graduating class of 750. And that kid was half Puerto Rican. *And* adopted. So I had never seen a beautiful black girl, my own age, in the flesh. Much less spoken to one. Much less one that could put her leg behind her ear while standing up. *And* smile at me at the same time. I want to say I was transfixed, but it was more like a blissful coma.

"I'm sorry," I said. "I didn't mean to bother you."

"It's okay," she said. "I'm done anyhow. I'm exhausted."

"Do you always practice this late at night?"

"I have to. I'm taking twenty-one credits and commuting back and forth to the Bronx. It's the only time I have."

"Damn," I said, mainly because she was intimidating as all hell.

"What are *you* doing out so late," she asked.

"I'm bored. And I'm still trying to learn this stupid campus."

"I know. It's big. And I have to walk all the way across campus to get to my car right now. It's like a mile away."

"I'll drive you," I said.

Just like that. What doesn't occur in eighteen years, happens in a snap at the end of a two-minute conversation. All the predisposed racial beliefs, all the manufactured prejudices handed out at my father's dining room table, fell away from me like puppies from a cardboard box. All of a sudden I'm watching long black legs, dancer's legs, bend into my father's hand-me-down car. The sort of thing that would've gotten me some crazy-ass looks in Bensonhurst, the neighborhood of my childhood.

"I can tell you're Italian," she said. "Because all Italian boys drive their Cadillacs."

"And I can tell you're black," I said. "Because all black girls call us *eye*-talians."

Me and Vivi Hicks from the Bronx laughed a lot that night. We also stopped the car and sat in the campus rose garden—which was kinda scary with its statues, trelliswork, tall hedges and crazy gargoyles—and talked to each other until two A.M.

"Since you watched me dancing," she said, "I need to watch you do something equally embarrassing for you. Then we'll be even."

I had no idea what to do except read a gooey short story I had just written for a creative writing class. It was some junk about a kid playing stickball and promising to hit a home run for his grandfather who's dying in a hospital bed across town. When I was through reading, she was bawling like a baby.

"God. When a guy can write, it's so sexy."

That's all I needed to hear. Before my notebook hit the ground, me and Vivi were having sex that was as awkward as it was awesome. It wasn't about inventing new positions or rewriting the Book of Tao, it was more about discovering a new world.

With too many different sensations for my mind and soul to register, I just tucked the night away as a "life-changing" event and took it out—still do, to this day—to remember how far away from home I was. I mean, Post was only forty minutes from my house—thirty, if the L.I.E. had no traffic—but I might as well have been in Siberia.

She was black. She was a dancer. She was older. She was from the Bronx. She cried over something I wrote. *She fucked me in the rose garden!* And because of that, my mind was made up. The next day I became a journalism major and a theater minor. And my curiosity for black women was born.

But the craziest part of the whole story? I never saw Vivi Hicks again.

I did, however, begin to settle into the myriad of journalism classes set before me. Reporting, Journalistic Ethics, Review Writing, Freelance Writing, blah, blah, blah. And what I quickly found was that every adjunct professor I had was either a former big-shot reporter, an aging author or a journalist still bringing in the bucks with freelance articles for major magazines. And all these guys had one thing in common: They loved to hear the sound of their own damn voices. So they'd talk and talk—mostly about overblown war stories concerning their coverage of this conflict, that conspiracy, this political scandal, that assassination and whatnot. So, it wasn't long before I started showing up for class about once a week and spending most of my time playing hoops with the brothers or watching the JAPs file onto campus via the Great Lawn. The bottom line was, I knew I could write and I knew I could bullshit my teachers into just about anything. Truthfully, that's how I always made up my schedule each semester. I learned the professors who were quicker to eat bullshit and I enrolled in their classes. Didn't even matter when the class was scheduled or where on our giant campus it was being held, since I knew I was almost never going to show up anyhow. In fact— you wanna laugh?—I remember semesters where I was enrolled in three different journalism classes all being offered at the same time in different classrooms. I was pulling down Bs in journalism, but in actuality, it was an A effort in terms of life experience in bullshitting authority. And that would soon come in handy.

Street-Fighting Man

Toward the start of my senior year in college, my father was losing a five-year battle with cancer. It got to the point that one night when I saw him limping up the driveway after another thirteen-hour workday, he didn't even ask me to take a few set shots with the ABA ball at our driveway hoop before heading inside for his late-night dinner and two Cutty and waters.

"What's the matter, Poppa?"

"It hurts when I raise my arms, that's all."

It hurt him because his cancer—a rare form of lymphoma that attacked his organs *and* skin—was stretching his skin as tight as a snare drum. Any sudden movements would leave a large and painful tear behind, which would bleed and burn before becoming as brittle as an old rose petal. Eventually, he had to stop working and check himself into a hospital. This is never good news when the patient is a stubborn old Italian man with no retirement plans, no pension and a lifetime savings account consisting of $1,500 stashed in a manila envelope behind a picture in his bedroom.

"Poppa, we gotta go to the hospital."

He finally didn't argue. "Let me have a scotch first."

It was his last one. What followed was a six-month stay at North

Shore Community Hospital in Manhasset, Long Island, in which doctors, internists, specialists and oncologists poked, prodded and pained my father, while making one solemn promise to his family. And that promise was that his disease would kill him. And it finally did, nine months after I left college.

Before that though, I decided to stop attending school and try to somehow earn enough dough to help my mother keep the house, a four-room colonial home in lily-white West Islip. It wasn't easy and it wasn't something my mother wanted: Her only son quitting college to help with the bills. Now I wonder, what was I thinking? Where does a twenty-year-old kid possess the balls to even think he can start earning $2,000 a week to pay the mortgage and everything else that comes from a family's lifetime together? You either sell drugs or enter a life of non-violent crime.

I chose the second option.

Casino Boogie

First thing I did was call my cousin, the family's black sheep because of his proximity to mobsters. Allie Boy immediately set me up in a Queens bookmaking operation, in which I would earn a small percentage of money from any new gamblers I brought into the house. The street parlance is called working "halfsheets." Essentially, it means that if I brought John Doe into the operation and he lost $500 in one weekend, the guy at the head of the operation would hand me half of that, or $250. And you might have heard of the guy at the head of the operation. His name was John Gotti.

I didn't have too much contact with Allie's boss, but I could tell he liked me and he understood what I was doing—dropping out of school to help my family. Once Allie Boy vouched for me and explained why his "good" cousin was working with them, John said it was good to have a college boy around. "I respect what you're doing for your family," he told me. "You was raised right."

It was right out of a movie. And then, of course, John's life would quickly become the stuff of movies as he stepped to prominence two years later as the mastermind in the gangland murder of Big Paul Castellano. But more on that fuckin' story later.

Working halfsheets was good for a while, particularly around football season. But I was still coming up short in terms of paying the mortgage. Of course, I was doing other things at that time—like stealing expensive shrubbery for a local landscaping firm, moving stolen cars from one town to another and stealing car parts for a local mafiosa. But that stuff was more of a hobby than a job. What I needed was a load of money to drop in the bank and forget about. I needed a score. And then I found it—a pile of fuck-you money in the form of a giant con.

An old friend approached me and asked me if I'd like to get involved in the sports tout industry. This was in 1986, when these "agencies" were opening up like Starbucks stores across the big cities. In short, the way it worked was I would cold call known gamblers around the country and convince them to let me handicap their games for them. I wouldn't place the bet or take their action, I was merely suggesting who they wager on based on my great knowledge of professional sports. Not to mention my propensity for bullshitting. In other words, I was advising them. And when you're a gambler on a losing streak—and I've been one—you don't only accept advice, you invite it into your home, feed it, tuck it into a warm bed each night and convince it to stay for as long as it likes. Of course, I always offered that help. But for a heavy price.

These gamblers would pay me commissions based on the dough I helped them make betting with their bookies. A typical relationship was 20 percent at the end of each week. So, if Joe Smith won $2,000 based on my selections, he'd wire me $400. Simple, right? But no two gamblers are alike. I quickly learned to get very exotic in my dealings. If I tell you I had Hollywood producers, priests in Philly, used car salesmen in Memphis, cotton farmers in Lubbock and Chicago clothing magnates on my list of regulars, I ain't lying. It took me about a week to figure out how to suck extra money from these guys before they even knew what hit them. I'd like to tell you the guilt was killing me, but that'd be a giant lie. And I don't lie.

An example.

Take that priest from Philly, Father Tom. Once I realized he was a solid payer and a man who stood by a deal made over the phone, I raped him. He knew me as Johnny Rourke, Frankie Nolan and Eddie Grant, never realizing each one of those men were all me. I'd installed three different phone lines in my office, called him from each extension under three different names and tripled my income in one afternoon. All I had to do was make sure Johnny, Frankie or Eddie's picks never conflicted. And Father Tom was one helluva payer. It wasn't uncommon for him to wire "us" as much as $3,000 to $5,000 a week. God only knows what church he was bilking. Did I win him money? For a while. But then it ends. The object is to work the scam for as long as you can, keep them paying you until they see that my "professional advice" really is no more scientific than flipping a coin. Heads I win, tails you're fucked.

Did I feel bad feeding the afflictions and addictions of degenerate gamblers? Sure, but not as bad as I felt watching my mother's giant Sunday feasts dwindle to pasta and potato and egg omelettes. And, in the case of Father Tom, I figured I wasn't doing anything that was going to secure me a spot in hell. I mean, I figured God would understand when I began my confessions with, "Forgive me, Father, for I have sinned. I lost Father Tom $3,500 on a two-team parley last weekend. But I have a giant get-out game this Monday night . . ."

Anyhow, I really needed money around the middle of '86. I had been going steady with that pretty girl I once admired through the window during sociology class my senior year and we were fixin' to get married in June. And before long we'd need to save for a house of our own. I still don't know why our parents thought a twenty-four-year-old boy and a twenty-two-year-old girl was a safe bet for a successful marriage, but they gave us their blessings anyhow. I only know my desire to marry her was bolstered on the day of our first date, when she walked up my driveway in a lavender pantsuit and I cried over how beautiful Jennifer Colletta appeared through my screen door. Anyway, like I said, I needed dough and fast. So I stepped up the speed of my bullshitting with two of the young industry's more dramatic cons. The people in the business remember it well.

First, I convinced an introspective but gullible lawyer from San Diego, California, to meet me and some colleagues of mine in Las Vegas with $50,000 in cash. My promise to him was to triple his investment after three days of precise and carefully executed gambling in sports books. Of course, my promise to myself was to grab the dough and take the next plane out of McCarran Airport back to New York, with 50K burning a hole in my pocket. But, what can I say, Sin City grabbed me—I ain't the first guy to fall for her—and I decided to stay a day or so, and hit the tables, fly in a friend or two, get some girls, shit like that.

In three days, I blew the money. Everything. I wish I could tell you I felt guilty, but I didn't. The men I was scamming during that time were the kind of men who were being taken on various levels by various men like myself. I guess there was a bitterness and a sense of entitlement that was growing in me ever since my father died. In my mind it just wasn't fair there were rich men out there willing to part with $50,000 on a whim when men like my dad were working thirteen-hour days for $50,000 *a year* and dying before their time. I suppose that's how I justified it at the time. Anyhow, there I was, with thirty-eight bucks in my pocket, sitting in my suite in Caesars Palace, drinking a Cutty and water and fiddling with the button on the electric blinds as the lights from the Strip painted the wall above my head. And I was wondering what I was going to tell the lawyer. Wondering, too, how the fuck I was gonna get home. Suddenly the phone rang. It was the lawyer.

"Hiya, Johnny. It's me, Lee. Just checking in to see how we're doing?"

"Lee, I'm gonna need another $12,000 wired to me tonight. Cash. How soon can you send that?"

"Oh jeez, Johnny. What happened?"

"Never mind that. Listen, I've got solid information on both games of the Blue Jays doubleheader and I will not hit these games without $12,000 of your money. I wouldn't dream of it. We're a team, Lee. I'm not going to lie to you. Right now, we've got nothing left. These things happen. But everyone whose money I'm wagering with has seen this before. They've been doing this with me for years. All of them sent me the 12K. Game One goes off in thirty minutes. How soon can you do this with us, Lee?"

This was a twenty-three-year-old kid talking to a fifty-year-old millionaire, mind you.

He sent me the dough via Western Union in fifteen minutes. I was at the airport in twenty-five. Home in five hours. The next day I gave Mom half the dough.

With a little cushion in the bank, and a steady stream of gambling cash coming in, I was able to flirt with the idea of writing for a newspaper once again—no matter how measly the wage. The paper was the *Huntington Record*. A loveable man named Jim Barbanel hired me and paid me $20 per article. And I only took that piddling job because I knew the old man had a hook into getting me hired as a part-time sports reporter at *Newsday*. Which he did, several weeks later. So there I was, making $10 an hour, writing about high school athletics at *Newsday*— Long Island's only newspaper—and just biding my time before some big editor would scoop me up and hire me full-time, give me benefits, vacation days, the whole nine.

Now, you might think a college graduate earning a whopping $10 an hour ain't anything to wet your pants over, but I'll tell you why this was a major victory for me. One thing journalism professors do, during every miserable semester of every year, is to dissuade you from thinking you will ever be a reporter working in the big city of New York. They actually prepare you to land an entry-level job in East Asswipe, Alabama, at $13,500 per. "I hope you're not studying journalism to get rich" was a famous call of those riotous professors.

A vision: I wanted to grab them by the lapels of their tweed sports jackets and say, "Yeah, motherfucka, I *am* studying journalism to get rich. I wanna be one of the goddamn best one day. Maybe have my own column right here in New York City. Maybe have more readers discussing my words in one ride on the A train than you've had your whole fuckin' life."

Of course, I never said that. I just set out to prove them all wrong. I decided I would not be one of the grads who worked for the *Homestead Gazette*, writing crime blotters about Miss Maple's calico cat getting killed during a Halloween prank. I decided I'd show all the fuckers and become one of my city's homegrown voices. An attitude they'd search for with the same gusto that they reached for their morning coffee. Canon, Breslin, Hamill, Lupica . . . Benza. All of them addressing the problems of the great metropolis they lived and worked in. Sounded like one big smile.

But first, I had girls' volleyball to write about.

A couple of years flew by at $20,000 per and Jennifer and I were happy enough. At least it seemed like we were. It wasn't a lot of dough, but next to nine-to-five in East Asswipe, it was like rolling sevens. Still, with no editor possessing the balls to pick me up and hire me full-time, the need to supplement my income was always wheezing at my back. Thank God, I still had the "action" of gambling giving me a hard-on every night and real wood-splitter every weekend. I looked at it as something to keep me happy while I fermented in my own dreams of future success in New York City. It was a helluva lot better than calling it what it was: It was me, lying to degenerate gamblers—people who needed serious help—just so I could live the life I wanted to live.

Anyhow, I was forever thinking of scams and scores, though my favorite had to be the time I struck up a "deal" with the most notorious gambler known to every salesman in the business. This guy risked more in a single day than you earn in a year.

The Elephant, as I will refer to him, was known to wager as much as $200,000 on a single game. I remember one random Thursday night during the college basketball season in which I convinced The Elephant to bet on twenty-five games. He actually had $1,000,000 riding on the games and I stood to collect 20 percent of his earnings from that one night.

I never did hit The Elephant for the ultimate score. But one week I earned him $60,000 and I woke up to a FedEx truck outside my house with the man delivering me a small box with $12,000 inside. I remember I threw the Benjamins on the bed and my wife and I fucked on them.

But it wasn't all fun and games. The notion of winning or losing that kind of money week in, week out, was hell on my relationship. My nerves were shot. I was not concentrating on writing worth a damn and began using *Newsday*'s phones as my gambling office, breaking in on early Saturday mornings—picking the lock with a credit card—and cold calling my gamblers with a bacon, egg and cheese sandwich in one hand and the betting lines in the other. It got insane. One minute I was speaking in hushed tones to The Elephant about getting him out of the $500,000 hole I put him in, the next I'd be complaining to my editor about losing a Saturday shift worth $90. My reality was warped. And, finally, with The Elephant in an insurmountable hole to the tune of $1.2 million, he finally disconnected his numbers and our fizz went flat.

But all good gamblers always have an ace up their sleeve. Mine was sparking interest once again with that California lawyer friend of mine. I mean, $62,000 is shit compared to $1.2 million.

The conversation began like they all did.

"Lee . . . how are the games treating ya?"

"That you, Johnny?"

It was easier than I thought. Lee and I began talking like a couple of guys over the open hood of a '72 Chevelle. The sixty-two grand never even came up. My kind of man.

I knew exactly what I was going to do. I was going to do two things. First, I was going to hook up Lee to a big bookmaking operation in New York City that I knew would take his action. Second, I was going to have him send me $5,000 in up-front dough, just in case he should lose some bets and never call again. I told him it would be a "good faith" gesture. And that's what happened. Lee sent me the five grand, no questions asked, and I phoned my cousin and told him of Lee's habit.

"He plays a lot?"

"Cuz, when this guy's hot, he throws down five and ten grand a game, no problem. And best of all, he's got the worst fuckin' luck in the world. We'll rape him."

"What if he don't pay?"

"He pays."

"You're *vouching* for him, then?"

I hesitated. "I'm saying he pays."

"You *vouching* for the guy?"

"Fuck yeah."

I didn't want to do that, but I had to. Vouching for someone means you are responsible for the guy should he flake on his debt. Though there's always a possibility of a guy flaking, I just couldn't see Lee going that way because of his propensity for shelling out money. He was a rich schmuck. But I also understood what it meant if he did flake—my cousin's boss would be coming to me for answers should Lee go bad. And, at this time—in early 1986—my cousin's boss, John Gotti, spoke in headlines.

"Should this guy go bad, you *and* your cousin will fly to California. And not to go surfing, *capeesh*?" That's the way John handled it when he and my cousin made a three-way call to my house.

Well, long story short, Lee started losing right off the bat and before long, found himself in a $13,000 hole. When that happened the operation cut him off—no more wagering until he sent them at least $5,000. After a weekend of intensive phone calls—like only a degenerate gambler can make—my cousin agreed to let Lee gamble to his heart's content, so long as he'd make a payment Monday morning consisting of the $13,000 plus anything else he lost.

"I sincerely swear I will," Lee promised.

"Should I believe this fuck?" my cousin asked.

"Absolutely," I said.

"You sure?" John Gotti inquired.

"I don't lie," I shot back.

Well, the luckless bastid dropped another $18,000 that Saturday afternoon, and that meant his Monday morning payment should have amounted to $31,000.

The next day the stupid bastard sent a check for $500 to my cousin's operation. Big mistake. A few minutes later my phone rang. Before a word was muttered, I could tell I was the last man hooking into a three-way call. I'd call it a conversation, but I never got a chance to talk.

"Shut up. Don't talk. Just listen." It was you-know-who.

"Call your fuckin' friend, the friend that you said was a man of his word—that fuck you vouched for—and settle this. I did not get to become who I am because of scumbags like him."

Click. Tone.

I tried to reach out to Lee but his home phone, cell phone, beeper and his car phone had already been turned off. He even stopped working at his office.

After weeks of agita, my cousin suddenly stopped harping on it. Just as quickly as Lee sprung into my life, he was suddenly out of it. A few months later, I sent a letter to the San Diego post office to inquire about getting a message to him at his home. Their letter came back to me stating his home appeared to be abandoned and no forwarding address was known.

I honest to God don't know what happened to him.

Eventually all the scams added up and I had earned enough dough to move me and Jennifer out from the apartment above my mother's house and into that starter home of ours. It was a cute little house and it was ours. We lived on the north side of town, right behind a tired stretch of stores that doubled as a hangout for the town's derelicts. We didn't mind though, because it was equally as close to her parents' house as it was to each of my sisters' homes. So we visited our families with regularity and in what has become the rule for all young newlywed Italian couples, we alternated Sunday dinners between the households. Never spending even one Sunday alone in our home used to eat Jennifer up, like it was supposed to be showing some sort of disloyalty on my part. But, hell, I always explained to her that we needed to be near our families on Sundays—recharge our batteries, get back to our roots, shit like that. I just didn't think there was any reason to spend a day like that alone— not with our families less than a mile away all venting the past week's worth of aggravation and joy and laughter to one another. Let's be where the passion is, you know? To Italians, it is the dining room table—the one room that always holds more drama than a small opera.

"Can't we spend one Sunday alone together? You'd think a husband would want that."

She was sort of right, considering my jobs and her jobs and schooling meant most of the week one of us would be coming home when the other was just stepping out to work. The first few years of our marriage consisted of reheated meals, stick-it notes on the fridge and both of us falling asleep before *thirtysomething* had even finished. We were tired, both of us working for what we wanted for ourselves, not necessarily for what we wanted for each other.

Naturally, this sort of behavior soon had each of us turning our heads and noticing that the world was a whole lot bigger than when we began dating—the night when I stopped my car at her stoop and wished her a happy birthday. She was sweet sixteen. So, in what seemed like no time at all, our little home echoed with the arguments of a deranged gambler who also faced the demons of not gaining on his dream to be a writer or an actor.

Jenn and I grew distant. I found escape in pickup basketball games at a nearby park. While she grew fond of playing the sad-sack soundtrack to *The Deer Hunter*, while crying to herself in the bathtub. We did all sorts of things to keep our minds off our decaying marriage. She joined a drama club with the teachers at the junior high she was working at. She stayed out late over coffee with friends. And every week there was a new diet sweeping Long Island that she and her friends dove into. Meanwhile, I remodeled the bathroom on a whim, put in a huge garden on the sideyard and banged in bigger windows around the house. I was speaking more to the girls at Home Depot than I was to my own wife. The point is, if I told you I wasn't hurting I'd be full of shit. Even though my ex-wife and I were through, and our sexual energy had been running on empty for quite some time, I can still remember the swarm of butterflies that developed somewhere between my belly button and my ass in the moment she hesitated when I asked her if she wanted a divorce.

"Jenny, no answer is as bad as a flat-out yes," I told her. "Just tell me if that's what you want."

Strange what you do in the very next minute after you hear news that will alter your young life forever. It's as inexplicable as it is perversely beautiful. Some people put their fist through a wall, curse each other or lobby accusations with the ferocity of two aging pros at Wimbledon. Me and Jenn jumped in the car, drove to Carvel and bought a couple of sundaes and ate them in the dark quiet of my sports car.

"Since when do you like mint chocolate chip ice cream?" I asked her.

She sighed. "That's our problem, Bo. Eleven years together and you still don't know what my favorite ice cream is."

She was right. There was no cause to fight or complain or even explain. A man should know what his wife's favorite ice cream is.

At any rate, details of anyone's divorce can get real boring real fast, so I'll spare you the day-to-day diatribes. What I will say about that woman is this: She still is the only one who knew me when. And there was never a point when she made me feel my dreams outweighed my abilities. She supported my beliefs while I paid her way through a master's degree on a con man's dime. Even on her way out the front door—with her last box of belongings tucked under her arms—she turned to me and said, "We're both going to get what we want, Bo. You're going to go off and find some beautiful model and I'm going to find a regular guy who wants to spend Sunday afternoons alone with his wife." She said this while our two dogs scratched at her knees and a smile fought through her tears like sunshine breaks through a rainy day.

Our divorce in 1989 put me in a bad state. I kept the house, moved two of my old buddies in, and began struggling to pay the bills with one less salary coming in. That same year I was also left to deal with a painful recuperation from extensive spinal surgery and the unexpected death of my mother. Cancer. All over again. And the way in which she went out gave me suspicions about God and heavy doubts on heaven. I had seen better days, let's put it that way. No one would've blamed me if I had climbed to a high tower with a high-powered rifle and just started blasting away. I already owned a few guns, but Long Island was basically a two-story town.

It's All Over Now

So, this is the way the summer of 1991 shaped up: Heavy D was asking his lover what were they going to do with the new love they found and Seal was telling us how crazy it is that far too few people want to fly. It was to shape up as my very own Summer of Love, but first I had lawyers to see and a divorce to get through.

I can't complain too much. I lost my sports car in the divorce, but won custody of my two Yorkshire terriers—Marcella and Mercedes, who suddenly became two five-pound piss and shit machines on account of the trauma of their parents' divorce. It was spite work, but somebody had to clean it up. I also had that damn dream home of ours, sucking every penny out of my bank account, but housing me and the tired asses of my two best buddies, John and Chico.

John had filed for divorce a few weeks after he came home from work early one day to find his wife's lover hidden in his daughter's bedroom. He beat the shit out of the guy, filed for divorce, grabbed his seven-year-old son, Pops, and drove straight to my house with the guy's blood still wet on his T-shirt. He moved into the spare bedroom.

Chico was a childhood pal who had just finished a five-month hospital stay after his girlfriend's cheating ways forced him to pump two bullets in his stomach in a suicide attempt. He eventually pulled the IV's from his arms, stole a car—white Benz, of course—drove up from Florida without stopping and knocked on my door with the hospital bracelet still on his wrist. He crashed on the couch.

And me? Well, I was trying to deal with the reality of my ex-wife making time with the square who taught Special Education in the classroom next to hers. A motherfucka who had visited my home and drank my liquor. Even though the ink had just dried on our divorce papers, her finding love so soon seemed a bit too fuckin' fast for me. So, let's put it this way—the house the boys and I lived in was filled with the riotous anger and laughter that only scorned men can muster. We were three men and a baby, with our backs against the wall and our balls tucked between our legs. One more hurt and the whole fuckin' world was gonna hear about it. But if I told you it wasn't the best damn time in my life I'd be lying to you. Chalk it up to misery breeding contentment.

Johnny decided to settle down with one woman, a nice Jewish secretary who he'd known for a while. Chico quit women altogether and became a misogynist. And I decided to go through them like water—falling in and out of love and letting my curiosity and my cock light the way.

By midsummer I had $13,000 in the bank—courtesy of one last gambling con—and a whopping $20,000 a year at *Newsday*. I'm seven years out of college, with no full-time job, no medical insurance, no benefits, no vacations, but a new girl every night. I think it was the vengeful residue of a guy who recognized that his ex-wife was now in love with Mr. Special Ed. And deep down inside, I was pissed at myself because I always had a sneaking suspicion about the two of them, anyway. It was only several months after she had moved out that I received news that she and Mr. Special Ed were engaged. And how did I get the news?

A vision: Your beautiful ex-wife moseys up your driveway, arrives at your front door, knocks once, walks in. She is carrying a large pot of sauce she's just made for you, but she's crying her eyes out as she steps into the foyer. "Bo, you home?"

She then proceeds to put the sauce in the kitchen and walk into the bedroom where you are watching Oprah deal with women who've left their men for their best friends. Your wife peeks in, sits on the side of the bed, breaks down and rains black mascara down her cheeks and onto her blouse. The tears are apology tears—the kind that take the longest to arrive, but rain like hell when they come. You are kinda pissed that she has interrupted *Oprah*, but hell, your life has become an *Oprah* episode.

"I'm getting married," she wailed, while sitting down on the bed, reaching out to hug me.

"You're supposed to be happy," I said.

"I know. But I feel like shit." Once again, the dogs were wild at her chest, licking her tears away. Boy, was I gonna be cleaning up shit tonight.

"Okay, Bapum," I said. Bapum was my nickname for her and I have absolutely no idea how I arrived at it. That sort of thing happens to every couple I know. "No more crying. I want you to be happy. Let's throw all this shit aside for a minute. If you love him, marry him and don't feel guilty. Don't worry about what people might think. Fuck what people think."

We hugged for a long time on the bed. Kissed a lot, too. Hell, I even thought of making love one more time for the hell of it, but that was never our strong suit to begin with, so why get all heated up? Instead, I asked her how much time she had on her hands.

"I don't know, why?"

"Come on. Cook us a little macaroni, would ya. I miss your sauce."

And we ate, drank some cheap wine from old jelly glasses and the dogs slept at our feet. They didn't even stir when it was time for her to split.

That episode reminded me of one very important lesson—opportunity doesn't always come in a box with a bow on it. All of the horrible circumstances and the rusted chain of events would finally lead me to my first full-time writing gig and the beginnings of the world I knew I belonged in. And, guess what? I didn't have to go to East Asswipe to do it. Just like I told you. I proved all the motherfuckas wrong.

Ruby Tuesday

All right, so, my wife quit me. I wasn't the first guy to have that happen to him. And like Jack Nicholson would tell me years later, "The best way to get over someone is to get under someone else." So I continued painting the town red, well, pink was more like it.

I was still socking away the hours at good old *Newsday*, but you have to understand, *Newsday* could've doubled as a goddamn insurance office. That's how staid and conservative the editors were. Even in the sports department—journalism's last bastion of political incorrectness, machismo and sexual innuendo—the editors would frown if they heard the word "damn" spoken too loud. They'd call you into their office if they heard that had you said "fuck." God forbid you sat there watching a track meet and you remarked how great Jackie Joyner-Kersee's ass looked. I remember I practically gave all of them a coma when I got my hands on the transcript from Mike Tyson's rape trial, stood on a desk, turned down the sound on the office TV and began to read aloud in Tyson's falsetto voice.

"And then, your wonor, Desiwee told me that she was on her pewiod."

You had to see the calamity to believe it, but the shortest editor in the joint came running out of his office, screaming, "You get down from there, *now*! This is a sports office, not a jailhouse." Blah, blah, blah.

Well, it sure felt like a jailhouse, I tell ya.

Anyhow, because of that little prank, me and a couple of the guys were hauled into the editor-in-chief's office and told that a female part-timer in the office wanted to file sexual harassment charges against us. We had no idea what the phrase meant, but we could tell by all the grim faces in that office that we were in some serious shit. The kind of shit you lose your job over.

"Apparently, there are other instances that this woman in your department finds offensive. According to her, your behavior is offensive quite often."

"Like?"

"Well, do you use the word 'fuck' in the office?"

"As a matter of fact I do," I said. "Just yesterday I said, 'Oh, fuck, the computer's shut down again."

"Um-hmmmmm."

"Anything else bother her?"

"In fact, she says you sometimes speak about your sexual conquests and she can hear you. Do you do that?"

"Fuck, no," I said. I was lying, but I had to lie. My sex life *was* exciting—doesn't that always happen when you get divorced?—and there were people in the office, mostly married people, who wanted to hear about it. There were people who downright asked me about it from across the room. I'm a kiss-and-teller. Shoot me.

Anyhow, the whole thing was as phony as it comes. It got to the point that we couldn't hang a poster of a female American Gladiator in the back of the office—that woman who felt sexually harassed asked that we take it down. And the little pussy editors at *Newsday* did what she asked. Everybody was afraid of the words *sexual harassment* back then. In the end, about five of us were written up. The girl? She eventually quit the paper and probably had no idea what sort of shit she had caused in her wake.

Meanwhile, I was becoming a good sportswriter in my own right. Sure, it was mostly high school or college events I was covering, but the reportage was strong and the writing style was cool and breezy. The only knock on me was that I always seemed to spend too much time in the loser's locker room. And that was a fair assessment. But the reason for that was, there's always more drama in the loser's locker room. A winner's mantra is the same every day: "We're just gonna have to take one game at a time . . . He really gives 110 percent day in, day out . . . We gotta get back out there tomorrow and do it again . . ." Blah, blah, blah.

That's probably why I never liked History class. History is written by the winners. And winners lie. You really want to know about history, go chat up the guys who lost the wars. They'll give you a story.

It was around this time I hustled up a few freelance articles to take the squeeze off me.

It's always best to write about what you know. So, I banged out an article for a cool start-up, *Long Island Monthly*, on my childhood pal Ronnie the coke dealer. I followed Ronnie around for a few nights, watched how he scored his coke, was there when he cut it up, waited with him for his buyer's beeps and rode shotgun with him on his deliveries. I called the piece "The Art of the Dealer" and it got me good notice. It kinda made Ronnie feel like a star of some kind, because I'd bring him around to parties and introduce him to my editors. "This is Ronnie, the runner," I'd say. And a crowd would gather around. "You lead one helluva interesting life," the editors would tell him. And Ronnie would blush. "Yeah, huh?"

Yeah, it was. While Ronnie did have a red convertible Corvette, a cigarette speed boat, a Ninja motorcycle and a Penthouse Pet as his girlfriend, he was always running from the law and taking long lams while the rest of us were planning backyard barbecues and trips to Yankee Stadium. Eventually, Ronnie went nose down like all bad dealers do—he was dipping into his profits too much to earn the amazing living he was used to. He crashed his car around a pole, sold off his boat to pay for the car and left his bike at a friend's garage after some Feds began developing a scent for him. His girl left him, too. Within a year, he turned up in Florida—I swear *Scarface* changed his life—and sent us all tickets to come down and party. He was legit, he told us. "I started my own credit company."

So, one weekend, with nothing better to do, me and Chico flew down to Boca Raton on Ronnie's dime to see our old friend after a year's lam. And, right away, the action starts. We were walking out of a restaurant—after a fancy lobster dinner—when Ronnie spots a brand-new white Mercedes-Benz purring at the valet stand. Within seconds, he hands the valet a twenty and tells us to hop in. And that's how, in a

devil's instant, some poor fucker loses his rimmed-out E Class to three
guys celebrating their best buddy's homecoming. Legit, my ass. We
hadn't driven a mile yet when Ronnie fishes out a vial of coke from his
inside pocket and asks me to hold the wheel while he starts spooning
the coke into his nose like I used to shovel Cap'n Crunch into my mouth
during my mother's gossip reports.

The new credit company he started? That was three guys he hooked
up with who happened to know how to produce phony Visa cards,
while poor saps like you and me paid handsomely for it. God knows
who paid for our lobster dinner that night.

Anyhow, when the three-hour joy ride was over, Ronnie thought it
would be a gas to drive to a local marina and let the Benz roll off the
dock and sink into the bottom of the bay. And that's just what we did.
And that's why, as much fun as Ronnie used to be, hanging around him
was like waiting to get fitted for prison grays. Less than a year later, that's
exactly where Ronnie ended up—doing a ten spot for credit card fraud
in Dade County. This is the first time I ever talked about that car theft,
by the way.

Again: Write about what you know. My next freelance piece was on
an old pal I'll call Vito Seno. Vito was a throwback, an old man whose
specialty was cracking safes and breaking-and-entering into anyone's
house he damned well pleased. When I met him he was a semiretired
thief living in Patchogue, who used to supplement his income by snitch-
ing to the cops on the incoming tide of black criminals who Vito felt
had "lowered" his art from a sweet science to something vulgar and
unrehearsed. He called them "colored cowboys" and told me none of
them could pick their way out of their own locked assholes. I used to
meet Vito for breakfast out on the east end of Long Island along with a
veteran cop I'll call Campbell. It was always the same diner, same booth,
same day every week. I used to call the place the Cops and Robbers
Cafe. And, in time, Vito poured his heart out to me about his life in
crime. It wasn't that he was proud of it—tying people up, ransacking
homes, impersonating a LILCO repairman in order to case a home—it
just was what it was. He needed to talk about it as much as I needed to
hear it. And even though he was "semiretired," I used to beg Vito to
take me out on a couple of surveillance runs. "Teach me the ropes.
Show me what you used to do. Show me how you did everything."

In time, he bent. One night he picked me up in his old Caddy and we drove up to the rich homes and apartments in Riverdale. Vito called this his old stomping grounds. "I hit this town like a plague back in the sixties," he bragged.

"How Vito, how? What'd you do?"

"All right, I'll show you. Keep your mouth shut and listen to what I tell you."

He reminded me so much of my father, it killed me.

Vito shut off the ignition and walked out to a ground-floor apartment. He beckoned me to follow him. We crept up to a window. "You see this tape here? This is the easiest burglar alarm tape to get around. I could reroute this with a paper clip and a piece of bubble gum."

"No way."

"Shut up, or I'll show you."

"You for real?"

"Gimme your gum."

Within a minute Vito had turned his back on me, fumbled around with the gum and a paper clip, and—voilá!—the window slid open with ease. The quiet night was not disturbed by any noise whatsoever.

"Still got it," he said.

A few more runs like this and I convinced Vito that a magazine would really be interested in his tale. In fact, I said, I know of one who'd pay me $2,500 to write it.

Vito thought hard for a moment, then said, "Gimme half of that and you got yourself a deal and they got themselves a story."

"Deal," I said.

"And don't think of reneging. Or I'll rob *your* house one night while you're sleeping like a lamb."

I sold the piece to *CrimeBeat* magazine and handed Vito his take a few weeks later at the same diner, same booth, same usual day of the week. I remember how he wanted me to slip him the money under the table, like we were both in jail or something. "When you spend forty of your sixty-seven years in the joint, some habits are hard to break."

His reputation as a thief lived on. And my reputation as a writer was beginning to grow.

Write what you know. I know, you're tired of hearing it. But it's true and it was totally paying off for me. I considered myself a freelance writer back then and I remember I said it like I was saying I was a great swordsman or something. "I'm a free*lancer*!" I'd say to anyone who'd ask. The extra income was good and it was a nice moonlighting gig on the side of knocking around *Newsday* for twelve bucks an hour and continuing my assault on high school athletics. I mean, what the fuck, how many times can you write about a kid throwing a touchdown pass?

Crime wasn't all I knew, you know. I knew a helluva lot about love and, since my divorce, I began to understand severe crushes and lustful letdowns. Most of my evenings back then were spent sitting in my sister Rosalie's kitchen and eating the dinner she was laying out for her husband and two sons. All four of us guys would immediately turn on MTV to watch *Club MTV* just for a peek at veejay Downtown Julie Brown and one of the show's paid dancers—a blonde bombshell simply known on the show as Camille.

Idiots that we were, we would literally tape the show just to catch the three-second glimpses of Camille gyrating and play it back—in slow motion, mind you—an hour later.

"Fuck! Look at her! Run it back! There she is!"

It was insanity. But I knew lust when it was calling me and her shit had me on redial every day of the week. "This show is killing me," I would announce. "I gotta get me a piece of that Julie Brown one night. And that Camille, too."

"Yeah, just you," my nephew Jack would say. He was at that stage where his uncle was always wrong. "With all the guys that are after her, you're gonna get her. Little old you from Long Island. She don't even know you're alive."

The kid was right. But I had a plan.

I queried a *Newsday* Op-Ed editor and asked if I could pen an open love letter to Camille, *Club MTV*'s hottest dancer. "Listen," I said. "I know it sounds crazy. But guys go nuts for this girl. Let me say in my story what we all want to say, but wouldn't have the balls to say if we saw her in person."

Well, the editor bought it. And to her credit, it was a female who made the decision. I didn't do it for the money—I think I got $250 or some shit—I did it to get near Camille.

Anyhow, the piece ran on Valentine's Day, and I ended it by saying I didn't ever want to meet her in the conventional manner. I wrote that

I wished to meet her by chance, in the same manner I used to catch her sexual moments on the TV show. "One day you will turn a corner and I will be there," I wrote.

Three months later, I'm waiting on line for a film in midtown Manhattan and Camille turns the corner. Out of nowhere. I swallowed hard and said, "Hey, I'm A.J."

A huge smile turned into a huge embrace turned into an exchange of phone numbers turned into a crush turned into dating and a friendship that's lasted years. But it wasn't long before the rest of the world learned about Camille. Her statistics eventually got *Playboy*'s attention and Howard Stern's admiring eye and huge airplay. As I write this, Camille Donatacci and her new husband, Kelsey Grammer, are honeymooning in St. John.

I don't care that I wasn't invited to the wedding. I knew the bride when she used to rock and roll.

Now, I got some balls on me. I'm feeling good. I'm still at *Newsday*, but I'm inching ahead of the pack with these freelance pieces. Not rich in the pocket by any stretch, but my dreams are gaining speed. Some editors at my paper's magazine section eventually call on me to write about other personal stuff. My mother's death. My father's death. My obsession with stickball. The sounds of summer. Even a nice piece on how I would never enjoy Manhattan with any other woman more than I did when my ex-wife and I were making our first forays into Big Town as smartass college kids. She has it framed in her home to this day. A nice flip of the finger to Mr. Special Ed, I might add.

Anyhow, now I decide to take on the big boys. I call *Esquire* magazine and ask permission to submit one of their monthly features, "Women We Love." Again, I swallowed hard and spoke to editor David Hirshey and queried him about writing a piece on MTV's Downtown Julie Brown. "I don't know if you watch the show or the network," I said, "but she really is hot as hell. The accent, the hair, the body. I think your readers would identify with my lust for her."

There was silence. And then Hirshey said what all editors say when someone else thinks of a piece they should've thought about months ago. Especially when they're a top-paid editor at a swanky magazine like *Esquire* and the guy on the other end of the phone is a part-time newspaper hack. "Yeah . . . you know . . . I don't think our audience would identify with a piece on Julie Brown. I don't think she's what we're looking for. But thanks a lot. Call us again."

Fucker. I knew what was coming.

Three months later, I picked up a copy of *Esquire* and there's Julie Brown written up in the mag's "Women We Love" section. I picked up the phone and called Hirshey. "Hey . . . it's A.J. Benza. I'm the guy who wanted to write about Julie Brown for you guys. Remember?"

"Right. Right . . ."

"Yeah, so what the fuck, man?"

He went on about how the decision to write about Julie was—amazing as it seems—being dreamed up in another editor's office and he had nothing to do with it. "These things happen," he offered.

Now, let's flash forward three years for a second. I'm at the *Daily News*, topflight gossip columnist and every time I had a chance to mention David Hirshey's name in an item I would purposefully misspell his name, Hershey, like the chocolate. And he'd always call me, whining, "If you're gonna mention me, at least spell my name correctly."

"Sorry, these things happen," I'd say.

Fuck him.

Remember I told you about bullshitting authority? Well, it came in real handy near the fall of 1991. *Newsday* was offering part-timers an opportunity to make extra cash by covering crime blotters. This was a big idea that some tight-assed executive dreamed up. Reporters would drive to several precincts around Long Island, flash their press card, take out the huge box of filed complaints and enter them in our laptop computers to be published for the paper's regional weekend editions. Well, hell, I threw my hat into the ring because there was an extra $100 per precinct you covered. I volunteered to cover four precincts, but there was no way I was driving to each neighborhood and going through the painstaking process of the above bullshit. So, what I did was I'd just create crimes that never actually occurred and report them as if an actual complaint had been filed. My bullshit ranged from, "A Maple Avenue home in Bay Shore was vandalized last Friday when unknowns gained access to the home's rear shed and removed a $1,000 power generator" . . . to "A twenty-three-year-old Patchogue woman was held up at knifepoint outside the Pathmark Supermarket center

Sunday evening when an unknown assailant followed her to her car and demanded she hand over all her cash and jewelry."

It was all bullshit. Not one crime was true. It got to the point, my friends couldn't wait to read the Crime Blotter every weekend because I was always using their homes as the ones that were getting vandalized, their cars as the ones getting stolen. It was a hoot. And I was $400 richer per week. But it didn't last long. *Newsday* eventually pulled the plug on the regional editions and the Crime Blotter page was killed. It could've gone on forever, there was no way they were gonna catch me. Another beautiful scam dying quicker than that stockbroker in Vegas. Oh well.

It was around this time I fell hard in love. Her name was Mary Bartolomucci, Italian/Irish girl with a quick wit, a killer body and an office down the hall from me at the paper's advertising section. As fate would have it, in the course of the same week, Mary's engagement went sour and my divorce became final. I eventually got around to asking her out for a drink one night, a Sunday. But first I had business to tend to. You're probably gonna hate this part of me, but it's bone and brittle in every single man you know. Even your daddy has some. It's just men don't like to admit to their dark side. Me? I'll admit to anything. It's the truth that's always gotten me in hot water, never lying.

I was seeing a beautiful and tough Italian girl from Staten Island at the time, Karen Cito was her name. She was my cousin's maid of honor, so the desire to date her came with a mandate from way up on top of my family's hierarchy. "Go ahead and date her, but A.J., if you hurt my friend, I'll fuckin' kill you."

And that was my cousin Barbara talking.

Well, I hurt her. Hurt her real bad. Why that happens to the good ones, I'll never know. Another unsolved mystery atop life's mountain of shitty things. Get Robert Stack on it.

I drove out to Karen's house off Victory Boulevard, an hour and fifteen minutes from my front door to hers late that Saturday night. The whole way there, I knew full well I was going to break it off with her to go out with Mary.

"Karen, it ain't working out for me. It's just not there anymore for me, baby. I don't know what to say."

"Is there someone else?"

"No," I said.

But there always is.

You hear what I said? Always.

I'll spare you the bells and whistles. Karen loved me like crazy and was loyal to a fault, but the wind cried Mary.

So Mary and I had our date. The night ended as we both made the other laugh through the open windows of our cars while headed south on the two-laned Route 110. Angry drivers were honking their horns behind us like mad, but love was brewing up ahead of them and there is nothing you can do in that situation. To this day, whenever I see a guy and girl talking through their car windows while driving down a highway, I never honk 'em. I just work the gas pedal gently and study their expressions and movements and I remember how that sort of feeling doesn't come around too many times in life.

Anyhow, eventually Mary and I heated up. One night, we had just finished having some fun and we retreated to the kitchen dying of thirst. I opened my refrigerator and all I had inside was a potato knish and some iced tea. That's it, I swear. Mary and I sat on the floor, petting my two dirty dogs, sipping iced tea and waiting for our knish to come out of the oven. I can't really lay any more importance on the event other than that, but I've gotta tell you, it was the best I have ever felt in my life and I was never more in debt, more scared of my future and more insecure about where I was headed in terms of anything.

There I sat, with this beautiful young Liz Taylor look-alike on the kitchen floor, propped up against the kitchen cabinets. "Mary, you know I'm falling in love with you, right? I'm down to my last knish, and there's really nothing else I can offer you, but I know the feeling and I'm falling in love with you."

She warned me not to. "I'm damaged goods right now," she said. "I'm still hurting and I need time to heal. But you're not ready yet either. You'll never be ready, A.J."

Smart girl.

Some six years after the fact I ran into her at a local pub. She's married to a rock and roll drummer now, with a house on Long Island and a bigger job at the paper. I walked her out to her car and I told her how I still think of her so often to this day.

"I think of you, too. But I think of how many more times you would have hurt me if I handed you my heart six years ago."

She was right. My desires would've started four-alarm fires all around her heart. From 1992 to 1997, I was a blur in every facet. Faster than a speeding Belushi, more powerful than a local mafiosa. Able to leap tall supermodels in a single bound. Look. Up in the sky. It's a bird! It's a plane!

Nah, it's a kid with a career that's about to take off. Mary was my last taste of home.

Factory Girl

had begun to travel into New York City a lot in those days—making my forays into the so-called hot clubs and restaurants at around ten P.M. and lingering on until the lights went on and the deejay was through scratching. I ran into a lot of characters back then—most of whom I've lost touch with since, most of whom I never wanted to see when the house lights went up—but it did create a colorful mosaic to be seen in night after night.

Forget *Newsday*. The sports department was going through a shift of power. Editors died, out-of-town hotshots were flown in, old-timers from *News*-side were moved over, full-time minority hires were mandatory despite my experience and seniority as a part-timer. Not to mention flat-out talent.

"You mean to tell me, we're going to hire a full-time high school columnist and a reporter as well as two reporters at New York *Newsday* and the hires have to be minorities?" I asked an editor one day.

"That's right. And there's nothing I can do about it."

"Doesn't matter that I know the beat. Know the coaches, the schools, the athletes, have the skills, the time in. None of that matters. The jobs have to go to minorities?"

"Yep." He was just as embarrassed to say it as I was enraged to hear it.

"That's *fucked* up," I yelled.

"Hey, pipe down over there," another editor hollered.

"Oh, fuck you, too. What am I doing here, busting my ass for eight years working shifts like a bartender, just so some female reporter from New Jersey or some black guy from Detroit can come in here and take the job that should rightfully go to me? How about cultivating some of the talent in the back of the room, instead of importing strangers?"

"That's enough, A.J."

"I got plenty more to say. Does anyone have any balls in this place to hear me?"

I was suspended without pay for a week for that one. But I didn't care. Pretty soon I was gonna leave this sinking ship.

I had gotten into the habit of finishing my six P.M. to midnight shift, maybe cutting out an hour earlier at times, and pointing my Toyota Corolla into the dark corners of New York City's nightlife. When the top editors weren't paying much attention, I would grab my buddies' attention—my partners in crime Gregg Sarra and John Valenti—by e-mailing them my intentions.

"Time to do the 50-50," I'd type out. "Cover me. I'll see you tomorrow."

Gregg and John were married with children so their replies were typical.

"Fuck . . . wish we could join you. You're covered, my boy. Bring home some stories."

The "50-50" was my lingo to tell them I was driving fifty miles in fifty minutes. All it entailed was me slipping out of the news room, hugging the wall the way a mouse leaves a hallway and sprinting down the back stairwell and into my four-door car. Then it was nothing but the L.I.E. separating me from a world I was dying to know about. I didn't know much at the time about the city's night people—outside of what I would read in Michael Musto's *Village Voice* column—but I wasn't going to deny the pull it had on me. That love affair began way back in college, when those theater majors would head out to the Ritz, Area, Palladium, etc. Our entry in was always based upon one of my friends "knowing" someone inside the club—a lighting technician, a promoter, a bartender. Sometimes the association game worked, sometimes it didn't and we would turn around,

light up a joint, and race back to campus. But I remember the knot
that would develop in my stomach as we all walked toward some bald
and burly bouncer with one hand on the guest list and the other on
the velvet rope. With each step, the music that was pumping inside
would send vibrations higher and higher up your legs until you'd be
standing on the rim of the huge crowd all waiting to get in and it was
as if your heart was taking its cue from the deejay inside. Within a
minute or so, it was beating to the club's rhythm and getting past the
velvet ropes was the equivalent of drawing a deep breath into your
lungs in the middle of a mountain climb.

"Private party tonight, people. Nobody's getting in unless you're on
the guest list."

I had heard that line before—too many times with my college buddies
alongside me. And the realization that I was going to drive fifty miles,
on a whim, mind you, with a great chance to hear some bald motherfucka tell it to me again was something that did make those anticipatory
drives a little angst-filled. But I drove on, sometimes alone, but most of
the time accompanied by an Indian girl I had met the week my divorce
was final. Simona had once helped me buy a nice pair of pants and a
pair of boots at a boutique in Greenwich Village and we immediately
hit it off. When I say immediately, I mean immediately. Like, the second
time I went in the empty store and tried on a pair of suit pants, Simona
came into the dressing room with me and did a lot more than chalk up
a hem line. Simona was a dark-skinned Indian, with uncharacteristically
thick lips and a long mane of black curly hair. She had brown eyes and
knew how to dress up her figure so that every curve was pronounced
and impossible to overlook. But she was no pushover, despite the fact
that she was alone in New York, working days as a salesgirl and going
to F.I.T. at nights. Simona was from an entirely different world than I
was. She had loads of very important friends who never wavered at the
sight of a velvet rope. So, with each passing week we'd make more plans
to go check out another of the city's clubs—be they aboveboard or
underground. The only problem was, she was almost always leading me
into a backroom or a velvet booth that was chock-full of her Indian
friends. Everyone would smoke cigarettes like crazy and buy Cristal
champagne like it was water and there I was with about $60 in my
pocket. But Simona never made me pay.

"Coke?" one of her friends asked.

"No thanks. I don't do any drugs."

That sure changed. But more on that fuckin' story later.

Anyhow, Simona and I developed a beautifully shallow New York City late-night relationship. She used me, I used her, and neither one gave a shit. But one night we were in the middle of some presex, candlelit conversation when Simona breaks the ecstasy with the one thing a guy never wants to hear, unless of course, Mrs. Right is saying it. And, I'll be frank, Simona was not Mrs. Right. No woman who does you in the dressing room of a Village boutique is Mrs. Right. She is Mrs. Right *Now*, maybe. But she ain't Mrs. Right. Anyhow, so there we are, in her Bond Street walkup, and she says, "You will marry me for citizenship?"

Ahhh, so that's what this is about. Gotcha.

I never did marry Simona the Indian, but I did finish the night's sex and stall her for a long enough time to make her think I was considering this wonderful idea of hers. I also managed to pull her chain long enough so that I had a closet full of designer clothes at a drastic discount.

Simona didn't take the rejection too hard, though, when I eventually did get around to telling her that I wasn't the marrying-for-citizenship kind. She simply and swiftly moved on to the next guy. And I moved on to the next girl and the next party and the next phase of my new life. But I was dressed better now. Looking back, Simona was more than a good lay and a free pair of shoes. She opened my eyes to a whole new world.

Waiting on a Friend

By the time that phase of my life was finally over—working halfsheets and gambling and all the peripheral evils—I had managed to make a good friend in my gambling partner, T.K. Tom Kennedy. He was ten years my senior and immediately saw something in me that reminded him of himself in his younger days.

"Remember J, as you are now so once was I. As I am now, so you will be. Remember, J, eternity." That's the kind of shit T.K. used to hit me with while he was driving his big old Lincoln and I rode shotgun.

I liked the way that sounded. It had a poetry to it, even if it was someone else's. So, I decided to invite T.K. on my journeys with me. Plus, there was something in him that reminded me of my father.

"I have a lot of goin' out to do. I gotta make up for lost time. You're welcome to come if those old legs of yours can hold out," I said to him.

"Brother . . . they've been good to me for forty-two years. They haven't showed signs of slowing."

So, T.K. and I began to hit the town. He would leave his home in East Quogue, Long Island, and pick me up in West Islip—about an hour's drive—and then we would turn the big lady toward the city. "You ready?" he'd ask me. " 'Cause I'm ready, motherfucka. I got $500 in my pocket and I'm ain't coming home with a penny."

And he wouldn't.

Our nights out were treated as events. But it was then that I had to deal with the regularity of being rejected at a club's door. Why? I was a nobody. Worse, I knew nobody.

"SORRY, FOLKS, GUEST LIST ONLY. PRIVATE PARTY TONIGHT."

When this first happens to you, you simply step aside and wander away from the calamity of the door and let the so-called beautiful people brush past you. And eventually, after talking to the doorman for a bit, you walk away defeated and try another club. After a series of turndowns, you find someplace that will allow you to walk in and spend your dough.

When it continues to happen to you—let's say, over a period of months—that's when your conversations with the doorman turn to bribes and pleas. Sometimes this works. Sometimes it doesn't. Either way, it's a helluva lousy way to begin a night—begging and paying somebody off just so you can have fun where some gossip columnist in his almighty column has deemed "the place" to have fun. Oh boy, did I learn a lot about that power. More on that fuckin' story later.

But there was one night in April of 1992 that I decided I wasn't going to take it anymore. And if anyone were to record one of the pivotal moments of my life, this would have to be the quintessential moment that laid the foundation for the House of Irony I was about to inhabit.

I had heard about *Vogue* magazine throwing its 100th birthday party at the New York Public Library. The whole fuckin' world was going and I wanted to be there so much I could taste the liver pâté *Vogue* editor Anna Wintour was sure to be serving that night. So, like usual, T.K. and I drove into the city—we got all fancied up in our Armani suits and shit—and we headed right for the library steps.

And there it was. Lights, cameras, action, DRAMA! I remember watching everyone—every big name in fashion—waltzing up the red carpeted steps and heading inside. Paparazzi popped off thousands of shots. "Naomi, this way!" "Cindy, where's Richard?" "Claudia, who are you wearing?"

It was insanity. And I had to get inside. But it was impossible. *Vogue* had hired a security team that could've schooled the Pentagon. T.K. had just about had it. "We saw everything we're gonna see, J. Let's go somewhere else."

"Fuck no. I'm getting in. The next time *Vogue* throws a party like this I'll be 132."

Just then, out of the corner of my eye, I see a grungy-looking guy kinda getting in the face of one of the security men. "You gonna believe that bitch? You gonna believe me or her? I'm Mickey Rourke. She's only *Mrs.* Mickey Rourke."

Actually, no one was really sure what the state of their marriage was, but what had happened was Carré Otis—Mickey's girlfriend and costar in *Wild Orchid*—had told security to ban him from entering the party. Apparently, the couple was feuding and Carré didn't want him anywhere near the joint. This caused Mickey to flip out. But when one of Anna Wintour's minions came to the door and flashed the thumbs-down, Mickey and his entourage walked down the steps fuming. And that's when he met me.

"What happened, Mickey?" I acted like I knew him from way back. Meanwhile, I was shaking in my suede loafers. The ones Simona the Indian had sold me. This was one of my favorite actors and T.K. knew it. Shit, I've been nicknamed The Pope ever since he starred in *The Pope of Greenwich Village*. Got me a Pope tattoo on my right shoulder to prove it.

"My old lady got me banned from getting in. Can you fuckin' believe that? I know you, don't I?"

"Nah. You don't know me. I just hate when a guy gets a hard time from his woman. Where's the party at now?"

"I don't know. We'll make some noise somewhere."

Instead of simply saying good-bye to a guy he had never met—much less knew—Mickey told us to hop in his limo and hang with him. "Come on. We'll end up seeing everybody later anyway. It's the way this city is. Everybody gets bored in a minute."

I couldn't imagine getting inside that party and checking my watch out of boredom. But Mickey's words would become so true in the years to come. We headed downtown—me, Mickey, T.K. and Mickey's minions—and watched Mickey close his eyes to Bob Dylan's "Knockin' on Heaven's Door." We eventually stopped at a spot on Sixth Avenue called Rex. It ain't there no more, but Rex was a very cool, funky spot. Beads in the doorway, a lot of red booths, low ceiling. You could get lung cancer just in the time it took to check your coat. I could've never gotten in there without Mickey.

"What's your name?" Mickey asked me.

"I'm A.J. This here's T.K."

"All right. So stick with me tonight."

It was the first glimpse I got of Mickey's dependency on other people. A few years later I would see how dependent Mickey could get with weeks of middle-of-the-night phone calls to me to help settle beefs with him and his girl.

So Team Rourke made the rounds through the club, just to let everyone know we were there, before we settled at a corner booth and waited.

And waited.

And waited.

T.K. was checking his watch constantly, giving me the raised eyebrows to split. "Fuck no, are you crazy," I told him. "I'm sitting here with Mickey Rourke and you wanna split?"

"Nobody's here but us," T.K. pleaded. "It's two A.M. We're beating a dead horse . . ."

And then it happened. The front beads parted and in walked Cindy, Naomi, Claudia, Linda, Christy. You name it. All of them decked to the nines and all of them headed our motherfuckin' way.

"Holy shit, J, it's on!"

In the years that followed, I gradually got over the vertigo that overtook me whenever a supermodel walked into a room. But that night was my first taste of beauty en masse parading into a small joint and paying homage to a man at my table. I say, "paying homage," but it was more like fawning.

So there I was, squished in a booth with the beautiful people. And, up close, they really are as beautiful as they seem. Don't get me wrong—they're full of shit like anyone else. But they are easy on the eyes and that can mesmerize you for a while.

Anyhow this was also the night when a couple of big supermodels decided it was just fine and dandy to show everyone in the room that a woman enjoys a woman every now and then. The refreshing burst of lesbianism—which was underground-yet-apparently-fashionable at the time—began at our table. And within minutes, two of the bigger cat-walkers were locked in a deep passionate kiss. One of them remains so TV-friendly to this day, our country's sponsors would've choked on their Kellogg's had they been sitting where I sat. It was beautiful, but I want to get something straight right now. I'm not necessarily into girl-on-girl. Actually, when the porno tape reaches those scenes, I reach for the fast forward button on my remote control. I could care less. It does nothing to stimulate me. But—I'm not stupid—I wasn't going to leave that club until the last girl trotted out.

Mickey was busy trying to stuff his hand down Cindy Crawford's jacket. When I asked why he seemed so obsessed with Cindy, one of the guys in his crew, Pinky, told me Mickey had hoped Cindy got the part in *Wild Orchid* before Carré was cast. I want you all to think I was cool enough to leave the room that night without doing something that was so utterly "civilian" of me, but I wasn't. I grabbed ahold of Pinky and asked him if he thought Mickey would give me his earring as a keepsake. Pinky laid high odds on that request since Mickey wore the hoop during *Wild Orchid* and he ordinarily gets very attached to stuff he wears in a film he liked.

"Fuck it," I thought. As soon as there was a break in the groping going on to my right, I grabbed Mickey and asked him the favor. I told him I'd trade him my hoop for his hoop. He looked at me curious, but he was smirking. "Why do you want to do that?" he said.

"Because you showed me a helluva good time tonight. I want to remember it. And I want you to know I'll return the favor one day."

With that, Mickey and I exchanged hoops. I wore it for years until it got caught in the hairweave of an ex-girlfriend I was kissing in the back of Sound Factory. That's a good story. I'll tell you about that one day.

But I wasn't done yet. I then asked Mickey to walk with me to the phone booth.

"Who we calling?" Mickey asked me.

"My ex-wife. She loves you. She'll shit if she hears I'm with you. Just say 'hello' to her for me would ya, pal?"

"Dial."

I'm sure Jenn's fiancé, Mr. Special Ed, didn't take kindly to the three-thirty A.M. phone call, but fuck *him*. Jenn played the call real cool, but the next day, she phoned me up freaking out.

"What was he *like?* I can't *believe* it!"

Anyhow, I felt like I was on glue when I walked out of Rex. And, quite frankly, I could've been. There was an impressive array of drugs available from people in the club if you wished to indulge. Me, I didn't do any drugs. Yet.

When T.K. and I walked out of Rex there was no way I was in any shape to drive home. All I could do was laugh out loud at the lunacy of the lifestyle behind that beaded doorway. T.K. and I grabbed a $40 room at the Chelsea Hotel, and had to share a hallway bathroom with some punk rockers. But I didn't care. I was way too excited to drive home and I needed a place to sit and let it all soak in. Not even the cockroaches on the wall would bother me. The night would eventually go down as my baptism of fire. I know I didn't give you much of a picture to go along with my peaked emotions, but I am biting down on my tongue— and have done so for years—when it comes to outing people's preferences for sex and drugs. When I left Rex and made a left up Sixth Avenue, I was really making a major turn in my life. I had just left a room where there were a thousand stories to tell, a thousand careers to diagnose, a thousand illusions suddenly backlit and I thought that corner of the world needed to be spoken about. At least it could be brought to life and delivered to the city's regular people—civilians like me and T.K. who just happened to stumble into the right room at the right time. But who was going to listen to me? And who was going to let me tell my tales? Really . . . who the fuck was I?

She's a Rainbow

think if you invest in women, it always pays off for you in the end. I don't necessarily mean investing money. Fuck that, I've heard too many horror stories with that kind of investment. And I know too many guys who saw little return. I'm mainly talking about investing *time* in women. I think investing time in women pays big dividends.

Working *Newsday*'s sports department meant short bursts of high-paced action. Answering phones, typing notes, reporting out a game story, checking spelling, getting quotes and editing. That chaos—with an entire phone system blinking red like a Christmas tree—was always followed with long stretches of boredom. No game results being called in meant plenty of downtime to read, write, bullshit, make personal calls or watch the sporting events on the big TVs all over the office. I remember looking at the clock and knowing I had three more hours before I could even think of hightailing it to NYC for some late-night fun. So, I would spend my time typing in ideas for freelance stories, writing bits of screenplays, compiling death lists and sending electronic messages to Linda Stasi.

Linda was the editor of New York *Newsday*'s gossip page, Inside New York. She was an attractive Italian woman who had the sarcasm, sex appeal and smarts that would make any man reach for her column with his morning coffee. Shit, most men would have liked to reach for her rather than their coffee—I was no different. But her sharp tongue meant she was to be treated with the same respect a snake charmer issues his serpent. Up until her column, I had never read a gossip column fueled by a woman's voice that didn't have an odor of posturing, self-promoting or formaldehyde, if you want me to be real. Every female gossiper was, well, old and devoid of sex appeal. For God's sake, Liz Smith hasn't given anyone a boner in a couple of decades. It took years for Cindy Adams and her surgeon to achieve a particular level of beauty. Rona Barrett's speech impediment could douse the fire in any man's trousers. And *USA Today*'s Jeannie Williams—though a good, old broad—writes with all the sexual style of a gas pump. Then along came Linda, fresh from a stint at several beauty magazines where she worked as an editor. I don't know where she developed her great sense of humor, but I know it had to do with growing up on Long Island, marrying and divorcing at a young age and then raising her beautiful young daughter, Jessica, on her own. Linda was a woman not to be denied. Her tongue was as quick as any man's fists—and in some cases just as honest and painful. Believe me when I tell you—line her up with the likes of those old Jewish comedians at a Friar's Roast and she would send the boys home laughing. And you can bet your ass, they'd invite her back.

So it was around this time that I became obsessed with Linda's column, which was cowritten by an old reporter named Anthony Scaduto and a young dry-humored Southern kid named Doug Vaughan. In my opinion, the three of them were kicking the pants off Cindy Adams, Liz Smith, Page Six and Richard Johnson's *Daily News* gossip column. And when it came to gauging a gossip page, those were the big four you tried to measure up to. I remember I would send electronic messages to Linda several times a week, and unlike other high-profile reporters, Linda would always return the messages by the end of the workday. I preferred communicating with her through our computers, because the few times I phoned her, Linda would answer her phone with the quickest "hello" in the business. Her speed put you off immediately.

"Hello!"

"Hi, Linda?"

"Yeah."

"Hi, it's A.J."

"Yeah."

"Got a second?"

"A second."

It was like that. So, anyway, a day after I stumbled out of the *Vogue* party, I managed to put together a message including everything I witnessed—everything from the drugs to the sex to the lesbianism, etc. It's not like I wanted everything to be written that way, I just wanted to let her know there was some stuff her hysterical and well-written column was missing. As much as Linda's commentary had politicians and moguls shaking in their wingtips, her column rarely hit on "The Scene." It was almost devoid of supermodel news, club news and the upsurge of youthful names who were peppering the world of New York City with their acting, artistry, music or plain old posing. So I sent her the message and waited to see what she had to say.

Within hours Linda phoned me up and asked if I'd like to help her out on her Inside New York page. "I can't write what you saw," she said. "It's too raw. And it's too personal. But I like that you saw it and brought it to life so well."

"Thanks," I said.

"I can send you out to events and you can report on them. Don't worry about writing. Leave that to me. You just go out and bring back the stories. Ask some questions. Stuff like that. And I'll write it."

"Where do I go? I can't get into too many places."

"We get all the invites. But I'd rather die than go out to clubs and parties. So, I'll send you out and you just tell people you're reporting for Linda Stasi."

"Cool."

"Here . . . here's one here. Do you wanna go to Grace Jones's birthday party at the Palladium?"

"Yeah. What time does it start?"

"It says ten, but she never shows up until midnight. So get there around eleven. And message me tomorrow with whatever you saw. Tell me what happened. We pay staffers for items, so we can give you $40 for every item you give us."

"Fuck the money. I want to work for you all the time. I want to be rescued from sports."

"We'll see what happens."

Talk about a new lease on life. Suddenly there was a sign of life outside the droll and boring walls of the *Newsday* sports department in Melville, Long Island. So I finished my five P.M. to ten P.M. bullshit shift in sports and hightailed it to the Palladium in my Toyota Corolla! My credentials would be waiting for me at the door.

I remember walking inside and not knowing a soul. And it was at that moment I developed a habit that would stick with me for the next five years of working the beat: When you feel lonely and completely alone, head to the bar and make a cocktail your best friend. Back then, gin and I got along just fine. It was light, usually mixed with tonic water, and I was able to down a bunch of them before feeling the effects. And, even then, it was nothing a quick espresso couldn't fix before the long drive home.

I had been there nearly two hours and Grace Jones hadn't arrived yet. In the interim, I had managed to make "friends" with one of the lighting guys—Jimmy Driscoll—who was kind enough to get me a backstage pass so that I could be near the real festivities when Grace finally did arrive. He asked me what I did and I told him I was helping out on a gossip page for New York *Newsday*.

"Don't fags and old ladies usually do that kind of shit?"

"Well . . . I dunno. I ain't gay, so maybe I'm changing things around here. We'll see."

Backstage was cool and it was certainly the place to be—with one of Grace's handlers barking orders to everyone around him. In the years to come, he would go through hard times, but he was always kind to me from the jump. He did me a huge favor that first night he met me. As soon as he realized I was working for Linda, he took me aside.

"Linda told me you were cute. She didn't tell me you were *exactly my type*. That bitch is gonna get it from me."

I played along. "How do you know you're my type?"

"Honey, that matters little with me. It's never about you wanting me. It's about me wanting you."

Then he laughed. He knew he was fuckin' with me and I guess he wanted me to know he knew. Whew!

Grace's handler took me to a distant room. "Somebody wants to meet you."

I'm thinking, "How could this be? No one even knows I'm here."

But as soon as he showed me who he wanted me to meet, my jaw dropped.

Some three years earlier I had fallen in love—well, hard lust—with an adult film star named Barbara Dare. I met her on a business trip in Las Vegas. I was working for a video magazine at the time and Barbara was there for the video convention that was being held at the convention center. She had been voted "Sex Starlet of the Year" by *Adult Video News*. I saw her signing autographs with a long beaded dress on and I almost shit. It's a rare day when a boy comes face-to-face with his favorite porn star, so I knew I had to do something outside the realm of asking her for her signature on some cheesy headshot her manager was selling for $5 a throw. So, I waited on line and when it got to be my turn to have her sign her name, I didn't present a photo. I just wanted to talk to her.

"I just want to tell you, when I put in your videos I never fast forward past anything you do. You could be tying your shoe and I watch it over and over."

"Oh, how sweet. Give me a picture, so I can sign it for you."

"Nah. I don't need a picture of you. But take my number and call me whenever you come to New York. We can have lunch or something."

I don't know who the fuck I thought I was kidding. I was a married man, living in an apartment above my mother's house, and here I was, hitting on an adult film goddess. But it obviously worked.

"Oh my God, look at you . . . you remind me so much of my ex-boyfriend."

"Who's that?"

By now, all the middle-America goons with their sweaty palms were getting angry at the time I was spending with her.

"He's an actor. Paul Land. He was in *The Idolmaker*. Did you see that movie?"

"Yeah, I know that guy. That's a compliment."

"So what do you do? Are you an actor?"

At the time, I was studying acting with Mira Rostova—who was once widely regarded as Montgomery Clift's confidante and lover. Mira was a heralded and reclusive Russian coach working and living out of a messy loft in the Flatiron District, and up until that day all I had gotten was a week on the TV soap *Loving* and a callback for *The Equalizer.*

"Yes, I'm an actor." Do you believe what a bullshitter I was?

"Do you do film?"

It was time to change the subject. "Listen, just call me. I'm also a writer and I'd love to do a piece on you and your industry. Call."

"Okay, A.J., I will. I don't get to New York too often, but when I do, I'll call."

I didn't believe she'd call, but it was a cool feeling carrying around the prospect in my balls for the next three years: A porn star ringing my line. It's every man's dream. Then, all of a sudden, she appears out of the blue at the Palladium.

"Holy shit. What are you doing here," I said.

"Well, I lost your number, so I figured I'd just come to New York and find you."

She was bullshitting, for sure, but she was giving me play and that's all I cared about.

Barbara went on to tell me she was out of the film business. I told her I was fine with that, and that now maybe my wrist would finally begin to heal. She laughed and said she was now making a living as a featured dancer at upscale topless clubs across the country. She had been performing at Goldfinger's in Queens earlier that night before she was dragged to the Grace Jones affair by her girlfriend.

And it was obvious by "girlfriend" she meant "girlfriend" like I mean "girlfriend" when I say "girlfriend."

"But she went off to find us some X and I haven't seen her in twenty minutes."

Suddenly, I am with a porn star who likes to indulge in drugs and women. I was a long way from watching *thirtysomething* with Jennifer.

It wasn't long before Barbara's dikey girlfriend showed up and was obviously unhappy with our friendship and the promise that it might flower before the night was through. Just one look at the girl and it was apparent Barbara was in it for curiosity's sake and the other was in it for life. When the diesel eventually pulled away, that meant Barbara was mine for the night.

Back in the day, the Palladium's Mike Todd room was the hot spot. Just outside of that room, the club was loaded with a number of nooks and crannies that lovers and druggies made a habit of visiting from time to time. Eventually, Barbara and I squeezed into one spot and talked the night away. At one point, we managed to stop talking long enough in order to consummate a feeling that had been brewing for three years. The simmer came to a boil that night—and neither one of us cared that Grace Jones had rode onto the Palladium's stage on a Harley Davidson and proceeded to sing several songs to her adoring fans. I just remember never being able to hear "Pull Up to My Bumper" without thinking of that night. Technically, that was my first night "on the job," but I was already being treated to some of the perks a gossip columnist comes to enjoy.

Suddenly, it was three A.M., and I had no story to bring back to Linda. Thankfully, though, Driscoll fed me some funny moments that he had witnessed—far too random to mention now—but good enough for me to bring back to Linda the following morning.

And that was the beginning of a long partnership between me and Linda and a strong friendship between me and Barbara.

A few more nights like that and a few more stories for Linda in the ensuing weeks led her to ask me if I'd like to sit in her office on Fridays and help her out with the Sunday and Monday workload. That wasn't hard to clear with the sports department since Linda's request for help came as a mandate from atop New York Newsday's hierarchy—one Donald Forst, the editor-in-chief. Forst spoke to the honchos at Long Island Newsday and within a few days some hotshot signed my release so that I could sit with Linda at 2 Park Avenue every Friday from ten A.M. to five P.M. and pitch in. The Friday gig went great for a few weeks until a few jealous assholes in sports wondered aloud where all the preferential treatment came from.

"You sleeping with Stasi?" one staffer asked me while we were playing charity basketball against the sports guys from WFAN.

"If I was fuckin' her, I'd like to think I'd get more than one day a week out of the deal," I said. "No. It ain't like that. Linda is like a mother and a sister to me."

And that would become the understatement of the year down the road, as Linda would become privy to every victory and catastrophe that found its way into my life. The truth is, she would become the most important woman in my life by way of just giving me a shot at something I always knew I could do—write a column for a New York City newspaper. Thanking people like that never comes out right. They don't realize they are responsible for so much of what you become. So, rather than try to thank her for all her help over the years, Linda and I shared a quiet understanding of my gratitude and love for her. It almost became embarrassing to tell her how much she meant to me at crucial times. So, a lot of times it went unsaid. Which is unfortunate, but so true of too many meaningful relationships in life. In the three years I worked alongside her, I think I hugged her and told her I loved her two or three times. It should've added up to two or three thousand.

Anyway, the point is I wasn't sleeping with the boss. But to deny that I sometimes dealt with a strong crush would be insane. That was something I wasn't scared of telling her either. And that day came when I stayed late on a Friday evening and one of the New York *Newsday* editorial writers, a real hot number in leopardskin tights and a snug black sweater, approached me with an invitation to a movie premiere. I turned her down right in front of Linda and Jane Frieman, who was then *Newsday*'s food critic.

"Why would I want to go to a movie with her, when I'm sitting with the hottest chicks this place has to offer?"

They loved it. And the closest Linda ever came to flirting back was to tell me something I never forgot: "You're the kind of guy, when he walks into a room, women fix their lipstick."

I thought that was the coolest line. Still do. Of course, I never witnessed one girl ever fix her lips at the sight of me walking toward her.

So now, I had me a regular gig every Friday, sitting beside Linda, writing bits of gossip for her column. Unfortunately, the column never ran my byline and hardly anyone in the building knew I was there under her tutelage, but the days added up and before long I had been there about three months—piping stories to her, reporting on rumors and making the nightly rounds. Making myself known is what it really boiled down to. Like I said earlier, who the fuck was I? I knew it was going to take time.

It was during this time I remember running into Richard Johnson, who then had a widely read column in the *Daily News*. Johnson and I both were attending a Ford Models party at Jim McMullen's restaurant, seated with old Eileen Ford and her daughter Katie Ford and son-in-law Andre Belazs, the hotelier. I barely belonged there to begin with, not really knowing a soul, but because the event included models I thought I ought to be there and take a story back to Linda. At the time—and still to this day—Johnson had a hard-on for Mickey Rourke real bad. When he wasn't calling him the "slimey actor" or "alleged pugilist" or "*Barfly* Rourke," he was berating his every move. It didn't matter if it was a new film or another boxing match Mickey was gearing up for. Johnson flat-out hated the guy and it was really a sore spot with Mickey.

"What's with this punk Richard Johnson?" Mickey would ask me as our friendship grew. "Why is he on my ass? Should I punch him out?"

"Can't hit a journalist," I told Mickey. "You can put the fear of God in him, even threaten him, but you're better off talking it out. Or else he'll be on your ass your whole career."

"What career?" Mickey would say. He was like that sometimes, very down on himself.

Long story short, I didn't like the treatment Johnson was giving him either. I'm loyal that way. But the topper came when Johnson challenged him to a fight—right there in his column. Johnson used an entire column one day to challenge Mickey to a boxing match. This drove Mickey insane, but he was in a no-win situation. Johnson is a tall guy . . . but Mickey would've flattened him in a second. It would've been two hits: Mickey hitting Johnson and Johnson hitting the floor. Either way, an actor can't accept a challenge like that. It's ridiculous and he'd never come away looking good. So, Mickey let his anger for Johnson implode. Johnson, meanwhile, kept right on egging him on, hinting to his readers that Rourke hadn't accepted his offer, that he was a coward, blah, blah, blah.

So, one night I see Johnson seated at that Ford Modeling party and I mosey over. At this point in my "career" he hadn't yet met me.

I tapped him on the shoulder. "Hey," I said. "I'm a friend of Mickey Rourke's and he's right outside in the street and he says he'd be more than happy to kick your ass after you're through with the party." It was a big lie, but I was having a good time amusing myself.

Johnson weighed the situation, but I could tell he was nervous. "Is that right?"

"I wouldn't lie."

"Well, I might be in here a while . . ."

Then I broke down. "I'm only messing with you," I said. "My name's A.J. Benza. I'm the guy helping out Linda Stasi over at *Newsday*. I just like Mickey and I always see you ragging him and it bugs me."

"Well, *he* bugs a lot of people," Johnson said.

"Whatever."

But before I turned away, I felt like I had to deliver some kind of message to this guy and I kind of know why. The truth of it is I always hated the photograph that ran along the top of his column. He looked so goddamn smug in it. When you get right down to it, whenever a columnist runs their own photograph with their column, their writing changes. I don't care what anybody says, you start to feel a bit more inflated with yourself and it comes across in the writing. Having your words read by the great city of New York is enough of a power trip, believe me. You don't need to have your mug up alongside it. Anyhow, that's what made me turn back to give Johnson one more for the road.

"Don't be surprised if I have your job and your office one day," I said.

"Oh . . . okay," he said, barely turning his head from the young Ford models at his table.

And one day I did just that. But more on that fuckin' story later.

To say Linda knew some powerful men was like saying Bill Clinton has had a few crushes he kept from Hillary. During the stretches Linda was on vacations, she would always have me fill in for her working alongside Anthony and Doug. She would graciously offer me her chair and her computer and any private number in her big, fat Rolodex. I would sit there, with the phone headset on, trying to compose a gossip item and her phone would ring. And ring. And ring. I never saw a phone ring like hers until I got my own gig a couple years later.

"Hello, this is David. Is Linda available?"

"No she's away. Can I take a message?"

"Just tell her David Dinkins called."

"Oh shit! Of course, Mr. Mayor. Fuck, I'm sorry. You got it. I'll put it on her voice mail right away."

Then, of course, all the others would chime in. Cutler, D'Amato, Cuomo, Trump, Wynn. The biggest of the big. The men who only need one name to be recognized. And I would sit there wondering what kind of world I was entering. A world where I was almost—but not quite—one phone call away from anything I wanted. Linda's power was engrossing. I wasn't beyond doing anything for her. So, aside from penning her gossip items from the world I was beginning to inhabit, I was more than willing to fetch her coffee and a soda every now and then. She had a thing for caffeine-free Diet Pepsi.

Linda's forte was politics. But more important, she had a penchant for shedding light on the effect local politics had on city dwellers. She was always hot to point out the hypocrisy that often got by the uninformed voter. And she liked to attack the big-shot pols from the head down. And that meant she'd start with their toupees. Or their combovers or their plugs. Or their hair replacement surgery. It didn't matter who she was slicing up. Everyone was naked in Linda's column. But more important, Linda was forever exposing herself, too. After a few weeks of reading the columns she headed, the reader got to know more dirt on her than on her subjects. And that's one of her special attributes I took with me.

Poor Manhattan Borough President Andrew Stein had to read about his hairpiece resembling a golf divet turned upside down more than you could imagine. And Linda, more than once, accused Rudy Giuliani of standing nineteen-feet tall in a windstorm thanks to his comb-over unfurling high to the heavens. But her columns weren't just about being funny. There was always a message in there somewhere. There was a reason for every joke, jab and joust. And then the next day, the lady wasn't afraid to take the hits from her subjects as they came. But she always warned me, "The hit never comes from who you think it will." I kind of knew what she was getting at, but it would be a few years before I really absorbed the lesson.

I remember the surge I'd feel whenever Linda would saunter in— usually wearing power black or red—and sit in front of the Xerox copies of all the competing columns I'd run off for her. Some days she wasn't happy, especially when it was obvious some publicist—who was most likely in our pocket—had hand-delivered a good story to another columnist. But Inside New York was hot back then and, most of the time, Linda would slug her last bit of coffee, shuffle the papers around in her lap and say, "We kicked everyone's ass today. Great job, guys." And then she'd turn to me. "Wanna go to OTB? I got a tip on a horse."

And there we were. Linda, my leader, and me, weaving our way through midtown's sidewalk traffic, looking to bet $20 apiece on a horse named Mimesis in the fifth at Belmont. On that particular day, the horse won and we each collected about $200 apiece. Not a bad little excursion. Linda told me the tip came from her buddy Carlo Vacarezza, a guy who—among other things—dabbled in horses with a stable at Aqueduct and Belmont and a training facility in Ocala, Florida. Carlo was once John Gotti's driver and was now running John's joint on the Upper East Side, Pulcinella—formerly the perennial mob hangout Da Noi. Apparently everyone knew this was John's joint, but me being from Long Island and all, what did I know about who had what piece of which restaurant? I just wanted to go to the place and show my gratitude to Carlo, by buying a few drinks at the restaurant one night. Well, gratitude almost turned into being grabbed by the throat and smacked around.

I remember walking in the joint unannounced with my buddy T.K. one night and chatting up Carlo.

"Hey, I work with Linda Stasi. I just wanted to say thank you for Mimesis?"

"Eh, what's a Mime's ass?"

"The horse," I said. "I want to thank you for the horse, Mimesis."

"Che gotza, 'Mimesis?' You mean, Mim-es-is."

"I thought it was Mimesis, like Mime-sis. That's the way the track announcer said it," I told him.

"She's a my horse. I don't care how the fuck he pronounces it. It's a Mim-es-is."

"Mim-es-is," I said slowly.

"Right, like you know, a Mim-es-is. When someone is someone you cannot beat."

"Nemesis?" I said.

"Right, Mim-es-is!"

Glad we cleared that up.

At any rate, I quickly became a regular at Pulcinella—stopping in late for some pasta or for a few Sambucas at the bar served by a blonde bartender we called Trish the Dish. One night, Trish thought I should meet the restaurant's sexy hostess, Lisa. "She's so lonely," Trish said. "Can't you take her out to some of these parties you get invited to?"

Lisa was Lisa Gastineau—the same stunning woman I used to see in the stands at Giants Stadium back when her husband, Marc Gastineau, was a popular Jet and the most notorious linebacker in the NFL. I remember every time he'd sack a quarterback, he'd lauch into his silly "sack dance" and the cameras would always cut to Lisa in the stands, wearing some giant fur coat and an even bigger smile. And me, being a bored married man living on Long Island, would naturally fantasize about women like that. What did it take to have them calling a guy like me?

Now, all of a sudden, I'm about to take her out. That's what a high-profile job in the big city does to you. It reduces the degrees of separation in a heartbeat.

After the phony introductions, Lisa launched into this sad song about being a slave to the restaurant and never being able to go out for a night. "And besides," she said, "no one will *take* me out."

Well I leapt at the chance. But it was more than just the chance at being seen with this beauty. There was something I liked about this chick. We were both the same age. We were both Italians. We were both enamored by celebrity. We both liked to laugh a lot. We clicked. One Monday night Lisa split the restaurant a little early and met me at the China Club. We had a bunch of laughs there. Drank some, danced a little, too. But mostly stayed perched atop the club's upper level— where all the VIP's have tables reserved for them—and talked a lot in each other's ears. Most of the talk was nonsense, but it was the kind of talk a couple substitutes for the hardest sentence to say in the world: "Do you wanna go to my place?"

Of course, my place was way out on Long Island and Lisa lived up near New Rochelle. So we had to settle on the Upper West Side apartment belonging to one of her girlfriends. After some more wine and some more laughs, Lisa and I moved to the couch. Like I said earlier, we clicked. Well, *we* clicked, but Carlo all but cocked his .45 when he found out that Lisa and I stole away for the night.

The next night, I walked into Pulcinella—after a long night of collecting gossip for Linda—expecting to throw a few back when Carlo called me into the kitchen.

"Come here," he said. "You wanna get me killed? Or do you want me to kill you? Which is it? Because if my friend finds out you were with Lisa, we're both in big trouble."

"Why is your friend mad," I said. "I had no idea Lisa was dating your friend. She never told me she had a boyfriend."

"Lisa is not dating anybody. *Anybody.*"

"All right, then what's the problem?"

"Lisa is John's girl."

"John's girl? *John's* girl?"

Mimesis he couldn't pronounce worth a damn, but I had no trouble understanding Carlo's pronunciation of D-A-N-G-E-R. Lisa Gastineau was John Gotti's mistress, and had been before John got sent away. And even with John in the Big House, the mandate was the same—prison bars or no prison bars—no one dated Lisa. No one. That was a little something Lisa failed to tell me.

I stayed away from the restaurant for a few weeks after that, but I bumped into her at a party tossed for fitness guru High Voltage at a place called the Country Club. "Where you been, baby?" Lisa said to me. She was wearing a black rubber Versace number and a long blonde hair extension that even Jeannie would've left in the bottle.

"On the lam. Jesus, Lisa, you almost got me killed. Why didn't you tell me you were John's girl? I know him. You know what a slap that is? Are you outta your mind?"

"Sweetie, I'm sorry. You were so green and I really needed a night away from the guys. But don't let Carlo fool you. You can call me. I can date. I can date anybody I want. You know how those possessive Italians get."

Yes I do. I *am* a possessive Italian. But following Carlo's message was a lot more appealing to me than lusting after Lisa. From that point on— though I genuinely like the girl—I always kept my distance. Listen, I'm not against stealing someone's woman away. The timing's got to be right. But John's girl, or ex-girl or whatever the hell she was, wasn't worth the risk. Those guys had always been too good to me in the past. Nothing's worse than living with the fear that the boys are mad at you, which I eventually went through. But more on that fuckin' story later.

You Can't Always Get
What You Want

never prayed Tony Scaduto would die. But I'm not gonna say I didn't go home at night and wish the man would hang up his typewriter, or at least walk away from the gossip pages. In my opinion, there was just no room for an aging reporter like him writing up gossip reports from the world of fashion, movies, television, sports and New York's nightlife. Outside of an occasional item on some union strike or a local political story, Tony would just sit at his desk and field boring phone calls while Linda and Doug toiled away and I was perched to take away his spot.

Tony was a fine reporter and author, but the game had passed him by. Getting him to understand who Suzanne Bartsch was or the significance of getting past the ropes at Soul Kitchen would be like trying to convince your white grandfather of Tupac Shakur's poetry. There was more than a generational *gap* there. It was a generational divide. Just seeing Tony sit at his desk with his ass asleep made me think back to all those journalism professors who bang you over the head about how difficult it is to break in at a major newspaper in a major city. What they never told us is that it has nothing to do with our "inexperience." It has to do with what the system does with guys like Tony Scaduto. These are the guys who go from a newspaper's crime beat to its lifestyle section to its Op-Ed page to writing obits *before* famous people die until they are eventually handed a cushy column like Auto Repair or Gardening or Chess—which nobody reads. Mind you, the guy's salary goes up consistently over the years until he is eventually making way too much dough for him to walk away from the paper no matter where they banish him. So, in essence, a young hardworking reporter like myself has to basically wait until guys like Tony die before we get a shot. Well, one day it almost happened. Tony's heart skipped a bunch of beats and he suffered a major heart attack. When Linda called me, I was so happy, I saved the message on my tape machine for about a year.

"Hi, it's Linda. Listen, I think Tony died or something. So come in tomorrow morning around ten. Bye."

I remember I got that message while I checked my machine at a pay phone on Bleecker Street, right across the street from Zito's Bakery. Up until the day I moved to Hollywood (six years later) and especially when I eventually got my loft in the West Village—I always walked to that pay phone when I had to make an important call in which luck would play a part. I'm insane that way.

The next day I walked in late, still a bit hungover from a night of partying, and Linda said, "Your prayers paid off." She was kidding, but she knew how badly I wanted his spot and she was helpless in the way of having him moved off of her page. It ain't like she hadn't tried in closed-door meetings with Forst. There was even a period when other columnists were complaining that they were not receiving their complimentary copies of hardcover and paperback books, so Linda asked that a hidden camera be installed in the mailroom to find the thief who was stealing from other staffers' mail slots. She even put up a sign she wrote herself stating, THIS ROOM PATROLLED BY A HIDDEN SECURITY CAMERA. It didn't matter. In two days, Tony was nabbed as the culprit and was suspended for a month *with* pay. When Linda heard the ruling, she went ballistic. "Well, then I'm gonna come in tomorrow and steal the refrigerator because I *really* need some time off."

Tony wasn't the only thief the camera nabbed. It also revealed the sad truth of a reporter named Jim Sleeper, who got his kicks stealing people's sandwiches.

"What the fuck do these fuckers have to do to get their asses fired," I lamented to Linda on the way to OTB one day.

She had no answers. She was just as frustrated as I was.

"If they would've fired Tony, he would've dropped dead of a heart attack on the spot," she said.

"Don't think I don't think of shit like that happening to him."

"Be careful what you wish for."

Now that it's all over and done with, I have to say Tony's book scam *was* a bit brilliant. He used to grab all the books that came in—and some columnists would have at least fifteen books a week sent to them for review purposes—and store them away like a squirrel stores nuts. Tony had books under his desk, in his drawers and in file cabinets all over the newsroom. And, little by little, he'd smuggle out several here and there and sell them to the Strand Bookstore. Over at the Strand, the second-hand bookstore, a brand-new $25 book might fetch you $10 or so. So God knows how much money Tony was socking away in addition to the money the paper was paying him to sit next to Linda. Talk about an earn. So don't ever wonder again why old motherfuckers go to whatever section an editor-in-chief banishes them to while young legs like myself can't get through the security gates. Everybody's got a scam too good to give up. Lucky for me, Tony's heart gave out before his scam got out.

Needless to say, Tony's phone rarely rang. But I steadily had *everybody* calling me. Within a week, with me sitting at his desk and using his phone, a big chunk of the city—or at least the night world I was running in—knew where they could reach me. Eventually, *Newsday* editors took Tony's voice off his voice mail and let me lay my voice in. It was an indignity of sorts, I know. But the column was getting sexier and people were beginning to respond to the new guy in town.

I still had trouble getting into certain nightspots. For whatever reason, there are always some assholes who mistake the guest list they're holding in their hands for the combination to the safe that contains their inheritance. And on occasion I dragged along Chico—who, by now, had grown accustomed to some of the perks his best buddy was getting treated to. One night, at SoHo's Merc Bar, I was stopped at the ropes and told the party inside was "private." Now, I had to be a little careful not to rile too many feathers until my position at the paper was a little more solid. But I was dying to get in. Word was, they had a black waitress who was so fine that even the reclusive Robert De Niro was making repeated trips to chat her up. But Chico wasn't having any of the bouncer's bullshit.

"Private party, huh," Chico said, wearing a big cross around his neck and a Muslim cap on his head. Chico was about 260 pounds at the time. "Okay, pal. Pick a window."

"What," the bouncer said.

"Pick a window. I'm gonna throw you through one of 'em so I want you to pick the one you wanna fly through. It's only right."

We got in that night. That particular bouncer, Jeff Gossett was his name, saw it our way.

Chico wasn't the only one looking for a new identity back then. I was doing the same thing. I figured I needed to distinguish myself and I went searching for new looks that would have people remember me. It's very difficult to stand out in the ever-changing world of New York's nightlife without looking distinguishingly different than the other people in my field. So, I took a look around and figured Richard Johnson had the suit and tie look down just fine. The *Village Voice*'s irreverent Michael Musto had the freak factor down pat. A balding head and a tagalong wife meant no mistaking *New York* magazine's Frank DiGiacomo. My partner Doug Vaughan liked crumpled cotton shirts and sport jackets and the accompaniment of a Jewish publicist in basic black. And the flamboyantly gay George Wayne stood out everywhere he went, unashamedly air-kissing and ass-pinching the rich and famous. That about summed up the boys in the band back then. Sure, there were a few guys who were contributing to the various pages around the city, but none possessed the same amount of clout as the aforementioned. Anyhow, the rest of the lot—Liz, Cindy, Linda, Suzy, the *Post*'s Beth Landman and assorted other women—were seen here and there. But it seemed to me, there was a path waiting to be blazed by a regular guy. It seemed to me—and tell me if I'm wrong—the group lacked a stand-up guy, a street guy, a regular Joe, someone who might keep a few of your secrets rather than blab every goddamn thing he heard around town. I decided that guy would be me, and the best reason I can give is it simply wasn't going to be a stretch. But I still needed to look different in order to stand out. Remembering a name is one thing. Not forgetting a face is another.

So I grew my hair and—cringe, cringe—went the way of a ponytail. I added a goatee. I stuck a second silver hoop in my right earlobe, like I wore sixteen years earlier, to accompany the one Mickey gave me in my left. I became obsessed with silver. So I bought one silver bracelet for my left wrist and one for my right, and then every few months—for whatever occasion—someone (usually a girl I was dating) would buy me another one. Soon, I was walking around with enough silver to open up a small shop in Mexico and keep tourists happy for a year. I wore nine bracelets, six rings, three Indonesian beaded chains and two hoops. I stepped in wooden clogs. In retrospect, I looked ridiculous—and don't think Linda didn't say so. But people remembered me.

So, the new me made the rounds every night like I had been doing for Linda on a sporadic basis. But now the invitations started to trickle in, the doormen opened the velvet ropes with a wink, club owners sent over a beer or two upon seeing me, publicists slipped me their cards, starlets slid on over.

In no time at all, the six weeks Tony needed to recuperate were up, and a crestfallen Linda had to tell me I was going to have to go back to gigging for her on Fridays only. But by then, Forst had given me my own phone line at New York *Newsday*, so I always felt like I had a life there no matter if technically I was only there one day a week. But then some magical shit started to happen and it's exactly the kind of fateful thing I've come to rely on in my life time and again.

Tony had another heart scare. Not an attack, but enough of a scare that doctors asked him to stay home for another extended stay. I don't know if getting nabbed robbing paperbacks fucked up his ticker for good or what, but all I know is I got the call to come up to the majors again. And, once again, I hit the town with a vengeance. Now it all seems like no time at all, but in retrospect, I had to log a lot of miles for the city to start to feel like my own. I began to establish a routine. I'd work for Linda from ten A.M. until six P.M. before I headed downtown for a quick dinner—usually in SoHo or the Village—and then off I went into the night, walking into club after club, chatting up everyone from beautiful people to the people the beautiful people didn't deem so beautiful. But I didn't give a shit, because I wasn't so many months removed from remembering what it felt like to feel unincluded.

Linda loved having young legs on the staff. She also loved having someone around who wasn't jaded or bored of the scene and was willing to go anywhere and ask any question to get any story. I remember spending an hour each morning opening Linda and Doug's mountain of mail and reciting to them the dozens of parties and events they were invited to. There were galas, art shows, swishy exhibits, concerts, Broadway debuts, giant film premieres, club openings, celebrity birthday parties, runway shows. You name it. If it was going on in the city, Linda and Doug were invited. And, to be blunt, they couldn't be bothered.

"Hey, Lin," I'd say, "Keith Hernandez is having a birthday party at 21. You want me to RSVP for you?"

"Hmmmm . . . I'm having an unnecessary root canal that night. Regrets."

"Hey, Doug, your invitation to Madonna's *SEX* party is here. You going?"

"No, thanks. How old is the out-of-Material Girl claiming to be this year?"

Meanwhile, I'd sit there almost cumming over the possibilities.

"You guys mind if I go?"

"If you *want*," they'd say, as if I were asking to wash their toilets.

They had grown to abhor the scene, which made me kind of wonder how they could've written about it so humorously and covered it so brilliantly without leaving their apartments at night. "It's all the same shit," Linda would say. "After a while, you'll hate it, too. Besides, that's why we have you here."

I couldn't imagine what they were talking about. What could be wrong with banging back a few beers with my World Series hero Keith Hernandez, or having a chance to actually speak to Madonna?

But burnout happens. More on that fuckin' story later.

The day came when Tony returned, but I found myself covering for Doug when he went on a three-week vacation to Thailand and, again, for Linda when she took two two-week vacations one week apart. Before I knew it, I had been helping out over at 2 Park Avenue for about a year. The column was snappier, Linda was freed up, Doug felt a bit more liberated and Tony, well, Tony was the same. Meanwhile, I was about to get my first big shot at impressing the bosses.

You can't ask for a full-time job every day. That gets boring real fast. And, on top of everything, you sort of feel like a pussy. A man wants

to walk around and feel like his work will speak for itself and the pro-
motions will come as they should. But the sad truth is, that's not the
way the world works. It isn't so much *who* you know over *what* you
know, it's more *how much* you can scream in that person's ear until they
throw their hands up and give you a shot. And that's what happened
with me and Forst's assistant editor and right-hand man, Richie Esposito.

Richie had the privilege of sitting in Forst's almighty office and tossing
the shit with him every day. There they sat, a couple of guys in power
suspenders, figuring what reporter to throw on what story, what columnist to lay on what scandal, what the front page—or "the wood"—
would look like or, most important, what to drink at Elaine's after all
the decisions were through. They'd sit there and toss a Nerf football
back and forth while they were steadily keeping New York *Newsday* a
powerful force alongside the *News* and the *Post*. It didn't matter that the
paper's dwindling circulation was draining its parent company, Long
Island *Newsday*, every day. What mattered—and what was really true at
the time—was that Richie and Forst presided over the best beat reporters
and columnists the city had. No shit.

Back in the day, I used to make sure I'd pass the almighty office on
my coffee runs and whatnot, just to keep myself visible. I didn't care if
I was wearing ripped jeans, sleeveless vests with no T-shirt underneath
and, again, all the jingling silver. I was desperate for Richie—who was
only a few years older than me, but held a big byline for years as a crime
reporter—to see me and chat me up. Maybe tell the old man I was okay.
Give him the big wink and thumb's-up or whatever it is superiors do
when they want to help along a deserving underling.

One day, Richie spots me and asks me to fetch him a coffee at Phillips,
a joint that preceded Starbucks and didn't fuckin' charge $3.50 for a
latte. I did my homework on Richie and found out he grew up in East
Harlem and was one of those guys who could've gone either way. In
other words, go legit at the right time, or stay on the corner of 114th
and Pleasant Avenue with his pals and eventually fall into a life of crime.
Richie, like myself, chose to go legit. That was my in. I figured I'd
eventually bring up my family's mafia history from way back on my
mother's side. But Richie surprisingly beat me to it.

"My friend John Miller says he used to see you at the John Gotti trial
every day. He says you were with *the boys* every day. How come?"

"I was supporting a friend," I said.

"Who's your friend?"

"John."

"*John's* your friend?"

"Yeah. My cousin works for him. So I would go and have lunch with him during the breaks, shit like that."

"You know him like *that*?"

"Yeah," I said.

"Come on. The coffee's on me. Let's take a walk."

I knew I was blowing Richie's mind, crime buff that he was and still is. But I wasn't lying. I had made friends with John back in 1990 and did sit in the courtroom at 100 Centre Street for many, many days until his lawyers Bruce Cutler and Gerald Shargel helped him beat the rap. As far as John was concerned, the shit about that Colorado stockbroker was forgotten. The fact that I came almost every day and showed him my support was of paramount importance to a man like him. In time I was often asked to accompany him, his associates and his legal team to lunches at Giambone, a legendary Italian joint on the Chinese side of Mulberry Street. It wasn't too long before this time that working half-sheets for him helped me support my mother after my father died. My appearance in the courtroom showed him I hadn't forgotten. And besides, do I have to tell you how cool it was having a friend as powerful as John Gotti? In the moments before the trial would begin, the elevator doors would *swoosh* open and John would walk out, flanked by Cutler and Shargel, and take his power walk through the double doors. His Brioni suits (always Brioni) were impeccably creased. His silk ties all hand-painted. His coif, almost lavender, didn't have a hair out of place. And, as if to punctuate the old school of gangsters he learned from, John smelled of Old Spice. More than once, court buffs who would line the halls of the court building would walk up to him for a handshake or words of encouragement. Black, white, Hispanic, man, woman—it didn't matter. Everyone, it seemed, wanted John to beat the rap. Even a disheveled drunken guy, leaning outside the courthouse steps, knew what he was witnessing—through his bagged vodka haze—as John stepped from his chauffeured Mercedes.

"John motherfuckin' Gotti. The man is bigger than President Bush."

With that, John peeled off a fifty and told the guy to get something to eat.

It was a fuckin' movie, all right. And with John winking at me, during breaks in some of the trial's more tense moments, I felt like a costar in the city's most gripping drama.

"Now, when you say you know him through your family, how do you mean?" Richie asked me.

"Richie, I'm not gonna give you names, all right? But John set up my cousin in an asphalt business and that cousin is on my mother's side. My mother's side, the Neapolitan side, was on the right side."

Richie understood. And slowly I told him the story of my grandmother Josephine Mastroianni—a distant cousin to Marcello Mastroianni—who had the miserable luck to land on Ellis Island with family orders to marry Nicholas Maione. Nicholas, the man to whom she bore her first five children, was a nice enough man, but I'd be lying if I said he was a looker. The only photographs I saw of him had him resembling the demon child of Will Rogers and Norman Rockwell. Well, legend has it Grandma took one look at him and protested. But just then, Nicholas's brother stepped in and changed everything with one sentence. He told Grandma if she didn't marry his brother and went back to Naples, he'd send word that she was a big *putana* in America. On top of the disgrace that would've been back in the old country, Nicholas's brother was Happy Maione—a gangster who would eventually become a terribly feared hitman for Meyer Lansky and Murder Inc. Good old Uncle Happy eventually got the electric chair for all those hits and— thank God—Grandma eventually had two children with another man after Nick fell off a building and spent the last few years of his life bedridden with Alzheimer's disease. Meanwhile, Grandma fell in love with a man named Manino—a tall, dark handyman who lived in the basement and helped with things like the rent and, you know, other things, while Nick was dying in bed. Anyhow, this is completely off the subject, but Manino was my mother's real father. That makes my mother a bastard. And that makes me a son of a *bastard*. I only say this to help correct all of you who've incorrectly described me as a son of a *bitch* over the years.

Anyhow, the point I was trying to make was that Richie was hooked, and with a little luck, maybe he'd hook me in to see Forst one day in the future.

A few weeks later, I had the good fortune of being present in the office when the story of Woody Allen falling in love with Soon-Yi Previn broke across the country. The newsroom was in a swirl. And though in the years to come I would be the bull's-eye in the middle of other media storms, I sat on the periphery of this one wishing I could do more. It's moments like these when reporters and newspapers are made, but Woody was not in the world I ran in. So my contacts were essentially useless, which meant I probably wouldn't be called upon to drum up any breaking news angles or sidebar stories. And that sucked because everyone wants their byline attached to a crazy story like that. And then Forst stepped out of his office and made his way toward me with that sleepy walk of his. I really think he hated coming near me because Linda and I were always laughing. And I think the guy would rather he be the guy laughing with Linda. It's always like that with me. Old men are always after the women I love. But more on that fuckin' story later.

"Hey, Benza, go rent a car and see if you can track down André Previn at his mansion up in Bedford, New York."

"When? Now?"

"No. After the *Post* and the *News* get there. Of course, *now*. And take your earrings out. This is a nice, rich town. I don't want you scaring anyone."

Previn is Mia Farrow's ex-husband and the adoptive father of Soon-Yi. Well, two problems. I had no credit card and I had no idea where Bedford was. The first problem was solved when an enterprising ex-girlfriend of mine met me at an Avis Rent-a-Car and put the car on the Amex card belonging to the sugar daddy who was keeping her. The second problem was solved when I got on my cellphone and had various friends who were familiar with the area guide me there as I drove. Bedford was and is a Twin Peaks–type town. It's an eerie place to drive into near nightfall. Hell, all places where the rich live are scary at night. Anyhow, I finally found the mansion but was met with disappointment when a huge wrought-iron security gate closed off the driveway to anyone and a posted sign advertised vicious attack dogs on the property. I don't know what the hell I was expecting. Previn is a millionaire. And millionaires tend to have gates at the ends of their driveways and guard dogs on hand. After a two-hour drive—not to mention facing Forst when I got back—turning the car around was not an option.

I pulled the car up to the gate and buzzed a few times, looking into the tiny surveillance camera. After a few seconds, some stuffy English majordomo barked into the speaker, "May I help you?"

"Listen, I'm a reporter from New York *Newsday*. My name is A.J. Benza. I believe Mr. Previn is expecting me. Can you buzz me past the gates?"

"I'm afraid I cannot, sir. Mr. Previn and the family are on holiday."

"Everybody is on holiday?"

"Yes, sir, that is correct."

"Mr. Previn had the foresight to go on holiday the morning of the day this story broke, huh?"

"Apparently so, sir. Good day."

"Wait," I said. "Can you comment on where they went on holiday?"

"No, sir. Now good day, sir."

"One more question. They all went on holiday? No one's home? Just you?"

"That is correct, sir."

"Even the guard dogs have gone on holiday?"

"What guard dogs?"

That was all I needed to hear. I popped the car in park, scaled the ten-foot fence and walked up the long, lonely driveway. And I began pounding on the door. After a minute or so, the majordomo popped open a hole in the door and spoke to me like we were in a bad Monty Python skit.

"Sir, please. You must get off the property. I'll be forced to call the police."

"Where'd the family go," I said. "Just tell me where they went and I'm outta here, pal. It's gonna be all over the papers tomorrow anyhow. Just save me the trouble and I'll do you a favor and leave."

"Sir . . . I will call the police. You are trespassing."

"Just tell me *where the fuck they went!* Don't think I won't stay here all night."

"Sir, I don't know."

"See, now you're lying to me. You *know*. If anybody knows, *you*

know. Listen, I hate that fuckin' Woody Allen for what he did. I'm with
André on this one. He must want to break the guy's skull and I can't
blame him. I'm having a hard time staying objective on this one, pal,
I'll tell you that. Now, come on, where'd they go?"

"They're in Europe," he said.

"Can you be any more vague?"

"England."

Bingo. I got my story. In the short time I was working as a reporter,
I had a suspicion none of the other lifers from the other papers would've
scaled that fence and gotten the butler to open the door and, essentially,
add another meaningful dimension to the unfolding drama. You might
be thinking the butler volunteering the Previns' location was no big
deal. But it was. You see, when New York City's four major dailies
began their coverage the next morning, and everyone in the city was
glued to the story, New York *Newsday*'s story—*my* story—went a bit
further than anyone else's story. And that extra inch of copy is worth a
day's head start for an editor looking to keep his paper ahead of the pack.

And for the record, I never took my earrings out.

Richie and Forst were happy, though you'd never really know it by
the looks on their faces. Editors generally allow themselves a few minutes
of happiness each day before they sink back into the grueling ritual of
filling the paper again and again and again. It really is a shitty job. Editors
age quicker than presidents do, but at least the commander in chief can
close his door and order up a blow job once in a while.

The next day came a mandate from Forst that I was to rent a car again
and drive to Drew University and find Soon-Yi in one of the college's
all-female dorm rooms and hit her up for a few questions. If I was to
find her, no one really expected her to say anything. Just finding her
was the goal. I figured what could be so hard? How many Asian girls
could be attending a college in Jersey?

Well, Jesus Christ, I don't know what rock I'd been living under, but
apparently most major college campuses are now populated by scores of
Asian-Americans and upon setting foot on Drew's spacious campus, my
pal Chico and I didn't know where to look first.

"Did we just walk onto the set of *Godzilla vs. Rhodan*?" Chico said.

We grabbed a black kid on a skateboard and offered him $10 to tell us where Soon-Yi dormed. "She the Chinese girl who's fucking Woody Allen, right? You the press?"

"Yes."

"You don't look like no press."

"We are."

"I heard about it. I didn't know she was here until yesterday. I don't know where she's at, but I can show you where a lot of Chinese girls live. Maybe she's there."

It was worth the shot. Where else were we gonna go? The little brother pocketed the $10 bill and skated away, leaving us at the back door of your typical American college dorm room. Once inside, Chico and I moved through the all-girl dorm with the precision of the Green Bay Packers defensive line. We just stormed the fuckin' place, knocking on closed doors, pushing in doors that were ajar, breezing into study rooms, interrupting meetings held in the lobby.

"Campus security," we'd say. We had it all planned. "As you're well aware, the press has been combing the campus for a glimpse of one of our students, Ms. Soon-Yi Previn, because of the allegations that she is having an affair with a Hollywood star. There are things we all need to know in terms of your student rights, Ms. Previn's privacy and the possibility of imposters posing as the press and, hence, posing a danger to Ms. Previn's security. Are there any questions and where can we find Ms. Previn to offer her advice in terms of her security?"

Not one hand would ever go up. Most of the time, they'd bury their faces in their books while we lied like lunatics. And, of course, no one ever offered us any help in finding the scrutinized teen. I don't quite remember how the story I filed that night read the following day, but I gather Forst was happy with my technique. It ain't like he called me in his office and told me. He just stepped out of his room the next afternoon and called my name.

"Benza!"

I turned and saw the Nerf football spiraling my way and caught it, careful not to spill Linda's latte. I tossed it back at him, hitting the diminutive editor right between the suspenders. There was no need for a thank-you. I got the message. As it turned out, that was the last thing Forst and I would ever share. Eventually I would set sail for the *Daily*

News—with Linda leading the way—as we left Forst behind in the sinking ship that New York *Newsday* would sadly become. I didn't know it at the time, but when I got right down to it, Forst's balls were no bigger than the editors I was working with on Long Island. When all the dust cleared—and I'll get to that soon enough—Linda had the biggest balls of anyone I worked for.

Play with Fire

It was sometime in the fall of 1993 that Linda was getting awfully upset and I was getting awfully antsy about the prospects of ever attaining a full-time job at New York *Newsday*. I remember following Richie into the men's room one afternoon and carefully timing my conversation so that he was standing there holding his dick with his back to me. By this time even Richie had taken to wearing suspenders just like his buddy Forst. From Pleasant Avenue to suspenders. It was depressing as all hell to me, really.

"Richie, what do I have to do to get a full-time gig around here?"

"I don't know. Let me talk to Don again and see . . ."

This time I cut him off just about the time he cut his piss short to avoid the uncomfortable conversation. "Come on, Richie, no more shit. It's just us—a couple of street guys—what the fuck is going on?"

Richie confided in me that that ridiculous sexual harassment incident back in Melville, Long Island, was hurting my chances of getting the nod in New York City. "The bosses in Long Island bring that up all the time, every time Don brings up the prospect of hiring you for Linda's page. It's hurting you."

"That girl was full of shit. Linda knows I don't mistreat women. That girl didn't like that she wasn't included in our clique. How badly is it hurting me?"

"I don't think you'll ever shake it. I think it will stop them from hiring you for as long as you're here. Scaduto could die and they wouldn't hire you. Listen, I can't really say now . . . but there is interesting shit brewing. As soon as I know, I'll let you know."

Richie washed his hands and I walked back to the cubicle I was still sharing with Scaduto.

Going to a Go-Go

It was Christmastime 1993, but the tone around the newsroom was anything but joyful. On top of the oft-reported rumors that *Newsday*'s hierarchy was seriously contemplating pulling the plug on its draining city offshoot, there were now rumors that a couple of multimillionaires were thinking of buying the New York *Daily News*. The famous tabloid had sunk to new depths ever since its last publisher, Robert Maxwell, tossed his fat ass off a yacht several months earlier and died. And now every gossip columnist in town included the reports that the brash Canadian businessman Conrad Black and New York's mysterious real estate developer-turned-publisher Mort Zuckerman were the men with the serious dough to do it. It seemed like sad news either way. No one wanted a Canadian owning the *News* and even fewer believed Zuckerman—a real estate giant who got a hard-on whenever he saw his name in print—could handle the job with the necessary class, panache and know-how. Well, for reasons that are too complicated to explain—but would, nonetheless, change my life forever—old Mort won the battle. He began to show his might right away with some high-profile hirings the likes of which George Steinbrenner was undoubtedly proud. Mort was slowly putting together an army to compete with Rupert Murdoch's *Post* and the fast-fading New York *Newsday*. I never imagined I'd be one of his soldiers. I had no reason to believe I'd be one of his soldiers. The guy didn't even know I was alive, I'm sure. But he wanted Linda—most high-profile men did back then. And like I said, Linda had taken me under her almighty wings.

Mort raided New York *Newsday* first. He lured Forst's top guy, Richie Esposito, out from 2 Park Avenue with a solid six-figure deal, signing bonus and a golden parachute should it all go bad one day. It was the kind of deal you read about and get sick over. In short, Richie was set. Mort then basically had Richie chip away at getting Linda—and her Inside New York column—to go on over to the famous *News* building on East 42nd Street. Forst didn't like working without Espo, his top dog. But newspapers don't usually treat you to lessons in loyalty. The friendships you make at a paper usually prosper from the glue of making news every day, of trudging off to a story together, of sharing contacts, giving out leads, etc. In general, being the voices of your great city. Hey, we make your subway ride easier and that's all we ever hope for.

Richie spent several weeks playing Cyrano de Bergerac for Mort, as the mogul made a run at the city's top female columnist. I didn't pay much attention to it—basically because of Linda's loyalty and love for working under Forst—until Linda took me over to OTB and spoke to me over the anxiety of hoping another one of the tips from her friends would pay off.

"So listen, I had dinner at Mort's house last night," she said, putting in a 2-7-3 exacta in the seventh at Belmont.

"Don't tell me you're fuckin' that old man."

"Please! He *really* wants to bring the column over to the *News*. He just thinks it's great."

"Well, what are you gonna do?"

"I don't know. Don doesn't know yet, but he will. No one keeps their mouths shut in this city. Especially the moguls. Anyhow, I told him if I come, I want to bring my boys—you and Doug."

I remember I was afraid to swallow, afraid I'd miss a word of the speech that was to change my life.

"What did he say?"

"He said, 'fine.' He's offering me a lot of money. A *lot*."

"Well, what are you gonna do?"

"I really don't know yet. But if I go, do you want to come?"

"Fuck yeah!"

"Okay, sit tight. I'll figure it out, bounce it off some people and I'll let you know."

"What about Zuckerman? Is this guy cool? Does he *get* it?"

"I don't know. He's a rich guy. They're all insane."

Three weeks went by and Linda, I remember, was in a very delicate state. Not that things were easy on me. I was belly-itching broke, mind you, and had taken up with Karen, the chick I dropped to be with Mary. I knew full well, if Linda took up Zuckerman on his offer, I'd have to drop Karen all over again: No way you can stay with one girl while trying to make your bones as the newest gossip columnist in town. There are way too many pretty publicists to date.

Then one day Linda left me a message to phone her at two P.M. I did the bad fifty-mile drive to Manhattan, got me a loaf of bread at Zito's Bakery and some Genoa salami, provolone and roasted peppers across the street at Faicco's and made my call at my lucky phone booth on Bleecker Street. The first two times I called, I only reached Linda's machine. So I leaned against the booth and tried to get my sandwich down and waited. A half hour later I got her.

"What's up?"

"Well, I'm gonna take him up on his offer. Your life is about to get very good."

Needless to say, that was the best sandwich I ever had.

"Call Richie and thank him. He was a big part of it. I got you $60,000 a year. Is that all right?"

Let me put it this way: I was down to the last $13 in my life. One year at 60K, not to mention a set of keys to New York City, was like hitting Lotto on a buck you borrowed from your worst enemy.

Mother's Little Helper

As much as I owed it all to Linda, there was a big part of me that felt my deceased mother had a lot to do with my sudden career swing. I cannot count how many days I would sit there brooding at the dining room table—bitching at my need to be creative and my desire to be known—and telling my mom of my wish to walk away from *Newsday*'s sports section and just find something else to do. Anything. Anything where the politics weren't so ridiculous and the people above you looked you in the eye and told you exactly where you stood.

"Creativity is a curse" was my big statement in those days. "Why couldn't I want to sell insurance or be a mechanic?"

My mother would put the water up, cover the pot and sit down next to me. "I don't want you to walk away from that job. You're gonna make it. Something is gonna come of it. I can feel it. A mother knows."

I'm not saying every chat with old mom was an epiphany or anything, but each one would at least make me proud to be doing something that she believed would lead to a bright future.

"I'm gonna tell you something you can never understand until you have your own child. A woman loves to have a daughter. But when she has a son, she never thinks that boy will do nothing less than change the world in his own way."

That's the kind of heavy shit my mother would lay on me. But then there were more important matters to tend to. "Okay, now do you feel like pesto or a little marinara sauce?"

She never did get to read one measly gossip report or see me on television or in the movies. But each step up the ladder was fortified with the intuition she spoke out loud with me at the dining room table.

All right. Enough with the mushy shit. On with the show.

Dance, Little Sister

Word got around the newsroom fairly quickly that Linda was leaving and she was taking her "boys" with her. I want to say morale at the paper was at an all-time low, but that would be a lie. Of course, there were staffers there who didn't want to see us or the column go, but then there were other staffers who couldn't give a shit for Linda and the boys who didn't write "serious journalism." Those were the staffers who secretly harbored dreams of getting the big, life-changing phone call from old Mort. It's like that whenever a rich guy is on a buying spree in New York City. No one wants to admit it, but they all sit by the phone and wait for the call.

From where I sat, I was a pretty good judge of who was genuinely happy for Linda and who wanted her to die before she filed her first story. And I was never bashful to tell her what I spotted from my vantage point. I think that's one of the reasons why she kept me around. I always had her back.

Tony Scaduto got so mushy when our last day rolled around that it made me feel bad about the way I used to wish strokes and heart scares on him. I hate when people do that to me. "Linda, I want to thank you for making work here so wonderful. You were great to me. I had a ball," Tony said. "And A.J., I see great things ahead for you. You're a real go-getter."

Oh, Jesus.

But the old good-bye party wasn't complete until Don Forst walked out from his office with about five minutes to go before we filed our last column. Staffers parted as soon as the diminutive editor waltzed over and stopped somewhere in the middle of the throng, snapped his suspenders and spoke directly to Linda. "This is the last time I'm gonna ask you—you coming in tomorrow?"

"No," Linda said.

"You calling in sick?"

"No," she laughed. "I'm calling in rich."

Then Forst walked over and shared a good long hug with her while Linda cried and laughed on his shoulder. It was a big deal, her leaving, I'm telling you.

Linda splitting meant more than just a half-page makeover for the paper. It meant New York *Newsday* lost its funny bone. It lost the only page a reader could turn to for a respite from the all-too-often shitty news that life in the big city brings to your eyes. And that's death. Just like *60 Minutes* needed Andy Rooney's inane but thought-provoking reports, a newspaper needs a page or so to let its readers laugh out loud rather than sucking their teeth over the latest tragedy.

So we left. We all took a few days to let it sink in and at the end of the following week I met Linda and Doug for lunch to talk over strategy. It was essentially going to be the same game plan. Linda was going to rely on me for my nightly leg work, and depend on Doug to supply his dry and witty commentary while she oversaw the whole shebang and gave every report her own special flair. But a funny thing happened on the way to the *News*. As Doug and I sat in some giant *News* office, being handed piles of insurance papers and contracts while everyone from Human Resources tried to make us feel at home, Doug looked at me and said, "I can't do this anymore."

"What do you mean," I said. "Tell them you want to do it tomorrow."

"No. I mean gossip. I'm done. I just don't want to do it anymore. I gotta call Linda tonight."

I want to say I was upset, but I don't lie. Doug's abrupt departure meant I was Linda's number-one guy. I don't care if it was by default. You think Lou Gehrig ever cared about Wally Pipp's headache? I just kept my mouth shut until Linda called me.

"Fuck him," she said when she phoned me. "It could've been great for him, but he wants to change careers. I'll tell you something right now, everyone who I've ever hired has gone on to big jobs making crazy money."

"I know," I said.

"Your life is about to get very good," she said.

"You already told me that."

"I mean *really* good."

"I know." I was scared, but I was more than ready.

I'm Free

Linda went off on a two-week vacation before we started the *News* gig. But she asked that I report there right away, make loads of phone calls, get my contacts ready and just let the city know what was going down. And that's what I did. I just banged out calls from my cubicle for six hours a day. From where I sat, I could see into the huge windowed office where Richard Johnson filed his *News* column every day and I remembered thinking he looked more like a banker than a journalist as he took turns speaking on his phone and typing away at his keys. And every day it was the same thing. The guy arrived at work around eleven and split around five or so. It seemed pretty boring in contrast to the loud, brash, laugh-a-minute world I'd just come from.

Either way, Johnson had recently left the *Post* for the *News*—pre-Zuckerman—for some big-ticket money from Maxwell. But word on the street, not to mention the newsroom, was that Mort wasn't happy with his column. And I don't know why. Say what you want about his work, Johnson always had a style. What you got when you signed Johnson was that he was going to attack everyone equally. He was an equal opportunity destroyer. You could've asked him to hold your newborn child on a Monday, but should you be in the middle of a scandal on Wednesday, Johnson was going to place your baby down and print the scandal. Sorry. It's that against-all-flags spirit—a social pirate, if you will—that made Johnson and continues to make Johnson one of the best. It just doesn't matter what benevolence you've accumulated over the last thirty days of your life, one phone call from Johnson and you'd get chills up your back trying to envision how he was preparing to turn your life upside down. I swear, I've been on both sides of his phone calls. Mother Teresa could have just patted down 100 kids with leprosy, but a message from Johnson would have had her combing her mind for the lone skeleton in her closet. And, believe me, she had some. We all do.

Anyhow, at the beginning, the *News* folks thought they'd have me and Linda working out of a cubicle in the back of the far-reaching *News* room. When I mentioned this to Linda—vacationing at home—she told me to walk into the afternoon meeting and tell them she'd quit without an office that would accommodate the both of us.

That's the way she is.

So, good soldier that I am, I did just what she said. I interrupted the meeting that the newly hired editors—Lou Colasuonno, Rich Gooding and Jim Lynch—were holding and I told them of Linda's demand.

"What do you mean, she'll quit?" Gooding asked.

"That's what the lady said."

"Is she serious?" Lynch asked nervously.

"Oh yeah."

"You know her. We don't know her," said Colasuonno. "What can we do?"

"You better get her an office."

Just from that one standoff I got the distinct feeling that that triumvirate—freshly raided from the *Post*—would be overpowered when it would come time to match wits and smarts and integrity with Linda. Three guys, with six balls between them, scrambling like little boys to keep the gossip columnist and her cub assistant happy. Something was very wrong here.

Before the trio could even secure the office, word came down that Johnson's days were severely numbered. For some reason or another, Mort wanted Johnson gone *yesterday*, but I got the feeling that Johnson wanted out sooner than that. It's always that way when you're working for an unappreciative rich guy. Undoubtedly, Johnson had printed something in his column that upset one of Mort's high-falutin' socialite friends, who never thought they'd be treated to such truths in the *News* once their wealthy and influential pal bought the paper for millions. I'm imagining what happened was, one of Johnson's items almost had one of Mort's pals falling off his polo pony in shock and a few irate phone calls to the publisher put Johnson on the chopping block. And that sucks. And that's the kind of guarantee Linda demanded from Mort before she signed her contract.

She told him, "No sacred cows. I know you have a lot of influential friends, but if the head of some company is an asshole, we're gonna say he's an asshole."

For Linda, Mort agreed. Apparently Johnson didn't have the deal ironed out.

With that news came the promise from the triumvirate that if Linda just held on, Johnson's large windowed office would be ours in no time flat. So, Linda played ball. And, as it turned out, I ended up in Johnson's office—in his chair as a matter of fact—just like I told him less than a year before that. I didn't bother reminding him, though. Johnson had already sealed a deal to edit Page Six. No sense making him an enemy any more than he was already going to be.

I remember watching Johnson walk out of the newsroom on his last day and thinking—no, *knowing*—I was going to take that same exact walk one day. Just then the *News* copublisher Fred Drasner and top honcho Eddie Fay said their good-byes to him and watched the elevator door close and send Johnson down.

"And that's that," Drasner said, clapping his hands. Fay was laughing and smacking Drasner's back. The two turned and practically bumped into me.

"Oh, Fred, this here's Benza. He's working with Stasi," Fay said. "A.J., say hello to Fred Drasner."

Before our handshake was through, Drasner gave me a once-over—carefully eyeing my ponytail, my earrings, my large flowing linen shirt and my wooden clogs—and barked, "This guy looks like half a fag." Then he turned to the elevator. "I'm gonna get coffee. Benza, you want coffee? How do fags like their coffee?"

I looked at Fay, who was laughing hysterically.

"This is the publisher?"

"Yeah. He's quite a guy," Fay said.

"You know, if somebody said that at *Newsday*, we'd be in harassment meetings for a fuckin' year?"

"That's why you're going to like working here. And, by the way, it could've been worse."

"How's that?" I asked.

"You don't look like a half a fag. You look like a *complete* fag."

Not a great start to a lasting friendship for most guys I know, but for me it played like music. I liked Fred's authenticity and Eddie's honesty. Fuck all the PC bullshit. Those guys were real. And they stayed real until Fred went bad on me three years later. Another rich guy turned phony. More than a year ago, Richard Johnson reported in Page Six that Drasner recently purchased a couple of ostriches for his big backyard in upstate New York. That story came on the heels of Drasner—an avid hunter—plugging a few dozen ducks with pellets while they were sweetly waddling in a pond. All of this brings up the interesting question: Does big money make you an asshole? Or do only assholes make big money?

Respectable

After several long and boring meetings, Linda and I settled on calling the column "Hot Copy." This came after several attempts from the triumvirate to call the column "Hot and Sassy" or "Apple Bites" or "Gotham City" as well as other equally corny names. After Linda threatened to quit a few more times, the trio decided on "Hot Copy" and away we went.

In true Stasi style, for our very first column Linda had everybody who "hated" her make comments in the column and then printed their sentiments word for word. And that's the way it began—the city's biggest names, the movers and shakers in the toughest city in the world, telling Linda to go to hell. It was brilliant and it set the stage for a brilliant run for a column that titillated, tantalized and taunted its readers every day. We never played it safe, and thanks to a trio of editors who were genuinely scared of upsetting Mort's newest big-money hire, almost everything Linda and I printed got into the paper.

More than once—hell, more than 100 times—word got back to us that some of Mort's pals were upset about the copy in a column that painted them as the phonies they were. But, to his credit, Mort held back from scolding Linda and the caravan moved on.

Back in those days, there was definitely a jealousy directed toward

our windowed office and it wasn't unusual to feel other reporters' eye-
balls boring holes in the back of my head as I leaned over my computer
to make a deadline. Some of these guys were seasoned reporters, or lifers
at the *News* while others were fresh from journalism school and carried
lofty bylines and burgeoning promise. Few of them enjoyed seeing me
hunt-and-peck my way to fabled glory at the *News*. Like I said earlier,
who the fuck was I?

There was one incident that got everybody's attention, though, and
obviously gassed my reputation as a kid who didn't take any shit and
was most definitely around to stay. I had written a column item about
a local lawyer who was very upset about the shooting schedule that the
makers of *Carlito's Way* were keeping on his Manhattan street. For days
on end, this lawyer would terrorize the production team by screaming
from his window during shooting, slapping terrorizing signs all over the
neighborhood and threatening to sue the movie studio for disrupting his
way of life and costing the local merchants a load of money they couldn't
make since the neighborhood's local traffic had to be redirected. I wrote
a solid piece, ending with the injustice that cops were called in and
eventually arrested this local lawyer for disrupting the shooting and hauling his ass to Bellevue for observation. It was fresh from being released
from Bellevue that the lawyer contacted me and I went to work on his
story. One day after the story ran, I got a call from "Victor," the *Daily
News*'s loveable Puerto Rican security guard, that the lawyer was here
to see me.

With all the crazies in New York City, you'd think there'd be a better
system for stopping a possible lunatic from meeting you at your office
and killing you while you walked out for a bad cup of joe at Au Bon
Pain. But there wasn't at the *News*. This was like *Talk Radio* come to life.

"Send him in, Victor," I said, figuring the guy wanted to thank me
for the piece.

A minute later the guy walks in and I usher him into the empty office.
Linda was off in a meeting somewhere—probably threatening to quit
again. From the moment I saw him and gave him the once-over, I knew
I was in for trouble. Despite the tugging story he gave me over the
phone, it was obvious that the guy was one of the city's loons. The kind
who think sidewalk pretzels are really a vehicle for the U.S. government
to spread deadly viruses and control the population. You've seen these

guys talking into their hot dogs, making very important phone calls to the Pentagon. On top of that, the guy was wearing rock-hard sneakers and was barely balancing the worst toupee in the history of the world on his head. It looked like that damn toupee William Shatner and Tony Bennett share, only darker.

"What can I do for you, pal?"

"Well, it's your piece."

"Came to thank me, did ya?"

"No. I came for a retraction. You painted me out to be a crazy man sent to a mental hospital." He kept scratching away at his temple like he was trying to pull out a tick.

"But you *were* sent to Bellevue," I said.

"True. Very true. But I went there willingly just to prove to the cops I wasn't crazy. See? See my point?"

I could see I was talking to the wall. Stucco had more sense than this guy.

"Listen, you're just an assistant," he said. "I want to talk to Linda Stasi."

"She's in a meeting."

Suddenly the guy got all ballsy and relaxed. He collapsed in Linda's chair, cracked open his *New York Times*, put his ugly sneakers on her desk and said, "I can wait. I have all day."

At this point I calmly pulled his wheeled chair away from the desk and rolled him out of the office and turned to finish my work. "Go home, pal. Before you get hurt."

A second later, he rolled back in backwards and spun to speak to me in my face. "What are you gonna do, hit me? Go ahead, hit me. I'll sue you and I'll sue the whole damn paper. You touch me and you're through. Please hit me. *Please.*"

"*Get outta here,*" I said. My fist was cocked behind my shoulder, waiting to drive this guy but good.

"I'm waiting for Linda," he said. "She'll like me, that Linda. I know I'm her type." As he's saying this he's rubbing his balls and rolling his eyes back in his head.

I grabbed his *New York Times* and tossed it in the garbage.

"Hey, that cost me fifty cents!" he screamed. By now staffers were rubbernecking to see what was going on.

I took out a bunch of change from my pocket and tossed all of it in his face, most of it ricocheting off his forehead. "Here's all the money in my pocket. Go buy a paper on me and use the extra money for a new toupee. You fuckin' look like Dondi from the comics."

And then he said something that set me off. It was stupid in retrospect, but what can I say—back then I had some insecurities about my hair.

"Why, you think your hair looks any better?"

Well, that did it. When your girl tells you to use a little less mousse, it hurts some but you listen. When some lunatic with a golf divot for a hairdo points out your hair trouble, you go for the jugular. I smacked him in the mouth—twisted his hairpiece in the process—and wheeled him clear across the office to the late Pulitzer prize–winning columnist Mike McAlary.

"Mike, what do I do with this guy? I want to open up his lip with another smack, but he's threatening to sue me if I hit him."

"Smack him again," Mac said. "I'll get Bruce Cutler to defend you in court for free."

Then I wheeled him into Linda's meeting with Gooding, Colasuonno and Lynch. Meanwhile he's kicking and screaming the entire time and the whole newsroom is both intrigued and in shock. "Somebody get this prick out of my sight or I'll kill him," I announced after wheeling him into the meeting unannounced.

"Who is he?" Linda asked.

"That lawyer we wrote about," I said.

"What did he do?" By this time security had been called and they were just arriving.

"He sat in your chair, rubbed his balls when he talked about you and he made fun of my hair," I said.

"Did you hit him," Linda said.

"Hell yeah."

"Good."

Security grabbed the guy, but not before his ego had to be smoothed over by a bunch of editors. Little did I know the guy was hiding a tape recorder in his pants and was taping the whole thing for possible legal action. Somehow Gooding convinced the guy to hand over the tape and he was escorted out of the building. I never heard from him again.

But a moment like that makes you look both ways before you leave the building every night.

Over the next few hours I received a series of electronic messages from staffers across the newsroom and sports desk and in various editorial offices. They were all congratulatory.

McAlary: "I want you on my team the next time I'm in a bar fight."

Mike Lupica: "Welcome to the *News*, slugger."

Charlie Sennot: " 'At a way to protect your post."

A tussle like that at *Newsday* and I would've been fired in a heartbeat. At the *News*, my newspaper heroes were lauding me. I was happy as a dog with two tails.

The next day I wanted to blast Victor for letting the guy past the security door so easily. But when I called, Victor was whooping it up like an immigrant who just hit Lotto. And that's because he *was* an immigrant who just hit Lotto. The fucker had just won a $2.2 million-dollar jackpot with his brother, an elevator man in the lobby of the *News* building.

"Helloooooo, Mr. A.J.," Victor sang into the phone. "Will you like to come outside and have a piece of my cake, Mr. A.J."

And out in the *News* hallway everybody ate off Victor's angel food cake. Reporters, columnists, editors, management, you name it. There was even a little cupcake for me, commemorating smacking the lawyer. "Two big wins for the *News* in a single twenty-four-hour period," Drasner announced. "Victor hit Lotto and Benza hit a lawyer."

Everybody was laughing. Linda turned to me. "Well, you just solidified yourself with the boys. You can't do any wrong with these guys now."

For a very long time I couldn't.

Ain't Too Proud to Beg

I t was both flattering, gratifying and scary as hell how sources began to find me.

My style was never to go out and solicit information from people. Hell, I never even carried a business card during the five years I wrote gossip. And don't even get me started with those pussies who carry around a pen and pad. It used to embarrass me to even be in the same profession. I guess I ought to feel sorry for a reporter who can't rely on his memory—not to mention his eyes and ears—to put together a gossip report, but I can't say I enjoyed being a part of a certain profession where both hands had to be clumsily occupied in order to do your job. If you're covering a press conference, bring along your miniature tape recorder. If you're covering a crime scene, then by all means grab a pad and pen. But if you're hitting the clubs, if you're planting yourself into the most private booths of the coolest spots in the fastest city in the fuckin' world, you'd better grab a drink and watch closely at what is going down around you. One glance down at your spiral notebook and you might've missed the cheater's kiss, the junkie's snort, the fighter's fist. And then you might as well have stayed home. See it, live it, be in it. Write it down tomorrow.

Anyhow, the method to my madness was to go out *every single night* and just let myself be seen. I figured putting myself in the right company of people and hanging out at the right joints would eventually pay huge dividends. And, over time, I was right. Little by little, the club world became mine.

Publicists were good to me in those days. Matter of fact, they stayed good with me. And here's a little something I figured out immediately about publicists—I could win them over in a heartbeat. It didn't matter if they were male or female. And I'll tell you why.

By most standards, male publicists regret the position they're in because the world of publicity is primarily run by women. The biggest stars in the world are all repped by older women—mostly Jewish women—who've been in the business a long, long time. So a twenty-five-year-old guy in that position is likely to buddy up to another guy in a manner that says, "Hey, I'm no pussy even though my line of work is mostly run by *yentas*." So that guy will go out of his way to make sure a guy like me thinks highly of his manhood. So, getting guys like this to fork over information on clients or just information in general was cake.

An example.

Random Male Publicist: "Hi, A.J., this is [insert WASPy name here] with Rogers & Cowan and I think I got something here you'd be really interested in. It deals with my client and his new film and it might work really well with your column, particularly because . . ."

Me: "Yeah, that's all good but listen, [WASPy name], you gotta tell me if you're fuckin' the receptionist in your office."

Random Male Publicist: "What?"

Me: "Your receptionist, that Puerto Rican-looking chick. You know who I mean, man. She's gorgeous."

Random Male Publicist: "Oh, you mean Rosa. Oh yeah, she's real cute. She's new. How do you know her?"

Me: "I picked up some credentials the other day and I almost shit when I saw her."

Random Male Publicist: "Yeah, she's hot as hell."

Me: "Are you hittin' that? I mean, because if you are, I'll back off. But if you're not . . . then you gotta hook me up."

Random Male Publicist: "No, I'm not with her . . . you know, we talk and all . . ."

Me: "I'm only saying that because when I was in the other day, I

could tell by the way she was talking about you. I mean, I didn't know
if you guys *had* dated or *were* dating. I couldn't tell."

Random Male Publicist: "Really? Like, what'd she say?"

Me: "I don't know, just random shit. I think she's into you though.
Anyhow, fax me your item, but listen, my man . . . I need some dirt on
somebody. You gotta find me some dirt. Find me dirt and I'll print your
lame item. And good luck with Rosa. Fuck man . . . she's so hot."

In most cases, not only was I able to reaffirm that guy's manhood,
but he'd be so hellbent to get me some dirt, he'd have a story for me
by that afternoon. So, I knew how to work the guys.

Working the girls was a little more interesting and more enjoyable.
Let me just get this fact out in the open right away. Publicists like to
fuck. Maybe it's the joy of all that expense account dough or the thrill
of whisking away to L.A. (or South Beach or Paris) to brush shoulders
with the high and mighty or maybe it's just an excuse to blow off the
steam that goes into publicizing huge press events. Whatever it is . . .
they fuck around. And if you're a moderately good-looking guy, making
the scene, you're gonna get lucky every now and then. However, if
you're a moderately good-looking guy, making the scene *and* in a position to help or hurt them, then you can almost name the night.

I didn't scream or rant and rave at publicists on the phone. I chose to
love and coddle them. I sent them flowers. I took them to dinner. I
wrote them notes. I left mushy birthday messages on their voice mails
at 12:01 A.M. I made sure their bosses—older female publicists—knew
they had terrific girls working for them. I never actually *dated* any one
of them in particular, but I saw a lot of them in private. And our secrets
stay with me. The only times things got sticky was when I had an unflattering item on a client of theirs that was going to find its way into
print.

"Listen," I would say, "it's gonna get in the papers anyway. You
might as well have me do it and not hurt them. You can trust me."

Most of the time, the said female publicist would tremble like mad
with the thought of an unflattering item on, say, Sylvester Stallone making its way into my column. The usual chain of events goes like this:
The said actor calls the head of the p.r. company and demands to know
why he's paying $4,000 a month to a company that can't keep a rumor
out of the paper. That call is followed by the company head calling the

said publicist into her office and demanding to know why her relationship with Hot Copy's A.J. Benza couldn't keep that story out of print.
After the company head threatens to fire the said publicist the next time
that occurs, she then calls to calm and reassure the said celebrity that it
will never happen again. By this time, the publicist will do anything to
keep an unflattering item out of the column.

Anything.

In other words, young publicists who work for volatile stars who are
constantly hounded by the tabloids are quite adept at placating columnists on the hunt for a damning story. Some of the biggest names in
movies, modeling and rock and roll sent me home happy and contented
many nights because they invested their money wisely in a publicist
who'd rather lay down for me than see the story in print and suffer the
wrath.

Back then, there was no such thing as going home lonely when I
knew there was always a publicist out there looking to protect her star
employer. All I had to do was make the rounds and find her. She was
usually the pretty blonde girl wearing all black, looking frazzled and
vulnerable, in the middle of some big fuckin' party at the Puck Building
or MoMA or Bowery Bar or Roseland or Laura Belle. You get the
picture.

Some Things Just
Stick in my Mind

For every five publicists I was fucking, there was always one who was out to fuck me. And I don't mean the ooh-aah kind of fucking. I mean, the hang-me-out-to-dry kind of fucking. It might have happened a few times in my tenure, but the one time that stands out the most had to do with a persistent little publicist named Ruben Malaret. Ruben was Cuban or Spanish or something like that and always handled celebs like Ricky Martin, when he was a soap star, or Puerto Rican singing and dancing sensation Chayanne. He was also an expert on Menudo trivia, so I'll let you be the judge on the kind of guy I'm talking about here.

For what it's worth, Ruben had given me some damn accurate and highly explosive stories through the first year we were speaking. His small stream of obscure clients were finding their way into the column and he was, at the same time, throwing me leads on juicy stories that often developed into lead stories. So everybody was happy. That's why I had no reason to doubt him when he called me with the biggest story I had handled yet.

"Hello, A.J. It's Ruben. You ready?"

"I'm on deadline. What's up?"

"You ready?"

"Come on. I can't fuck around, man. Whattya got?"

"You want to know who Cindy Crawford's fucking around with?"

At the time, Cindy was very married to Richard Gere, but there was always the matter of the gerbil rumor making good gossip. So maybe, just maybe, Cindy wasn't happy. And maybe, just maybe, life in the Habitrail wasn't as swell as people might think. So I listened.

Ruben insisted that Crawford and Chayanne hit it off at a National Children's Leukemia Foundation dinner at New York's Marriott Marquis and that Cindy had asked the foundation to book her a room there so as to be nearer the singer *People* magazine was about to crown one of its "50 Most Beautiful People." Richard was out of town and Cindy was mad that Richard was not planning on being on the West Coast when she was to arrive there the next day, so she stayed the night in New York. So, from Ruben's tip we let the story out that maybe, just maybe, Cindy and Chayanne were hanging around. I had no reason to disbelieve Ruben. As I said, he had never lied to me in the past and eventually a source builds up enough credibility and you don't feel the need to double- and triple-check every lead they give you. Besides, I called Cindy's agent, Michael Gruber, and he declined to speak to me. So, hey.

Nine days later, Ruben calls again. This time he says he has proof that Cindy was in Beverly Hills scooping up a few gifts from Fred Hayman's and having them FedExed to Chayanne's South Beach condo. Ruben told me Cindy scooped up a silver Cartier musical-note money clip and a Fred Hayman black leather wallet. Further, he added, Cindy was ordered to attend the Oscars with Gere a couple of days before the shopping spree, to kill the rumors. He said he had proof that Cindy's assistant "Lisa" had just phoned Chayanne's assistant and gotten his address.

"Ruben, this is big. If you're fuckin' me on this, I'm gonna kill you. You know that, right?"

"Come on, A.J. Have I ever lied to you? Wait . . . have I ever been wrong about anything I ever told you?"

Truth is, his reputation with me was sterling. I agreed to run the story—with the proper calls to Cindy's publicist, Annette Wolf—as long as Ruben could prove that the jewelry Cindy purchased was actually going to Chayanne.

"Hold on," he said. "Listen to this."

Ruben then switched me back on the phone and I heard a third line ringing.

"Who you calling?"

"I'm calling Cindy's assistant as a woman from Fred Hayman's jewelry department. I'll pretend that Cindy suggested I call her and tie up the loose ends."

"All right but . . ."

"Shhhhhh . . ."

Just then a female voice answered the phone. "Hello, this is Lisa."

Then Ruben went to work. "Hello, Lisa? This is Hillary Anson with Fred Hayman in Beverly Hills. We just had Cindy in here and she wanted you and I to speak to finalize this sale. She had to run."

"I know. I know. I was expecting your call. She told me."

"Now Cindy bought a silver money clip for $75 and a black leather wallet for $115. If you let me ring up that total and you could give me her American Express card, we'll be all set."

"Oh, yes, of course. I'm sorry, Hillary, can I ask you to hold on?"

"Of course. Take your time."

With just the two of us on the line, Ruben could hardly contain himself.

"Jesus, this is good. How the hell can you speak like a woman so well?" I asked him.

"I can do a lot of things." Ruben chuckled.

"All right, I'm sold. I'm gonna hang up. Call me when you're through."

When I contacted Annette Wolf for a comment, she was ready for me. "This is complete bullshit the whole way around!"

If I hadn't heard what I heard with my own two ears on that phone with Ruben, I would've believed Annette and the story would've died that day. But the hunger for a big scoop obviously dulled my senses. We ran the story and it basically made the sweet and beautiful Cindy Crawford—America's homegrown beauty—despise me. And, if you've learned anything about me—the last thing I want to do is alienate a beautiful woman. Let alone the finest white girl in the country.

Of course, nothing ever came of a Crawford/Chayanne affair. The rumor died the next day as it got no play in the tabloids—who, at this point in time, were having a grand old time copying Hot Copy exclusives and running them in their rags as if they were their very own. It was sickening. Annette Wolf cringed whenever I rang her and the notion of walking up to Cindy at a party to chat was out of the question. For the next three years, Cindy and I only came face-to-face once. And that was at a party for her fitness guru, Radu. The rumors at that point were that Cindy and Richard were finally on the outs for real. My job was to hit the party and corner for a second, get a comment and split. We already had a photographer who had snapped her photo on the way into Nino's Restaurant, where the party was waiting. The press wasn't invited, but I was a personal friend of Nino, the owner, and he always had a seat and a free meal for me.

A vision: You watch Cindy walk in, the very vision of the kind of beauty and wholesomeness that buckles your knees. You watch her kiss Radu, as the trainer lifts her up over his head for all his pals to see. Even Regis and Joy Philbin put down their fried zucchini to laugh and applaud. You watch Cindy sit on a friend's lap, talk animatedly to almost all who come her way and you watch her generally cast the kind of shine to that room only superstars can muster. I mean, it's one thing to see her on TV chatting with David Letterman. But when you are close enough to smell her perfume and reach out and touch that damn mole of hers, you start to develop a form of Bell's palsy of the face and body and you cannot move. You just see Cindy in slow-mo and you sit there happy and contented like a cat who's found a sun spot on the kitchen floor.

But you have a job to do. So you shake out of it—the sweat, the hesitation, the embarrassment, everything—because your photographer got the shot and your editors are expecting a story. And it takes everything you have to walk toward her, but as you do you notice she is not wearing a wedding band and suddenly the story is half-written. Now all you have to do is ask her five words: "Hey, Cindy, where's your ring?" That's it. Five lousy words and your night is over. Even three words would work. You could even say, "Where's the ring?" Actually, two words would be sufficient. At a time like that, you could just make eye contact with her and say, "No ring?" and that might even get a response out of her. In a real panic, you could hold up your own ring finger and kind of shrug your shoulders, as if to say . . . "Forgetting something?"

You wouldn't have to say anything, just a glance and a nod and a shrug. That's not so hard to do, is it?

But you don't do any of that because you never have a chance to. Instead, here comes Cindy in all her grace and charm and ball-aching beauty walking right toward you. She sees you—knows exactly who you are and knows she has to approach you and disarm you immediately if she is to have any kind of fun at this party for her dear friend. And here comes Cindy and she sees you looking at the finger and when you look up at her face—that beautiful fuckin' face—she is one foot away and looking you right in the eye. But she's not mean or vindictive or anything you'd expect. She is, instead, walking toward you like a wounded animal. Worse, a wounded woman. And Cindy Crawford plants her body in front of you so you can't move now and she doesn't move until you shake off the awkwardness so your eyes meet her eyes and all of a sudden the giant billboard of beauty that is Cindy Crawford speaks softly into your face.

"Please don't ask me that question."

You walk away from the party, out into the misty rain falling on First Avenue and the story means shit to you. In fact, you wish you were out of the damn business altogether because the first person you meet in the street is the rain-soaked freelance photographer who knows his shot doesn't get printed if you didn't ask the damn question. But you always ask the questions. That's why the photographer isn't hawking you. That's why he winks at you as you hail a cab to get the hell out of there. But tonight you didn't want to ask the question. Tonight you were *The Deer Hunter* and you couldn't pull the trigger on Cindy Crawford. All you cared about was that you were close enough to smell her breath. And it smelled like lavender.

Fast forward two years later—a lifetime of gossip gained. Hell, a lifetime of everything lived. I'm cleaning out my desk, freshly fired from the *News* and about to take the same walk I watched Richard Johnson take. And my phone rings and it's "Hillary Anson"—the lady from Fred Hayman's in Beverly Hills—calling to say she is so sorry I am leaving the paper. "I think what happened to you is ridiculous," she says. "That Pete Hamill is no good."

But before I could shake away the daze of trying to remember who was talking to me, Hillary's voice crumbles and breaks apart into a man's voice. A laughing man's voice. And suddenly the voice is a familiar one. Suddenly Hillary became Ruben Malaret right before my ears.

"I'm just busting your balls, poppi," Ruben says to me. "This is a blessing. You're gonna go on to bigger and better things. I just wonder what columnist I'm gonna work with now. You and I were great together."

"That whole Cindy Crawford/Chayanne thing was *you*?"

"Come on . . . you knew it was me."

"How the fuck did you do two female voices at the same time so differently?" I was astonished and ashamed.

"Watch," he said. "I'll do it again." And with that, Ruben launched into a bogus discussion between "Lisa" and "Hillary" again. And I never felt better about leaving a room in my life. I can't blame Cindy Crawford for hating me one bit.

Exile on Main Street

Eight years ago, $60,000 and an expense account was a big deal. But more important than the dough—and the fact that Mort Zuckerman was, in essence, financing my dating life—was the fact that I was holding a set of keys to the city. And to a frustrated kid who used to tremble at the sight of a velvet rope and a beefy bouncer, there ain't a better feeling in the world.

By this time, I had finally sold the house that was draining me dry on Long Island. The market was bad—so bad that the house I once bought for $149,900 was not going to fetch me the $135,000 needed to satisfy the mortgage loan I took out. The offers I was getting were in the $120,000 range. And there was no way I was going to be able to come up with the $15,000 to satisfy the bank. So I made one last plea to my broker—who was not very skilled at bringing prospective buyers into the home but was quite adept at taking snapshots of each room every time he visited so that the home could go into those cheesy real estate catalogues you see in 7-Eleven. One day, I invited him over and casually left my father's .44-caliber handgun on the table.

"What's that?"

"That's the gun I'm going to kill you with if you take one more fuckin' snapshot of the fireplace, that's what that is."

Okay, I'll admit it, I was watching *Goodfellas* too often at the time, but I was in a tight spot: Tired of the Long Island to NYC commute and coming home every night at the ungodly hour of four A.M. and unable to beg, borrow or steal the $15,000 the bank was going to start screaming for if I took the last offer of $120,000 for the house. Finally, I just wrote a series of letters to the bank, explaining my plight (divorced, one less salary coming in, bad market, mulling over foreclosure, etc.) and after four months of haggling they just took the $120,000 and never bothered me again.

So Chico and I went and crashed on my sister Rosalie's couch a couple miles away. It was the two of us, my sister and her husband, my two nephews, my two Yorkies and her *fifteen* Yorkies—Gypsy, Alfie, Ruffiana, Gucci, Baci, Bella, Tina, Rocco, Bubida, Chico, Cisco, Don Juan, Marcella, Mercedes and my puppy, Cesare. It was *The Simpsons* meets *The Odd Couple* meets *Mutual of Omaha's Wild Kingdom*. It was a pleasant eight-week stay until I stumbled upon an apartment for rent on Madison Avenue in Manhattan's Murray Hill section. Normally, I wouldn't dream of moving into a neighborhood where most every woman had the gout and every man was a retired doctor. But when this appealing-looking fortyish woman named Sophia spotted me in a deli and asked me if I'd like a massage at her shop on Madison Avenue, I went for a walk. She took me to a nice apartment building, into her penthouse suite, lit a joint for us and proceeded to go to work on me. (WARNING TO ALL WOMEN: This is the kind of insane shit your man does, but never tells you.) I swear I only went because she looked like she slipped out of Jacqueline Bisset's family tree and hit a few branches on the way down. On top of that, she was what I call a "footnote person," those annoying enough to quote the last intellectual conversation they had had, but not brave enough to formulate a thought born of their own mind.

Within a few minutes, Sophia tells me she owns the penthouse but is going to rent out the eleventh-floor duplex within a couple months. The duplex, it turns out, was where she was running an escort/massage service without the building's landlord knowing about it. I told her I was looking for a place, but couldn't pay more than $1,500 per month for an apartment. After we did some negotiating, Sophia decided to give it to me at my price as well as offer me her penthouse when she summered in the Hamptons. I stopped her before she tossed in her Mercedes and her teenage daughter in the deal.

I'm not going to lie to you: Sophia was a nut, a flat-out loon who only Catherine O'Hara can play when someone greenlights the movie of my life. And the notion of living in the same building with her after our little massage session would have been awkward, but when someone offers you a Madison Avenue duplex for $1,500 and summers in her penthouse suite for free, well, you shut your mouth and open your checkbook before her high wears off.

Chico and I jumped right into the invigorating rigors of city life—with me walking to work each day with a coffee and my paper tucked under my arm and Chico taking a managing position at Scores, the topless mecca and my home away from home. The dogs had a more difficult time, though, as they were not used to shitting on the busy streets of Manhattan. They say you can't teach an old dog new tricks, and that's true. But you also can't teach an old dog how to walk with a leash if they've been used to running around a yard on Long Island. For several days, I literally dragged my pedigreed Yorkies down the busy stretch of Madison Avenue between 39th Street and 37th Street, right in front of Ian Schrager's posh Morgans Hotel. And for the first two weeks—three times a day—I watched patiently as neither of the two moved their bowels. It was like they were on a reverse hunger strike. They were used to seeing grass. They didn't know what to do on concrete. It got to the point that I even stopped bringing out paper one day. And, of course, that was the day both beared down and decided to leave steamy, curling mounds of shit right in front of the Morgans's busy door.

Not picking up after your dog is punishable by a fine in most parts of the city. Along Madison Avenue, you get the gas chamber if your neighbors really push for it. With nothing in sight even resembling a paper towel or old newspaper or cupcake wrapper, I was forced to be inventive. I dug deep into my pocket, fighting off the evil glares of passersby and bent down to scoop up each mess with a dollar bill. It's all I had on me.

"Do you believe this shit," I yelled up to Chico, who'd been watching from the window. "What if I only had a twenty on me?"

"What if you only had four quarters?"

•   •   •

The months rolled by and Chico was making more money than God. Scores was a gold mine and everybody shook down everyone. The security guards shook down the dancers. The managers shook down the security guards. The owners shook down the managers. And the mob shook down the owners. But there was so much money to go around, no one was mad at anyone. Me? I was racking up the words at the *Daily News*, making an even bigger name for myself within the club world and having a ball like any bachelor would with what amounted to two apartments and a Rolodex that was starting to bulge with some of the city's more beautiful people. Private numbers and all.

I picked up where I left off on Long Island, taking women home at all hours of the night and sending them home before I headed for work the next morning around nine. If Chico wasn't bringing home a few girls from the club, then I was usually dropping into any number of hot spots around town and keeping the rotation well-oiled. Back then, my starter was Shann, the Jamaican singer who was waiting tables at the Copacabana until her deal at Sony came through. Shann was beautiful, especially when you saw how happy she was at home in her sad little four-storey Chelsea walkup where the brazen cockroaches would stay put on the stucco bedroom wall for hours because the summer heat was even too stifling for them. Shann was new in town and had just quit experimenting with a woman lover for two years. It didn't take long after she decided to swear off women that all the men came running. Toward the end of our very open-minded love affair, even Robert De Niro got into the act—calling her from the set of *A Bronx Tale*, asking her to come by and help him with the soundtrack. More than once, we'd be in the middle of a session and the phone would ring and it would be De Niro, attempting to ask her out with his shy and uneasy—but adorable—manner.

"Hi . . . Shann. It's me . . . Bob. Hello. I was wondering . . . I'm still here on the set . . . I thought maybe . . . If you were home, you might want to . . . I dunno . . . come by. Whatever you want . . . You can call me . . . I'm here . . ."

"What's it like to date him? What does he do? What does he say? How does he treat a woman?" I was drunk on the notion that Robert

De Niro, my idol, was sharing a woman with me. And on this particular night, I was sharing her bed.

"He's very respectful of me," came Shann's Island-flavored reply. "He's sweet, very sweet and very handsome and intense. But he's very different than the explosive man you see in the movies. He's very gentle."

And I was very lucky. But Shann and I were history not too long after I lost my hoop in her weave during a wild makeout session at the Sound Factory.

Tuesday nights were always good to hike up to the Country Club to see the young, crazy Colombian Sonia. I called Sonia my "Upper East Side project," because the twenty-year-old cocktail waitress lived on East 112th Street with her three-year-old son and would frequently get roughed up by the boy's drug-dealing dad over visitation rights. Sonia was a wonderful girl, despite how terribly sad her past, present and future looked. But few of my friends understood what I saw in her beyond a beautiful little body, adorable face, infectious laugh and a desire to jump on restaurant tables and dance to Latin grooves. I just loved that she was a survivor and that she wasn't above doing anything in order to keep food in her boy's mouth. That was noble to me and nobility is one of my turn-ons. We quietly fell to pieces after five months or so and last I heard, Sonia's mom is raising the boy back in Colombia and Sonia is busy dating rich men who pay her so they can be around her beautiful little body, adorable face and infectious laugh. She stays home on 112th Street and waits for her pager to beep.

I also made some time with a girl named Janine, fresh from San Francisco and looking to break into journalism. We met at a charity function at Tavern on the Green and I had the good fortune to be seated next to her. After a hundred laughs at dinner and afterward over some drinks, Janine and I began dating. However fun the dating was, we were never really able to have a solid run since Janine was completely open and honest about not being emotionally separated with her ex-boyfriend, Matt. This Matt was a struggling actor/writer and was really playing with Janine's heartstrings. And if he decided to fly in and see her on a whim, then I'd be the guy left in the lurch at the last second. I wasn't really mad at her for it—hell, there were plenty of other girls around—but I liked to think

Janine and I had a legitimate shot for a long-term thing. But she used to try to explain her unpredictable thing with Matt this way:

"He writes a lot," she would say. "And he loves for me to read what he writes. He trusts my opinion and right now what he's writing is very important to him."

"What's he writing?

"It's kinda like an autobiography. But it's kinda not?"

I couldn't understand that a kid in his early twenties had the ability to write an autobiography, much less compile a life with enough memories to fill a book.

"He's writing it with his friend," Janine would say. "It's really good."

Well, the stop-and-go quality of my relationship with Janine was enough for me to walk away from it with my heart still intact. And the fact that Matt remained a mystery was fine with me. Eventually, Matt broke Janine's heart when his life took off and he went on to see other women. Several years later when a film called *Good Will Hunting* hit like a hurricane, I learned Janine's Matt wasn't any ordinary Matt. Janine's Matt was Matt Damon.

I just talked to her about it the other day. And it's funny. Now I'm obsessed with him and she can't bring herself to talk about the guy anymore.

I also had me a ball with a Broadway showgirl for a stretch. Kimmy was a dancer in *Crazy For You*, which was playing at the Shubert Theater. After taking in the play with Chico one night, I pointed her out in the middle of a huge dance number.

"Holy shit . . . look at that blonde. We gotta wait by the stage door and see her."

"Come on, Pope, every girl in the cast is blonde. How you gonna find her?"

After the play we made our way to the side door, bought a street pretzel and waited for what seemed like an eternity. Finally, I spot the blonde walk out and hail a cab. So Chico and I do the same thing with the taxi behind her. "I'm gonna say something I always wanted to say," I told the driver. "Follow that cab."

"You're really a sick bastard," Chico said. "You're not a lover, you're a stalker."

"I just want to see where she lives."

I had to. There was something fresh and adorable about watching Kimmy be the last one out of the theater, walk to the curb with her little blonde bob and long leggings and Capezios and whistle for her cab to stop. It was obvious to me that Kimmy was a Midwest girl living out her dream to make it on Broadway. And here she was, on a cold wintery night in Times Square—after another sell-out performance in a Tony Award–winning play—sticking two fingers past her red-lined lips, whistling to hail a cab. It was the kind of moment she probably dreamed about all her life. And it showed in every move she made. And it was sexy as hell.

So we followed the cab. And though I did get a little nervous when it headed into the Lincoln Tunnel, I stayed calm enough to assure Chico I just wanted to see her home. When it finally came to a stop on a little dark street in Weehawken, I told my cabbie to stay put as I got out to talk to her before she got to her door.

"Hey. Don't be scared of me," I said. "I just saw you in the play and I had to find you outside the door and see you out of your costume. I'm not some crazy stalker—though I know this is probably kind of scary for you—I swear I just wanted to see how pretty you were from up close and not from twenty rows back."

Kimmy was understandably stunned and surprised but not necessarily scared.

"And you followed my cab home?"

"Yep. Me and my friend Chico." Then I called out for Chico to say "hi."

"Hello."

"Hi, Chico," Kimmy said. "Well, what's your name?" Her hand was twisting her doorknob.

"I'm A.J."

"Hi, A.J., I'm Kimberly. My friends call me Kimmy. I'm not sure what my stalkers call me."

Fuck . . . now I'm thinking beautiful face, gorgeous body *and* a sense of humor. I was hooked.

"I'm kidding," she said. "You don't look scary, but you'll understand if I don't sit out here all night and talk to you, wouldn't you? I have two shows tomorrow and I need to sleep."

I couldn't argue with the girl, but I knew I had to see her again.

"This is nuts, but you want to have a cup of coffee or something sometime? After your show one night maybe?"

"Maybe," she said. "I'm a spontaneous girl. Let's see how it goes."

For the next two weeks, I parked my car in a Times Square garage and walked up and down 44th Street. I remembered Kimmy walked out around 10:50 P.M. on the first night I spotted her, so that's around the time I did my walk-bys. Finally, at the start of the third week, I "bumped" into her as she and her legs made their way toward the neon chaos of Broadway.

Kimmy was warm and inviting and we walked to Howard Johnson's for coffee and some apple pie à la mode in a window seat. After an hour or so, I learned Kimmy was from Milwaukee and *Crazy for You* was the first gig she ever auditioned for. She had only gotten the part eight days after she packed a truck with her dreams and drove to the big city. "So this is what you always dreamed of, isn't it?" I asked her. "Coming to New York City, working in a big show, sitting in Times Square and letting your dreams sink in."

"That's what a lot of girls back home dream about," she said. "What do guys in New York City dream about?"

"Getting a showgirl," I told her.

For the next several weeks, I did my nightly rounds at all the town's hot spots but now I had me a tall Midwestern stunner on my arm. Kimmy could never stay out too late on account of all the energy she needed to conserve for the show, but she did like to pack as much fun as she could in the length of time she'd stay out. One night, she invited me to a party another actress was having at her East Village apartment. The loft was packed with showgirls. It was like a cattle call, only all the girls had full-time gigs in a Broadway show and were making the kind of dough they always dreamed of, so you can imagine the spirit in the room was high. Midway through the night, Kimmy introduced me to her pal Marla Maples, who had just gotten the role in *The Will Rogers Follies* and was the toast of the town, what with her crazy affair with Donald Trump. After I explained to Marla that my column and my editor were practically shills for Donald's shenanigans, she felt at ease being around a gossip columnist.

"Trust me," I said. "My editor is very good to your boyfriend. We only write good things about him. He tells us a story, we write it." Marla seemed happy with that.

Later in the night, I found myself occupying my time with what became a new habit. I had a penchant for entering a stranger's house, excusing myself to the bathroom, and ransacking the medicine cabinet. At first, I did this at the urging of a male friend who told me he did it to see if the woman he was sleeping with was on any kind of medicine, ointment or antibiotic used to combat any number of sexually transmitted diseases. And that's the reason why I did it . . . at first. Hey, you can never be overinformed is the way I see it. So with each house party I'd hit, I'd excuse myself to the bathroom, turn on the water to drown out the unmistakable sound of a stranger opening a medicine cabinet, and start rummaging. And I'd look for anything that had any strength at fighting an STD. Flagyl, Vagisil, Zovirax, Valtrex, penicillin, etc. You name it, I searched for it. You think looking down a girl's blouse is personal? Try looking inside her medicine cabinet.

But just as some say marijuana eventually leads to harder drugs, maybe searching for penicillin leads to Percocet and Percodan fascinations. I don't know. All I know is, it was around this time that I began to form a relationship with prescription drugs. I was never hooked, but we got along, let's put it that way.

Anyhow, I remember I walked away from that party with a pocketful of Xanax, Valium and Percocet. I also found a handmade ceramic cross—which belonged to the girl giving the party—that I draped on Marla's neck as I left the party and headed back to Weehawken with Kimmy. Marla thought the gesture was sweet, never knowing she then spent the rest of the night wearing a piece of jewelry it looked like she had stolen from the chick throwing the bash.

"What a sweet gesture," she told me. "Why are you giving me this beautiful cross?"

"Because you're gonna have one helluva cross to bear with that boyfriend of yours," I told her. Several years later, the old man was my cross to bear. But more on that fuckin' story later.

Kimmy and I had a good time for the short burst we were together. Our schedules were tight and she eventually found herself a man who also wore Capezios for a living. Someone she could go home with after the show ended and spend the better part of the next day with. That was always a problem for me. But, at any rate, give or take a few hostesses, waitresses, bartenders, actresses and models, that's how my romance rotation rounded out as my gossip career at the *News* started to heat up.

Hang Fire

Linda and I anchored the ship for two months until it was time to bring aboard one more writer. She had originally asked for a staff of three and Mort agreed. She was just biding her time before she found the right writer. A select few came in and out, some we took to dinner—some I took out alone for obvious reasons—and we would quiz them on their knowledge of the city and its movers and shakers. More important, we also wanted to see if they had a sense of humor resembling ours. There aren't many people as fucked up as me and Linda when it comes to laughing, we were just trying to find a third. One by one, all the hopefuls who came by failed. Some miserably and some by inches. More than an ability to write and a funny bone, what Linda was looking for was someone who possessed the necessary contacts to follow a lead on any story that came across our desks—no matter how huge or how small. And, quite frankly, the next person aboard would also be more like a glorified assistant. Maybe you didn't hear—I was through fetching coffee.

The tryouts were tiresome and we were *thisclose* on giving up on adding a third player to the team when Linda got a call from Michael Lewittes—a publicist for p.r. powerhouse Howard Rubenstein. Throughout my stint at New York *Newsday*, Michael had probably been one of our greatest sources. He would never hesitate to phone in various oddities he witnessed while out on the town or lay a tip or two on us all for some preferential treatement for some of the clients he represented. And that give-and-take is essential for any gossip column to fly. More so, sorry to say, than an ability to write.

Linda laid out the job details—lots of legwork, long hours, attending a million events a week, assisting her, tough deadlines, as well as menial things like making Xeroxes, fetching coffee, etc. Not to mention, the money was shit. I don't even think the kid was offered $35,000 to start.

"I'll take it!" Michael said. "Anything to get out of p.r."

"What do you think?" Linda asked me. "He's hungry for the job. He knows a lot of people . . . Do you get along with him?"

"Me? Sure. I like him. He's like Woody Allen."

"My God . . . the kid graduated from Yale! What's he want with this job?"

Two days later, Michael got the call up to the majors. He quit Rubenstein, no doubt stunning his rich Park Avenue parents in the process, and came aboard for shit money but a shitload of possibilities.

"Why would a rich Jewish kid from Yale want to work for a couple of crazy Italians," I asked him over several drinks that very first night.

"I want to laugh," he said. "And besides, there may come a day when I need some people killed and I know you guys will point me in the right direction."

That was the beginning of a beautiful threesome. It didn't take long before the city stood up and took notice.

Michael was a kid who knew the classics in and out, could recite Shakespeare, hum a few bars from most concertos and he could also get ready for a black-tie event quicker than the stiffest WASPs I knew. It was obvious to us that Michael had been held down at Rubenstein, an organization run by one of New York's biggest blowhards and star-protectors, Howard Rubenstein. Howard's sanctified son Richard—a kid who was once the spitting image of Seinfeld's neighbor Newman—was the employee Michael reported to every day and, it became apparent, there was no love lost between them. When Michael quit, it was Richard who began to spread evil rumors about him across town. Rumors too stupid to remember now, but a vicious rumor in New York City is like a hacking cough in a crowded elevator: After the rumor hits, there are very few people who want to be near you. It took about two weeks of swirling rumors for Linda to pick up the phone and call Richard directly.

"Richard, I've been good to you. I've been good to your father. I've been good to your clients. If this shit doesn't stop with you and Michael, I'm going to start firing my missiles on all the evil shit I know about your clients and your family. And you don't want that."

That was that. The rumors stopped. And Michael began to carve out his own reputation and niche in the close-knit and catty community gossip reporting was and is.

Michael's hire started to pay dividends right away when he brought in two solid stories his first week aboard. The first had to do with TV producer Steven Bochco developing a little show called *NYPD Blue* and Michael's take was that this Bochco show was going to be his most blue. Of course, the story was denied by major network executives who are paid to thwart every gossip columnist's advances. But we went to press with it and eventually ABC announced it as true. That's not such a huge, terrific story in the grand scheme of things, but I bring it up to illustrate how many times a gossip reporter is accurate, but their stories are shot down repeatedly. If you think about it, who the fuck really cares that we broke the story of Bochco's new show before Bochco's production team decided to send out a neat little press release? In the end, most of the time it's not so much breaking a *big* story as much as it's just breaking any story at all. The need to be the first to tell a story to your readers consumes you.

Michael's second scoop was a neat little piece, but he struggled with it only because it dealt with a true story concerning an acquaintance of his. The acquaintance was former Yale graduate Nancy Jo Sales—the same woman who would slice me up in a *New York* magazine profile several years later. But more on that fuckin' story later.

It came to Michael's attention that Nancy Jo had enjoyed a special pen pal friendship with Woody Allen when she was a teen. Normally, that would be considered sweet of any busy professional to write a thirteen-year-old girl and motivate her to write, go to the movies, attend a good college and read a lot—mainly Marcel Proust and see a lot, including Orson Welles's *The Lady from Shanghai*. But since Woody had since admitted to essentially screwing his girlfriend's adopted daughter, his letters from long ago to Nancy Jo took on a new meaning. At least to us they did.

Initially, Nancy Jo was all right with handing the letters over to Michael because she had already sealed a deal over at *New York* magazine to write a piece herself. She was figuring a little attention in our gossip page might lead to more readers picking up *New York* when her article hit. So, Michael brought in the letters and—how do I put this?—we went wild. We couldn't wait to break the story and I'll tell you why.

There's nothing better than exposing and burying hypocrites and phonies. And, judging from Woody's "love" for Soon-Yi *and* these old letters to Nancy Jo, Woody never looked more suspicious. It wasn't that his letters had a sexual connotation, but who the hell knows how peds work? Anyhow, the point is, Nancy Jo got cold feet at deadline and made a call to Michael begging him to drop the story. She claimed the execs at *New York* mag would kill her piece if it broke in our column. Michael went from being the hero to the goat in one afternoon when he sulked from his cubicle into our office and cleared his throat.

"Linda, we've got to kill the piece."

"Are you crazy? It's our lead story. It's five minutes to deadline and all the editors are crazy for this story. What the fuck happened?"

Michael wasn't sure, but he explained that it was either Nancy Jo who had gotten cold feet or her editors were giving her hell. Either way, Linda didn't give a shit.

"This girl is your friend?"

"Well, I know her . . . I mean, yeah. . . . you could say we're friends . . ."

"Good. You call her and tell her if we pull this story your editor is going to fire you."

Michael turned away and headed back to his cubicle. His face was the same color as his beige khakis.

"You being a little hard on the guy, no?" I asked Linda.

"I have to be. This is the biggest story in *New York* tomorrow. If we roll over on this one, and it runs somewhere else, we'll be the biggest shitheads in the city. She'll buckle."

Nancy Jo never buckled. That is to say, all she could do was continue
to beg for the story not to run. But when Michael hung up and told
Linda, "Okay, run it," he knew the business he was now in just broke
up a friendship. But, more important, Linda knew she had broken in
Michael.

"Michael, I wouldn't lie to you," Linda said. "She'll talk to you again.
It's not like you uncovered some deep secret in her life. She approached
New York to write this as a freelancer, for chrissakes. We're going to
look great tomorrow and she'll forgive you."

Michael's third story—and probably his biggest of all time—was
breaking the news of Jerry Seinfeld dating young Shoshanna Lonstein.
Several nights before the actual story broke in the tabloids, Chico and I
attended a Knicks game with Michael, Linda and Linda's daughter, Jessica. Sometime before tipoff, with the Knicks hosting the Bulls, word
came down that Senator Al D'Amato wanted us to join him in his
skybox. None of us really wanted to go because we had just begun
scoring really good tickets for Garden events and it was our belief that
real fans didn't sit in fancy skyboxes where shrimp cocktail is served.
Long story short, Linda, Michael and Jess went up to see D'Amato while
Cheek and I stayed put. It took about fifteen seconds for me to see this
beautiful and busty brunette seated next to Seinfeld on celebrity row.
"That must be the young chick he's supposedly dating," I told Chico.
"We gotta get a picture of this."

Needless to say, everyone snapped a picture of the couple. But it was
our column who identified her—and you can chalk it up to the busy
networking of young Jewish professionals. A beautiful young Jewish girl
like Shoshanna was not the kind of story my sources could help me
break, but it was right up Michael's alley. So Michael began calling some
of his synagogue friends and before you knew it, he had a name and a
home number to walk into Linda's office.

Initially, Linda was dead set against running a story that featured a
multimillionaire dating a girl who was barely legal. "I've got a daughter
the same age," Linda said, "and I just can't bring myself to report on
it." But once Seinfeld and Shoshanna were cool with making public
displays of their love, Linda lowered her sights. But first Michael had to
get a comment from Shoshanna. So we waited for the end of the day

to make the speaker-phone call. And her and Michael's exchange ought to illustrate how young she was at the time.

"Hello, is Shoshanna in?"

"This is Shoshanna."

"Shoshanna. This is Michael Lewittes from the *Daily News*. How're you doing?"

"Good. We don't want home delivery."

"No, no. I'm a reporter. I'm calling to ask how long you've been dating Jerry Seinfeld. That is you, right? We don't have the wrong Shoshanna Lonstein, do we?"

"No, it's me. I am."

"How are you guys getting along?"

"Fine . . . ah, I have to go now. We're eating supper right now and my parents are going to get angry about me being on the phone."

Click.

Tone.

Headlines.

It turned out to be the very night Seinfeld was at her parents' home for dinner.

In 1993 there weren't too many stories or scandals we didn't have a good handle on, to say nothing of a fresh slant or a wild take on. We were definitely defined by our ability to break stories as much as our humor, sarcasm and ability to float a story in the column for weeks on end. Kind of like a running inside joke that only our everyday readers were in on. An example:

The editor-in-chief of the *Weekly World News* was Eddie Clontz. The *Weekly World News* is that insane newspaper that swears about the man who dug a hole straight through to China or the housewife who carried her mule's offspring in her womb. For whatever reason, nobody could say the name Eddie Clontz in our office without all of us cracking up hysterically. It got to the point that I put a banner across my wall that screamed, "Get Me Eddie Clontz!" In time, we even used to add his name to the illustrious list of celebrities attending an event. We'd write, "Last night's premiere of *Carlito's Way* also featured Arnold Schwarzenegger, Bruce Willis, Demi Moore and Cindy Crawford. But no one shined like Eddie Clontz, who arrived alone and left midway through the film." Nobody knew what we were talking about, but we were dying every morning when we opened up the paper.

A publicist for the film would call. "Do you know why Clontz left?"

"We have no idea," I'd say. "But you better do some checking. You don't want to rankle a powerful guy like Clontz."

I swear, *nobody* knew who the fuck he was but they would all die at the thought of him leaving their event. That's a phony publicist for you.

Finally, the night arrived for all of us to wet our pants. There was word that former President Gerald Ford was going to attend some sort of snooty party at 21 and Michael jumped into his black-tie to attend. Literally every reporter was crawling out of the woodwork to ask Ford something, *anything*, about his feelings for new Prez Bill Clinton. But I practically begged Michael to sneak one question. "If you get anywhere near him," I said, "please ask him how he feels about Eddie Clontz."

Michael laughed and said he'd be happy if he could get within ten feet of the guy.

I pleaded as he bolted. "You *have* to. You have no idea how big we'd be tomorrow."

Well, late that night Michael managed to squeeze his 128-pound frame into the throng and poke his notebook into Ford's view. After Ford was gracious enough to answer all of Michael's generic questions on the country's state of affairs under Clinton, he grew the balls to pop the big one.

"And finally, Mr. President, what are your feelings on Eddie Clontz?"

Michael said everyone stopped writing and just looked at him like he was an idiot. Just then Ford chirped up, "Don't know yet, but I'd sure like to meet him."

Sure, they're all honest when they're *out* of office.

The following day we ran Ford's quote on Clontz and ended the piece by writing, "Ford wants to meet Clontz? Get in line, pal. Get in line!"

Again, I'm sure nobody got it. But it made us pee. And not enough columns do that. And that's what the three of us swore we'd try to do every time out.

Get Off of My Cloud

The two people most responsible for our column's success and my own visibility were Michael Jackson and O. J. Simpson. It would take a year or so before Simpson hit the headlines, but in 1993 Jacko began to steadily unravel. And we were there to record every history-making second of it. What began as an innocuous mention in our Sound Bites sidebar column—usually reserved for paying back publicists for giving us stories in our main column—turned into, perhaps, the biggest story in my tenure as a gossip. You know what? Outside of O. J. Simpson's murder trial, it absolutely was.

We had gotten word from a very reliable source—a *very* reliable source—that Michael Jackson had a new little friend he liked to pal around with. We were hearing he took the little kid to Disney World and Euro Disney and sometimes just liked to stay home and order pizzas so he and the kid—and sometimes the kid's entire family—could watch television or rent some videos. Our ears immediately pricked up. I mean, if he wants to show up at an awards show with Brooke Shields on his arm, we really can't say too much except to comment on the general's jacket he's wearing or his disappearing nose. Hey, we even cut him some slack when he started dragging around that midget Emmanuel Lewis, because, hey, maybe it was some sort of celebrity bonding. Even the friendship with the monkey was as intriguing as it was stupid for a while. At least the monkey was relatively healthy as opposed to his other pal Liz Taylor, who took more falls than Gerald Ford and more pills than Betty Ford. But when he invited a thirteen-year-old boy to his home and locked his bedroom door, that's when we developed a problem.

Anyhow, no question the report was true. And it didn't come from any top-notch Hollywood detective or business insider or anyone deeply entrenched in the business of show. It refreshingly came from an old Jewish man in Nassau County whose wife was best friend to the sister of the mother of the little boy who was befriended by Michael. It sounds a bit convoluted, but it's not at all. And it all checked out fine. See, the mother would innocently tell her sister of her son's good fortune in meeting Jackson. And then the sister would tell her best friend across the country about her nephew's new friend. Then that woman would hit the pillow at night and tell her husband what she heard was going on at the Chandler home. He, in turn, would phone us. The pipeline was innocent enough, but we didn't think the actual story was innocent at all. So we went at Michael hard and as a result were the first column to mention the boy's name—Jordan Chandler—long before the rest of the country. We did this because when we first heard the story we ran it as a "Michael's-got-a-brand-new-friend" kind of item. Then, in the days to come, our source told us the blockbuster news that this kid's family was going to drop a big bombshell on Jackson in the form of a sexual molestation lawsuit. So we had actually mentioned the kid's name before he made his feelings—or lack of feelings for Michael—known.

I don't care who I ever wrote about in my tenure. Nobody ever generated more hate mail than when we'd feature Michael Jackson in our column. The only "celebrity" who came close was whenever we'd poke fun at the Pope's "gaudy" robe and Popemobile. Those stories bombarded our mailbox, too. But Michael has at least twice as many supporters as the Pope. At *least* that number. Any anti-Michael stories we printed made us subject to calls for our ouster, hateful letters from readers printed within our own newspaper and even death threats. What the fuck is wrong with the country that a columnist can't view Michael doting on a pubescent boy behind a bedroom door the deeds of a weirdo? And it wasn't just outsiders lashing out at us. I can recall two huge arguments within my own family regarding articles we wrote about Michael. One day, in the middle of a cousin's wedding, my nephew Jack—who was twenty-three at the time—lashed out at me.

"The guy just missed out on childhood. He wants to have one. It's all innocent."

"Jackie," I said. "I'm not anti–Michael Jackson. Christ, I wanted to *be* Michael Jackson when I was eight years old, but if you suddenly befriended the thirteen-year-old boy next door behind a closed bedroom door, and played games with him, I'd personally break down the door and kick your ass. And you're my own blood."

"Oh yeah! Then kick my ass now! You're so fuckin' bad!"

I mean, it was insane.

But it's important to point out that there was an incredible number of insiders who were calling and delivering the goods on Michael every day. And, despite who might lay claim to breaking that bombshell of a story, the fact remains Hot Copy practically had a hidden camera in that home thanks to the meddling mind of our little old Jewish connection. We were so inside on this story, we almost couldn't look at it squarely after a while. Things really got bizarre—and a bunch clearer, to be honest—when my phone rang one day with the high-pitched cries of none other than Michael's sister LaToya Jackson.

"Hello. Is this A.J. Benza?"

"Yeah. Who's this?"

"This is LaToya Jackson."

"Yeah, okay, Jack . . . nice try, ass."

Click.

But a minute later she phoned back—and it really was her—and I let her talk and talk. I was still kind of green enough in the industry to get excited over a phone call like that and it was mind-boggling to me why LaToya would want to chat me up and not another more respected columnist. I remember as she choked her way through the soul-cleansing phone call, I was paging through an old *Playboy* layout of hers. She's a weird one, but she still turned me on.

"I see you. I read the column. And you know what? You are the only one with the nerve to say the truth," LaToya began. I couldn't help myself from thinking that she was playing with one of her silly pet snakes while we spoke. "My brother has a problem. He always has. He needs help."

LaToya would then speak breathlessly for minutes about the beatings Michael took as a child from the hands of his father, Joe. And how, as a result, he went into a shell and is now in search of a pain-free childhood.

"But that's what everybody says," I told her. "What are you telling me that's different? What do you know?"

LaToya then gave me stories—stories we never printed. She told me she was scared for Jordan and did not doubt his molestation claims one bit. "I wouldn't be surprised if others come forward, too," she said. "This is bigger than everybody thinks."

Say what you want about her silly little nose, her burlesque shows in France and her marriage to manager Jack Gordon, the truth of the matter is LaToya was cryptically accurate when it came to news regarding her bizarre brother.

Anyhow, throughout my entire tenure, getting a tip on Wacko Jacko would always have me cracking my knuckles with anxiety and delight. And there was a time when my sights were set so hard on him that he actually quit paying support to the woman who bore his brother Jermaine two sons. And that woman, in turn, had no choice but to quit speaking to me. After all, her sons had to eat. Yeah, Uncle Mikey can get pretty ruthless when he wants to. But more on that fuckin' story later.

Monkey Man

I look back and I cringe now at all the support and black ink Linda gave to Donald Trump, New York's most pompous ass and self-promoting press whore. I can't say I didn't understand it back then—and I still understand it now in the grand scheme of how a gossip column stays in touch with big scoops—but it makes the hairs on my back stand on end nonetheless.

Here it is in a nutshell: Weight moves weight. Big names know big names. For Linda and the column, befriending a guy like Trump meant that the column would have a bigger insight into other stories breaking around the city every day. No question a guy like Trump can tip you off to huge real estate stories, political scandals and such. And it was also a way for Linda to get hand-picked invitations to all sorts of highfalutin events where other men with big influential names showed up with their big cigars and inflated egos. And there wasn't a week when Trump didn't phone us up with a tip or two or didn't extend an invitation to dinner or a party to Linda. I never had a problem with big-name people dishing dirt on other big-name people. It happens every day in the gossip business. *Every day*. And you wouldn't believe the names involved. The people who have six underlings flag a call before they take it are often the same people who think nothing of picking up their phone and dropping a dime on a former friend, costar, agent, manager, whatever. The problem I had with Trump's tips was that the billionaire always had to be paid back in the most smarmiest of ways. He needed boldfaced headline paybacks. Whether it was him tossing his name in the ring to buy a new building or him promoting another boxing match at a tacky Atlantic City casino or him dissing his ex-wife Ivana, Trump called for big placement in the column every time out. And Linda gave it to him principally because he was dropping dimes on a lot of people who eventually became big scoops for the page. And, God forbid, he had a new girlfriend he was squiring around. The column was filled with references and pictures documenting his latest affair. Trump lives a life under the mantra, "I am written about, therefore I am." This guy doesn't check his pulse in the morning to see if he's alive. He checks the papers.

The cache of Trump calling to speak to you wears off in a few months. Once you look past the bad puffy comb-over, yellow hair that reeks of Aqua Net and the eyebrows that haven't seen a tweezer since Nixon was in office, he can be very engaging, very complimentary, even a little charming. But if you're smart and you shake out of it, you realize it's mostly a façade and that everything he says, every second on the phone with you, is just to ensure that the next thing he needs written about himself will make it in the column without a publicist's push. And that's the way the relationship goes with him. He works the press like a hooker works the streets. And when you have a gossip column that's generating major interest and churning out big breaking stories, you put up with Trump's P. T. Barnum act. But Trump treated us to some of the biggest scoops we ever had and we treated him like a god. It was only after I stepped away from the biz and he stepped in between me and a girlfriend that I had thoughts of pushing him off the roof of one of his gaudy skyscrapers. But more on that fuckin' story later.

Our cream puff treatment of Trump actually kept us ahead of the entire city when it came to the saga of his relationship with Marla Maples. Why? Because Trump told us everything himself. As a result, Hot Copy was first to break the news of Marla being pregnant and our "Momma Marla" front page remains one of the highest-selling papers in *Daily News* history. Subsequently we were also first to break The Donald's marriage proposal and the wedding plans and Linda was the first columnist allowed in the hospital when the Georgia Peach popped out baby Tiffany. It was all heady stuff—the kind of stuff the lower- to middle-income *News* readers loved to read about. Linda was also invited to the couple's garish nuptials at which Trump quipped to the crowd, "When you're talking classy weddings, you're talking this wedding." Jesus Kah-rist. But that's The Donald, take him or leave him. Me? I'd like to take him to the middle of a city without a gossip column and leave him there. Watch him wither away.

Memory Motel

The months rolled on and Hot Copy kept up a fabulous pace at breaking stories while keeping the city laughing and infuriated at the same time. In 1994 the three of us hit the ground running. Our roles were clearly defined and there didn't seem to be a day when one of us didn't have our finger on the pulse of some great happening or secret. Linda and Michael might not peg 1994 as their personal best, but for all that I witnessed, experienced, avoided, recorded and longed for, it was the beginning of the wildest time of my life. And no one sucked more life out of that year than I did. I don't know what occurred that set the tumblers in motion, but I'm experienced enough to know that there's always an imperceptible pivot at which point things start turning your way. For a baseball player, it might be an infield single in the middle of an 0-for-21 slump. For a hoop star, it might be a slam dunk on a scoreless night that sends the crowd into a fury. I don't know, it's almost impossible to tell. But there's no mistaking feeling it once the tide begins to ebb and flow to your rhythm, rhymes and reasons. I do know that by early 1994, I finally had a spot to hang my hat. I ain't talking about my Madison Avenue duplex either—which by now also housed my nephew Jackie on the Levitz couch as he bartended and auditioned his way toward his dream of being an actor while I, more than happily, paid his way. No, I'm talking about the dream all writers of the city have in terms of having their very own "joint" to call their own. A place where you escape the madness of your beat, where you take your interviews on your terms, where the risotto is cooked just right and the kitchen never closes until you've taken your last bite and pushed your plate forward. A place, as foolish as it sounds, where everybody knows your name. That place, for me, was Boom—a Euro-hip restaurant that would magically transform into a sweaty and exotic haven around midnight and stay that way until four A.M. or so. The maestro was Rocco Ancarola, a beautiful Italian man who spent his youth in South Africa and always harbored dreams of coming to America and being an actor. That dream fell short, though he did do a terrific turn in a Madonna video once—but, instead, he only turned out to be one of the greatest restaurant front men the city has ever seen. Hollywood's loss was New York's gain. And I have no problem admitting to anyone that Rocco Ancarola, among other things, taught me how to love women.

I had been blindly hanging out at Boom for a time, shamelessly flirting (and getting nowhere) with its beautiful raven-haired Puerto Rican bartender Lina, when—in the middle of a frenzied night—a Boom regular named Joey Coffee grabbed me and told me, "Rocco is back in town! You've got to meet Rocco."

It took a lot to pull me away from Lina back in the day, but the bar was packed and Lina was too busy for my intentions, so I left my espresso and Sambuca and went to find Rocco—the mysterious owner I hadn't yet met but had heard legions of stories about. He was like Zorro, what with his legend and all. Back then, the crowd Boom attracted was far more eclectic than anyplace else. There were artists, photographers, models and actors as well as transvestites, junkies, fighters, lovers and royalty. And the mix worked just fine. But best of all—there wasn't one fuckin' suit in the place. Anyhow, the crowd was thick as stew the night Joey grabbed me by my arm and guided me to the curtained CD room to introduce me to Rocco. And there he was, standing on a wooden box, barking instructions to his waitstaff and blowing kisses and compliments and winks to the crowd before him. The CD player was spinning a sweaty song belted out by a Brazilian beauty named Daniella Mercury and Rocco watched as his crowd began to whip into a frenzy.

"Rocco," Joey shouted over the roar. "This here's A.J. He's with the *Daily News*. Say hello."

"Why aren't you dancing?" Rocco admonished me. "I see you looking at Lina. Take her on the bar and dance with her. This song is *amazing!*"

"You do it," I said, as the bar was six deep.

"I'm busy. Give me five minutes."

With that, Rocco parted the curtain just enough to show us the back of a very beautiful woman who was unmistakingly pleasuring him as he spoke to us. Then he winked, laughed a little boy laugh and ducked inside again. Five minutes later, he was out, slipping through the crowd and jumping up on the bar to dance with my Lina. Five minutes after that, Rocco pulled me up and gave me a twirl with Lina for a song or two, as the beauty kept her hands on the chandelier and ground her skirt against my body to Prince's "Sexy Motherfucka." Bottles fell, glasses broke, cocktails spilled and reputations were set in stone. And my awe for Rocco was born. The friendship remains a constant. I never did ask him who was giving him head. Anyhow, Boom was my home away from home and the setting for many memorable nights. It was almost always a backdrop for my wild times. It's still the first place I check in with every time I fly home.

Rocco introduced me to a myriad of people. And on those nights when it seemed a bit awkward to seat a gossip columnist at the same table as, say, a private rock star or a press-shy movie actor, Rocco did so without a moment's hesitation. "You're my best friend," he'd say. "If they don't like it, they can leave."

Rocco knew my tactics were different than the other gossips. And he was certain his diners would feel the same way. And I believe all of them did except for a few. But one particular night I felt especially uncomfortable sitting at the same table as former First Daughter Patti Davis—the intelligent, rebellious and outspoken daughter of Mr. and Mrs. Ronald Reagan. I kind of felt a bit overmatched. So I politely declined and me and Chico took another table nearby. Sometime during our dessert, Chico got involved in a shouting match with a couple of guys at the bar. As is often the case with Chico, shouts turned into threats and threats turned into shoves and within seconds the three of them were in a full-scale swing out several feet away. There was little I could do other than wait for a precise opening to grab a chair and crack it over one guy's back. I did. And several seconds later, the injured guy's pal saw it our way and the two of them headed out the door. Chico and I sat back down to our crème brûlée and green tea ice cream. A few moments later, Patti came by and made some cracks that she could've helped us if we needed any backup. I remember she was big into working out back then—readying for her *Playboy* pictorial—and she was flexing her biceps and abs for us. The girl was hard as rock and having a good time with us. But more than that, I think she was turned on by what she saw.

Several days later, Patti left a message on my office phone asking that we have dinner one night soon. I know she needed some good press behind her what with her nude layout and an upcoming novel, *Bondage*, but the phone call suggested more. At that point in my career, it was a pretty big phone call to field. And an even bigger dinner to make. I let Linda listen to the message on my voice mail and asked her for her take.

"She wants to sleep with you," Linda said.

"Nah."

"Yes."

"Yeah?"

"Yes. I'm a woman. I know. She wants to sleep with you."

"All right," I joked, "I'll do it for the good of the column."

My sweet and short romance with Patti began innocently enough. Dinner at Orso, a walk in the rain and a kiss on the lips as I placed her in a cab back to the Essex House. Conversation with Patti was heavy and deep. At the time, her dad was at the very beginning of suffering from Alzheimer's disease and Patti was looking to smooth out her on-again, off-again relationship with her mom. She was also readying for the release of her very sexual novel and was bracing herself for the expected backlash of her *Playboy* layout. But in the weeks that followed, the backlash hardly ever came and the public—even her dad—respected her decision to pose. And it wasn't only because she looked absolutely beautiful, I think the public finally caught on to Patti's renegade spirit and began to treat her like some sort of national treasure. Think of it, how many children of former presidents are ever heard from again? Outside of John Kennedy, Jr., and Patti, they're a fairly quiet bunch.

Needless to say, Patti was in good spirits every time a publicity opportunity took her from her Connecticut home and placed her in front of the big cameras in the big city. Sometimes I was by her side, particularly the time we stayed up all night at the Essex House and walked over to 30 Rock for her *Today Show* appearance. It must have been five A.M. as we began our walk and Patti tried to give me some insight into how difficult it was to walk alone, holding a man's hand, without scores of Secret Service agents looking over her. I dug it, too. It ain't often a guy gets to date a president's daughter. And, I ain't gonna lie to you, every one of my friends knew. But, hell, I would've dated Patti if she poured coffee at Starbucks. She is a cool chick and has a lot more "guy" in her than you know. Anyhow, after a few months, our fizz went flat. I know why, but it's far too personal to say. At any rate, it has to do with me being immature with a woman's feelings and that type of thing doesn't happen too often. I've tried to get back in touch with her through a mutual friend several times over the years. But Patti won't budge. I like her more for that. And I miss her friendship.

Talkin' about You

Not since Hedda Hopper made the cover of *Time* magazine in 1947 had gossip columnists carried such high profiles within the media and around the country. At the start of 1994, New York City's newspapers had as many as twenty gossip columnists running around the city, breaking stories with the delicacy of a repo man making off with your brand-new Bentley. And when you figure in the tattletales at the weekly and monthly magazines like *New York* magazine, Esquire and *Vanity Fair*, the count could almost double. Television was also ringing in with *Entertainment Tonight, Hard Copy, The Gossip Show* and *Inside Edition* offering up their own scoops on Hollywood's elite. Right around that year, there was also word that Knopf was close to publishing Neal Gabler's tome on the granddaddy of gossips, Walter Winchell. Further innuendo had the great Martin Scorsese ready to direct the film version. To paraphrase Buster Poindexter, the gossip industry was . . . fuckin' hot, hot, hot.

For some odd reason, this was also around the time Linda told me privately she wasn't long for the job anymore. She told me in confidence that she'd finish the contract Zuckerman gave her and then, maybe, ask to be moved to the news side. "I think I'd like to write twice a week," she told me. "Write about whatever I want to write about. I'm tired of this stuff. I've done it for five years already." She told me she had about a year left in her. In the meantime, she said, it was time for her to let me step into the spotlight a bit more. "You're ready," she said.

First thing she did was bring me to the set of *The Joan Rivers Show* and listen to her tell Joan, in so many words, that I was her successor and to please have me as a guest on the show as often as they had her. Joan was quick to please and booked me the next week for her regularly featured "Gossip, Gossip, Gossip" segment on her Friday shows. The weeks went by and I was a hit. Joan and I spoke the same language. And I knew I was on to something when, during one commercial break, Joan spoke directly to the audience during commercial break and told them: "This kid is going to be big. You mark my words." Then she turned to me in a whisper, "You're different than everyone else. Stay different. Ugh . . . what a pleasure. A male gossip columnist who isn't gay. Please!"

Then a producer piped in, "We are twenty seconds to air, Joan . . ."

"Hold it," Joan whispered to me again. "You are straight, right. I mean, I have no problem with gays. None at all. But you seem so straight and I just wouldn't believe it if you were gay . . ."

"Ten seconds . . ."

"You're not gay, right? Please don't take this the wrong way. If you're gay, that's fine . . ."

"Five . . ."

"I have no problem with it. But nobody would believe . . ."

"Three, two . . ."

"Hello, we're back with A.J. Benza, gossip columnist for the New York *Daily News*. Now let me ask you something, why do you think your style is so popular?"

"Well, Joan," I began, "it's popular because I'm different than most other gossip columnists. I'm a kid from the street. I'm not a rich older woman. I'm not a snob from London. And I'm not a gay man."

"Oh, stop it. Who would ever think you're gay?"

Joan was always good to me and the best thing she might've ever done for me was have me open on the show that Howard Stern was going to speak about his new bestseller *Private Parts* before a couple hundred of his screaming fans in the studio audience. Though I realize Joan was throwing me a big bone by booking me, I also realized I could've choked on that bone had I not let the audience know that I was there for the same reason they were. A few seconds after Joan introduced me, I opened the segment by saying, "Let's make this quick. I came here to see Howard. Screw me."

She loved it. The crowd loved it and even Howard was appreciative of it backstage before he went on. Despite the way he acts on radio and television, Howard is a thoughtful and honorable man. He always remembers the little guy. "Hey, thanks for taking care of me in your column," he said, as he autographed my book. "You're one of the only gossip columnists who's on my side. Plus, you're not a homo."

Hands of Fate

N ow who's this guy we're meeting," Chico asked me as we cut our way through the crowded and oh-so-fabulous lobby of the Royal-ton Hotel.

"Some guy who says he produces *The Gossip Show* on E! and he wants to meet me about getting a spot on the show."

"This guy flew in from Hollywood," Chico asked.

"Yeah."

"Just to see you?"

"Yeah."

"I don't like it. It smells. Something's wrong."

"Would you relax," I said, while spotting the show's producer Gary Socol in the middle of the scene.

"Just watch it with these Hollywood guys. They're all cocksuckers. I'll be at the bar if you need me."

As harsh as it sounds, Chico's advice is right on the nose with most Hollywood types. But he was way off with Socol, the unassuming and peaceful producer who would change my life before the ice in my Cutty and water had melted.

I had heard a little about E!'s *The Gossip Show* before I met with Socol. I knew it was on that channel that was hard to find and I knew it was the same channel that had just signed Howard Stern to a nice fat contract. I immediately figured it wouldn't be a bad business decision to align myself with any network that had the foresight to sign the King of All Media. That was the initial thing that showed me someone at the network had balls. The second thing was the way Socol approached me. He seemed a little intimidated initially, but before our conversation was through Socol told me he wanted me to be a part of the show and he requested one thing.

"Just be yourself," he said. "Don't tell *secrets* like a lot of the others do." He was rolling his eyes at the thought. "Just talk the way you talk. Move the way you move. And you'll be fine."

That's easy enough, I told him.

"The last thing we need is another effeminate man dishing dirt. Just be A.J."

Socol told me they would initially put me on the air once every two weeks and see how things went. The camera crew would come to my office and I would be paid $110 per appearance. Seemed easy as pie.

"He flew all the way in for that," Chico asked.

"Yep."

"That town is fuckin' nuts."

It is. But that town helped launch me into the homes of millions of people on a weekly basis. And before long, the show's popularity grew and it went from a weekly show to a nightly show. And not long after that, I was the only correspondent to appear four times a week. Even the queens Liz and Cindy never got more than three. But the biggest boom of all occurred when the show would air right after E!'s live coverage of the O. J. Simpson trial. Every day, for millions of transfixed viewers across the country—smackdab in the middle of the gripping trial—a promo for *The Gossip Show* would air with me telling America to stay tuned for our show. And stay tuned they did. America was turning on the trial, but stayed tuned in for their dose of gossip immediately following. It was kind of like a palate-cleansing slice of ginger between giant gulps of sushi. And think of my reports as the dab of wasabi that is sometimes hard to get down.

My reports were honest. They had an edge. And, because I was beginning to get closer to the subjects I was writing about, they ringed more true. It was, like I told Socol, easy as pie. All I did was sit in my office and pound at my keyboards until the E! crew would arrive. They'd put a mic on me, swivel my chair around and just let me rant for a minute or so. And before long Socol pushed my salary to $250 a pop. So, do the math. That's $1,000 a week—every week—just to perform a simple extension of my grueling job. So, say what you want about Hollywood, but that town basically almost doubled my salary—practically matching my yearly take at the *News*—just for five minutes of my time each week.

So there I was, less than two years removed from my last $13, now a six-figure fool. I was set to get *fucked up* on fun.

Under Cover of the Night

No two ways about it, the *Daily News* had a certain swagger to it at the time. The roster was impressive and filled with hardcore writers with stiff city voices and the knack to punch out poetry in the face of a relentless deadline. Outside of our column, we had giant names like Lupica, Dwyer, Daly, McAlary and Kriegel, guys with the kind of guts that usually beget glory—or at least the hard truth. Hell, even the behind-the-scenes guys had the kind of names and personalities you didn't want to fuck with. Guys named Big Mike, Gypsy and Billy Martin. Guys with a story working for the newspaper that broke the big stories.

We also had Fred Drasner running in full stride now, looking to pummel the competition in radio and TV spots that were always screened for you in the privacy of his office when he could find you in the hallways and kidnap you. "Come here, come here. Got a minute? You're gonna love this shit." And there he was, playing stickball on a Brooklyn street, knocking the "spaldeen" "two sewers" away. Or he was on the radio, following a moving sports article read by Kriegel, where he would bark: "That's Mark Kriegel. He writes for us. The *Daily News*. We're the most New York you can get." And for a good stretch, we were. But to say we weren't flowered with a little English flair and sensationalism wouldn't be fair to Zuckerman's startling and ballsy hiring of the British wunderkind Martin Dunn as our editor-in-chief.

When Zuckerman lured the thirty-eight-year-old Brit away from his *Boston Herald* gig to sit in the big chair at the *News* Building in late 1993, it was a move some newspaper hacks sneered at. Outside of the usual petty jealousies, there were concerns and moans that the job might be better suited for someone who had been at the paper for years. Perhaps someone with broader New York sensibilities and, at least, roots that had been set in the city's concrete jungle. Others inside the paper were just flat-out pissed off that they had been passed up for a guy who knew more about Piccadilly Square than Herald Square. But they were dead wrong. They didn't see the flash behind Zuckerman's gesture. I did, and I waited for Dunn to kick into gear.

But Dunn never had it easy at the paper. Aside from constant chastising from Zuckerman and various "whine-and-jeez" meetings with various reporters, Dunn was accused of being aloof with his staff, never addressing the newsroom as a whole and only given to snatches of conversations with underlings. But if he is going to be accused of that, then he must also be accused of injecting the *News* with big-headline, page-one splash and pushing to make the paper more appealing to women and—and here's where I prospered—allowing the paper's entertainment writers to flood the desk with ideas and stories pertaining to our culture's obsession with celebrity. Bottom line, Martin Dunn was guilty of expertly commanding his troops in a full-scale tabloid war between the *Daily News* and the *Post*. A winner was never officially declared, but the war gave all of us a shot to show our armor and raise our swords. Generals Rupert Murdoch and Mortimer Zuckerman looked on as we kicked each other's asses up and down the newsstands every morning.

Dunn and I hit it off from the jump. The very first story I came to him with was my contention that figure skater Nancy Kerrigan was carrying on an affair with her very married manager Jerry Soloman. I told Dunn I had sources tell me of a secret videotape that showed the lovebirds holding hands as they walked in the woods. Now, I know managers are supposed to offer their clients guidance and support, but this seemed a little much. I told him my source—a tabloid TV producer—couldn't run with the piece because his boss had a close friendship with Soloman. He was giving me the story to run with as a gift. "Impress your new boss. I just want to see the thing in the paper," he told me. In fact, they all say that.

Of course, Dunn loved it and immediately told me to fly down to Virginia and see if I could do a little work on the piece. Bolster it up, report it out. Basically, get closer to it and not have it hanging there in a gossip page. "This is wood," he told me. "All right then . . . get a flight and go."

That sounded wonderful, but American Express had just taken their privileges away from me and my Visa card was socked to the limit. So I walked back into his office, a big deadbeat facing a big deadline

"What is it then," he said, one part Benny Hill one part Herman's Hermits.

"I gotta borrow your Amex. I don't have a card."

"Oh, bloody hell. Don't you have a corporate card?"

"No. They never offered me one."

"Well, first thing tomorrow we'll see about getting you one. But use it for snagging stories, not for shagging girls."

Long story short, I never made it to Virginia. It was late, we feared the story might not hold and we had a Washington reporter shuffle off to Virginia and confront Soloman's wife in the driveway of their giant home. Not the way I would've done things, but it wasn't my call. At any rate, Ms. Soloman wholeheartedly denied having a problem marriage and my inquiries to Soloman were met with strong denials and letters from his big-shot attorney threatening lawsuits should we go ahead with the story. Just when it looked like we were at a dead end, I ran an end-around and nailed it.

With the help of Lonnie Hanover, Scores's publicist who was also working publicity for the giant restaurant Metronome, I was allowed to sneak into the post-show *Saturday Night Live* party for the show that Kerrigan had just hosted. Lonnie let me in a back door and then it was up to me to confront Kerrigan in the VIP area, ask her the big question and get the hell out of Dodge before her handlers started having babies on the spot.

Lonnie took me aside. "All I can do is let you in. If they make you, you're going to have to be tossed out and I have to act like I don't know you or how you got in. You understand?"

I knew the drill. It wasn't the first time someone had opened up a back door for me.

As he said that, I watched Whiskey Bar owner and Cindy Crawford's former boyfriend, Rande Gerber, peel up West 21st Street in a fancy sports car, put the car in park, shut off the lights and remain there halfway between Park Avenue and Broadway.

"Hey, there goes Rande Gerber," I said.

"Oh, forget about it . . . It's a great party," Lonnie said. "*Everybody* is inside."

Anyhow, as I'm heading to the rear door, I spot Cindy Crawford—who was still married to Richard Gere at the time—fall into a cab and head west on 21st Street. Then I watch as the cab stops right next to Gerber's sports car and Cindy gets out and falls into Gerber's passenger seat. And then they kiss before peeling away.

So, on the way to a giant story, I have another beauty unfold right before my very eyes. Instantly and subconsciously, I start to think that tomorrow's column will have not one, but two stories big enough to lead any goddamn column in the country, let alone Manhattan. It's in moments like these that you spend the rest of the night relaxing or partying like hell. You know your work is done. It's like making quota a day early. But I still had a major story to break.

Once inside the cavernous Metronome I was hardly anonymous. But I meandered to the bar, downed a Jameson and followed the masses to the back VIP area, which was cordoned off with a rope. As I get there, I spot Jimmy Judo, a guy who used to work the rope at China Club and he immediately winks and lets me walk right in. Now all I have to do is ask Nancy any question pertaining to her relationship.

"Hello, sweetheart, you were great tonight on the show," I said, another lying voice in her pretty little ear.

"Oh, thank you so much."

"So how you handling the big city?"

"Oh, it's big but I love it."

"Is it hard with everybody coming at you?"

"Actually, people have been very supportive of me."

I could see the flaks starting to spring into action. You don't hear the words but you can see them flashing across their little furrowed brows.

"Wait a minute . . . isn't that the gossip guy . . . how did he get . . . *security,* we need security here . . . !"

"Nancy, one more thing," I said. "Is it hard being away from your boyfriend Jerry?"

"Yeah . . . it's kind of . . . well, we're really not . . . He's my manager. Who are you?"

Then I was gone. I had my story. As far as I was concerned, I looked into Nancy's eyes when she fumbled the boyfriend question and that was enough for me. Unfortunately, it wasn't enough for a front-page story, but it would fit nicely in the column. And we ran it through fierce denials and threats of huge libel lawsuits.

"I hope you're right about this one," Dunn told me. "Mort will have your ass if you're not."

Anyhow, we weathered the storm and in a matter of days more proof came to light that an affair was going on. Several weeks later, Soloman and his wife separated. Not too long after that, Soloman admitted to being in love. Today Jerry Soloman and Nancy Kerrigan are married and have a child.

And that's exactly where we're at with Rande Gerber and Cindy Crawford. They, too, are married with a child, though my inquiries to Cindy's agents the morning after the *SNL* party had them in a fury. "How dare you! Cindy is a married woman. That was not Cindy Crawford you saw in that car," they said. "We will not sit back and take this. Expect to hear from her lawyer."

I never did. They knew that I knew what they didn't want anyone to know. They were doing their job, but I did mine better.

Those two scores solidified my position with Dunn more than anyone else. With him in my corner, there was no telling how far I could go.

When the Whip Comes Down

I ain't lying when I say the *Daily News* was hot. And we were consistently kicking in everyone's asses in terms of breaking stories and extended second and third-day coverage on major events, crimes and disasters. It was almost as if everyone turned it up a notch at the exact same time. There was a buzz about us. And we all began to feel like little stars when Ron Howard asked to observe us in action so he might get a better feel for what a newsroom is for his upcoming flick *The Paper*. So for a period of several weeks we sat at our keyboards as the likes of Glenn Close, Marisa Tomei and Michael Keaton sat in our offices and listened in our meetings while doing their research. I wasn't lucky enough to land a cameo in the film—which a number of our editors and columnists did—but in the several times Howard took me aside for questions, I must have made a little impression on the guy. Because it was a little over a year later he and the great Brian Grazer cast me in another one of their films. But more on that fuckin' story later.

Around this time, television crews from most of the tabloid shows began to ring my phone on a daily basis. It was like clockwork, actually. I remember typing stories out and knowing in the same second I was dotting my "i's" and crossing my "t's" which show producer would be ringing the following morning. But back in the day, *Hard Copy*'s hardboiled British producer Susan Crimp was a mainstay on my phone machine.

"This is A.J. Benza at the New York *Daily News*. Leave me something good at the beep and I'll take care of you," is what my voice mail spit out.

"A.J.? Susan Crimp here, darling. What say we come by around noon for a look at your Naomi Campbell catfight story? It's fuckin' brilliant, doll. I'll bring the contracts. Say $250?"

At the beginning, I used to jump at the chance for a quick $250 just for five minutes' work with a television camera in front of my face. But I got wise once I realized that most of these shows' producers don't have a clue what to air every night until they sit down with a cup of coffee and cigarette and plow through the gossip columns. And once I saw that most of their segments stemmed from what they read that very morning in the gossip pages—and Hot Copy was leading the charge—I stuck them up for more money.

"Susan . . . A.J. here. Glad you liked the Naomi story, baby. But $250 ain't what I was looking for. That's not even scale, kid. Let's make it an even $500."

Usually, she agreed. And each time she agreed, I'd up my ante every time she called. It got to a point I was getting $1,000 a visit, sometimes for measly thirty-second sound bites. Even when she balked at a request for higher payment, I would pay it no mind and simply fill out the contract while she was packing up her gear and scribble in "$1,000" next to the amount of my fee. Far as I know, she never figured it out. Every week, another few checks would arrive: Amount Paid—$1,000. And that was just the deal I was working with Crimp. Don't forget, I also had producers from *Inside Edition, Entertainment Tonight, A Current Affair* and *American Journal* paying me, as well. Let me just say this: I started to like TV a lot.

The money was good, so it was around this time I sold the last remnant of my married days and got rid of the four-door Toyota Corolla—which Jennifer had picked out—and took over the lease on a buddy's Nissan 240SX. It was sportier to say the least and I liked the renegade spirit of driving a stick again. Plus I never again had to feel funny if a valet came around a corner with my car. Not that a Nissan is necessarily a chick magnet, but a four-door Corolla has them looking for the baby seat from three blocks away.

All that media attention surrounding Dunn's arrival and Howard's successful opening of *The Paper*, brought more attention to the gang on East 42nd St. Aside from profiles in *New York* magazine, *The New York Times* and countless other periodicals, it wasn't long before Dan Rather was interested in shining the light on our paper with his top-rated CBS news show *48 Hours*. The show was basically going to illustrate a day in the life of a powerful tabloid and was set on spotlighting several of the *News*'s high-profile reporters and columnists. Some of us who got the call were Rob Speyer, a cub reporter off the streets of New York who preferred covering crime to sponging off the millions his father made being the Speyer half of New York City's megapowerful real estate firm Tishman Speyer. The show also counted on trailing tough-talking female columnist Amy Pagnozzi, Irish columnist Michael Daly, Belgian-born beat reporter Jose Lambiet and the triumvirate behind Hot Copy— Stasi, Lewittes and yours truly. And it was after this point that things began to truly turn for me—as a columnist, as a New York personality, as a guy who was about to blow up.

Linda's segment of the show was simple enough. Our leader sat on her desk and explained what it is that we were doing at the time. "It's not gossip" was Linda's battle cry back in those days. "Gossip to me is unsubstantiated bullshit and that's not what we do. We check everything nine ways to Christmas before we print it."

Was it "society" reporting came the query.

"No. No. No," Linda said. "I could care less what society people do. I'd die of boredom letting you know what it is they do."

Then what is it, the *48 Hours* reporter wanted to know.

"We break news and we spin it," Linda said. "There're too many serious pages in a newspaper. We break news and find the humor in it."

Later in the show, two different camera crews followed "Linda's legs"—me and Michael—on our after-hour rounds around Manhattan. Most of Michael's night was spent sharing a quiet meal in SoHo's Mez-zogiorno restaurant with Pacific publicist Peter Seligman, who, during dinner, was dropping a dime on Nancy Kerrigan's alleged nasty personality. My portion of the show was decidedly different as the cameras began filming me in my apartment before they followed me to Scores and then Boom before retiring to the trendy Casa La Femme restaurant on Wooster Street. What the cameras uncovered was my closeness to the "employees" at Scores (shapely girls as well as guys with crooked noses) and my ability to get permission to take two knockouts along with me for the rest of the night. So there we were—me and my pal Danny Montanez—escorting two of Scores's finest girls (Lonnie and Tamara) as we watched them topless table-dance at Boom and do the same at Casa La Femme, where we met up with Madonna's boy-of-the-moment, male model Johnny Zander. Suddenly, my segment of the show was not only about my ability to get inside the "in" spots and dig up information on celebrities, but it also illustrated my ability to bring a party with me wherever I was headed. No doubt there were guys all over the country watching me as I visited Scores on their television sets and then there I was bringing Scores's finest with me to other establishments. I didn't realize how powerful or seductive that image was going to come off until I viewed the program on television several weeks later and I watched the cameras catch Tamara (who went on to become a *Penthouse* covergirl) and Lonnie caress each other's bodies as they held on to a chandelier in the back booth at Boom. And even more so when our segment ended as me and Danny threw our arms around the strippers and faded from view on a dark SoHo street.

There's no other way of putting it: That show made it feel incredibly cool to be working for the fourth largest paper in America. And any young journalist with any aspirations at all would've killed to have my job. And I would've killed anyone who tried to take it all away from me.

Not too long after that, the unthinkable happened—Linda up and quit. Even though she had told me in confidence that she was leaning that way, the news still killed me when it finally went down.

Linda had been given a new column some months before. Her assignment this time out was not gossip by any stretch. It was more in line with what she was stronger at anyhow—and that was putting her own unique spin on the ironies that weave their way through the topical news that affected all of us. Whether it be a national story or something that only pertained to a small part of the city itself, Linda's job was to smother the story with her sarcasm, pin it to the mat with her pithy reportage and blow away the competition by balancing wit, understanding and a no-nonsense mentality. All the while remaining completely subjective, as all great columnists do.

The column, which usually ran once or twice a week, was a success as far as I was concerned. I remember laughing out loud every time I read it just as I do now with her TV column for the New York *Post*. Even though Michael and I were now sharing an office and Linda was sitting in a cubicle outside Dunn's office pounding out her own column, the new arrangement was kind of sad. I felt like Linda had been traded to a rival team. Every morning when I read her column, I felt like a ball player who checks to the previous day's line scores to see how a former teammate played. Even though her own gig—outside of gossip—was what she wanted, it was still a very different atmosphere without her around us anymore. It was a weird predicament to be in—as much as I wanted to shine outside of Linda's shadow, it was a bit scary not having Mama Bear in the lineup every day. I mean, I'm sure Scottie Pippin always wanted to sink the winning bucket, but not at the expense of Michael Jordan sitting on the bench.

Anyhow, unbeknownst to me and Michael, Linda had been having some harsh words with Dunn and some of the other suits at the paper. It was mainly about her column not running on any kind of regular basis and the fact that it sometimes appeared as far back in the paper as page forty. "What the fuck am I, a sportswriter?" Linda would ask sometimes.

No one is really certain what happened when she up and quit and I loved her too much to pry when she left the office one day with tears in her eyes. My guess is that Linda felt the male columnists were always given preferential treatment and back in those days the *Daily News* truly was a boys' club. Once she asked me, "If I were a white, Irish, male columnist, do you think my column would ever run further than page eleven?"

She might have had a point. But I figure it was a point the brass didn't want to hear her make anymore. And one day when Linda threatened to quit over something pertaining to her column's placement, Dunn called her bluff. And, staying true to her proud fighter mentality, there was nothing left for Linda to do but make those words come true.

At any rate, because of the way she stormed out, Michael and I never really shared a moment with her to thank her for all the nurturing, tough love and the legitimate shot she gave us. I kept the chainsaw I gave her and left the broken bits of porcelain coffee cups that she once smashed against the wall on my desk. As a final tribute, I even framed some of her best hate mail and kept it hanging on my wall. The halls were never the same without her laughter. She would call from time to time and say, "Great column today, boys," but it rang a bit hollow. She was calling the *News* from her home now and we were right at home at the *News*.

Happy

One half-hour to deadline was not the time for anything else but toning up the column items that Michael and I were compiling for the next day's read. It was in that tense time that I would let my phone ring off the hook while I gave everything the once-over, made sure everything was jake and punched up a joke or two.

An example.

Me: "Hey, Michael, I want to begin this item with a funny fuckin' line. Come on, gimme a hand. Okay . . . The rumor about Pearl Jam's surprise concert at a downtown nightclub is spinning faster than . . . faster than what?"

Michael: "Ah . . . faster than William Shatner's hairpiece in a wind tunnel?"

Me: "Bingo!"

One half-hour to deadline was like verbal surgery for us, so it was important we paid no mind to our ringing phones. But one afternoon, in the middle of writer's block, I reached to quiet the incessant ring.

"What?"

"Mr. Benza?"

"Yeah!"

"Please hold for Brian Grazer."

I have a lot of friends with fucked-up senses of humor. This was undoubtedly one of them, probably Chico, impersonating the powerful spikey-haired Hollywood producer just to rankle me at deadline. I waited for "Grazer" to click on.

"Hey, man, have we met?"

"Yeah. We met at Sav-On. In the hair gel aisle."

Click. Tone.

A few seconds later my phone rings again. This time I press the speakerphone button, ready to really bust Chico's balls.

"Come on, fucker. I can't do this. I'll talk to you later."

And then I hear the faint voice of the female secretary who had called me seconds earlier. "Is there a better time Mr. Grazer can call?"

I was baffled.

"No. Put him through."

A few seconds later I hear Grazer—and at this point I know it's not Chico—clicking on. "I'm gonna make this quick," he said. "You want to be in my movie?"

"This really Grazer?"

"Yeah."

"You ain't shitting me?"

"No. I'm casting my film and from time to time I catch you on *The Gossip Show,* and I don't know . . . I think you might work in my film."

"Hold on," I said to him before turning to Michael, beaming like a little boy. "Hey, this is Brian Grazer asking me if I want to be in his film."

"You sure that call isn't for me?"

"I'm serious, ass. What do I do?"

"For starters, get him off hold and talk to him," Michael said. "This is not the kind of guy you put on hold."

I clicked back on. "Okay, yeah. That sounds good. What now?"

"I mean, you want to pursue acting, right?"

"No, I want acting to pursue me."

"I like that," Grazer said, continuing the seduction on his car phone. "Well, I think I can make that happen. I'm doing a film called *Ransom,* with Mel Gibson and Rene Russo. Their kid gets kidnapped. It's a real great thriller. Listen, I'm coming to town tomorrow night. Let's have dinner. In the meantime, I'll have my office fax you over the sides for the role. Read it and we'll talk tomorrow."

I put the finishing touches on the column, but at that point I didn't care what it was going to read like, to tell you the truth. I was going to be a star for God's sake. Brian Grazer said so. I waited an hour after I put the page to bed for the fax machine to crackle with the sides to my meaty role. Michael, being the good friend he is, waited along with me.

"This is history," Michael said.

"Yeah, but history was written by liars," I said.

"Do you think they'll let me have the column when you go off and become a movie star?"

"Michael, you can have my Mercedes if you want, pal."

Just then, the fax began to spit out the pages. First the cover sheet came through, from the offices of Imagine Entertainment. Cool. Then the second page came through nice and clean. Heaven.

And that was it. Two measly pages. Two. Actually, one page if you don't count the cover sheet. On top of that, the part highlighted was for "Deli Boy," and the character's only line was "You want cheese with that?"

I dreamed of a *meaty* role, not a role in which the character handles luncheon meat. What the fuck was going on?

Michael was dying inside, but he stayed as dry as any Yale wiseass. "Remember—there is no such thing as a small part . . . But sometimes there really are some meaningless, forgettable roles."

After laughing my ass off, I took home the news to Chico and Jackie, who were playing Nintendo on the couch. "Can you believe this fuckin' guy calls me and offers me a part in his film and I'm the guy slapping together a ham on rye?"

Jackie was still starstruck, nonetheless. "Dude. That's one more line than Kevin Costner had in *The Big Chill*. I say we go out and celebrate."

And we did, visiting the Japanese joint on Madison for shiatsu massages with "happy endings." There's always something about a pretty little doting Japanese woman telling you over and over, "You so strooooong."

I decided to take up Grazer on his offer and I met the diminutive bigwig for dinner at the Bowery Bar the following night. I brought along JohnnyBoy for a little support and, in time, a few other people found seats at the table like Alan Finkelstein, Russell Simmons and Annabella Sciorra. Grazer showed up with his girlfriend Gigi Levangie, a pretty one who remained very complimentary the entire evening. "I'm the one who always told him about you," she repeated to me several times. We sat around laughing, eating dinner and rubbernecking another Thursday night in Manhattan into oblivion. Two hours later, Grazer finally brought up the film.

"So," he said, patting me on the leg. "What'd you think about the part?"

"Well," I deadpanned, "there are several ways I can approach the character. But I see Deli Boy as a very intense sandwich maker and I intend to really shake people up with my choice." I then launched into a deranged Robert De Niro impression.

"You want cheese with that? You heard what I said? You like my cheese? You hate my cheese? Does my cheese bother you? You're gonna find your dog dead in the hallway, you *son of a bitch!*"

Grazer was laughing, but it was clear he had no idea why. "What are you doing?"

"Delivering my line," I said. "The sides your office sent me were for a part called Deli Boy. It had one line."

"Okaaaaaay. There's been a mistake. I want you to read for one of the *kidnappers*. I'm terribly sorry. I'll have my office straighten it out in the morning."

I was feeling like a big shot that night, so I remember picking up the $250 tab for everyone's dinner. To this day I still can't believe that I'm quicker to the pocket than any millionaires I've ever sat down to eat with. Anyhow, I decided to hang around and shoot the shit with JohnnyBoy well after Grazer left. It was around one A.M. when fashion photographer Sante D'Orazio came by our booth to chat with JohnnyBoy. I had never met Sante before that night, but I had written about him dozens of times. It was hard not to. Sante was a good-looking fashion photographer who had the enviable position of shooting the world's most beautiful women in the most exotic corners of the world. Aside from that, he practically had a corner on the *Sports Illustrated* swim-suit shoot as well as the Victoria's Secret catalogues. As if that wasn't enough, Sante was very rich and was also married to supermodel Kara Young, a woman I always held as the most gorgeous model on Earth. In fact, hers was the kind of beauty that uncharacteristically tied my tongue in knots.

At any rate, Sante was coming my way and Kara was following him and I was kind of in a coma.

I don't remember too much of what was said inside that tight booth that night. I just remember JohnnyBoy making the pleasant introductions and Sante thanking me for a recent piece I had written about him. And then the beautiful couple said "ciao" and made their way past the thick crowd, hugging good-bye to owner Eric Goode, nodding good-night to doorman Jeff Gossett and turning left on East 4th Street and into the blue-black Manhattan night. And I remember turning to JohnnyBoy and very calmly saying, "How well do you know Sante? Is he a really good friend of yours?"

"Nah. Not a *good* friend, buddy. Just a friend. Why?"

"Because I'm gonna take his wife away, Johnny."

"Okay, buddy."

And about a year later, I did just that. And for more than two years she was the love of my life. But more on that fuckin' story later.

The next morning I couldn't have cared less what was happening in New York City. It would all have to wait. I was sitting on some very important sides from Los Angeles and gossip took a backseat to my dreams of being in the movies. When I finally got them, I was both relieved and scared shitless. Grazer came through in a big way. The seven pages of sides in my hands did, indeed, have some meaty dialogue to them and I only had a couple of hours to digest them before booking it up to 10 Columbus Circle to read. What Grazer forgot to tell me was exactly who I was reading for and that mattered to me since I had never read for a movie role before.

I don't remember the cab ride uptown, I was too involved getting familiar with the script. "If you hear me talking back here, don't worry about it," I told the disinterested hack. "Reading for a movie. Yep . . . big movie role. *Big.* Big as they come."

I would have shit my pants way ahead of time if I had known I was going to be reading for Ron Howard. But there I was, without enough time to even find a men's room in the entire building before an assistant called out, "A.J. . . . Ron will see you now."

What could've turned into a disastrous situation was sweet as pie since Ron handled me like a virgin at a family picnic. "So Brian tells me you're a natural," he said.

I didn't know what to say except to be completely honest. "I don't know about that, Ron. If I were that good, you'd a picked it up and put me in *The Paper*, right?"

"Hell, I didn't know you wanted to act back then or I might have."

He makes you feel real easy, this guy. And when he talks you can't help but feel you're sitting right there in Mayberry and he's gonna offer you a piece of Aunt Bee's apple pie.

After Ron described the role, he urged me to "just be yourself" and "have fun with it"—the most overused (but truthful) expressions you ever hear when you're staring into a camera. And so I did. And when I was done, Ron leaned back and smiled.

"Hey, wow, you can do this. You can really do this."

He then asked me to read again, but this time as the other kidnapper. And I did. And when I was done, Ron leaned back and smiled even bigger.

"Gee, A.J. That was really good. You should really pursue this. I'm not kidding."

He actually says things like "gee." The guy makes you feel so at ease, I almost asked to read for Mel Gibson's role while I was there.

"Okay, well, we'll be in touch in a few days and let you know what we're gonna do."

"Like what," I said. "A couple of days?"

"Um-hmm. Like two days or so. Thanks again."

Boom. It ends that quickly. But then the real cramps begin.

I didn't hear anything for two weeks. And I couldn't call anyone either. I had no agent yet. I had no manager. I wasn't even in SAG yet. I was only in that spot because Brian Grazer and his girlfriend liked me on *The Gossip Show*. After I officially gave up hope and told my friends to do the same, my phone rang late one afternoon—again bull's-eye on deadline.

"A.J., I have Brian Grazer calling."

Grazer's familiar voice clicked on. "Okay, I'm gonna make you a star," he said.

"No shit?"

"No shit. Ron said you were great."

"Jesus, that's great," I said. "What role? What kidnapper?"

"You're not a kidnapper. The kidnapper roles went to Donnie Wahlberg and Liev Schreiber. But Ron wants you in, so we wrote in a part. That's what took us so long. You're playing a reporter, essentially you're playing yourself. You sneak into a fancy party at Mel's penthouse, you bother Mel and Mel and his goons throw you out."

I wanted to tell Grazer that I didn't sneak into fancy penthouse parties and I had never been thrown out of anyone's home since high school, so I wasn't, in essence, playing myself. But, let's face it: The guy just gave me a major break and for that I would owe him for a long, long time. So big deal, I was playing myself. He could have told me I would be playing *with* myself and I still would have shown up at Kaufman Astoria Studios on shoot day with bells on.

Some Girls

My love for the Playboy Mansion must be a Pavlovian thing, dating back to the days when my Sicilian father plastered old *Playboy* centerfolds above my crib and bassinet, despite the shrieks of terror from my dear Neapolitan mother.

"Al . . . he's not even walking or talking yet."

"Who says that's the first thing he's got to learn?"

Maybe after fathering two daughters, Poppa was exulting that he had finally had a son at age forty—and goddammit he was finally going to celebrate the sounds of another man in our tiny Bensonhurst, Brooklyn apartment. Who cares if I shared a room with my seventeen-year-old sister Rosalie and eleven-year-old sister Lorraine at the time. No time was the wrong time to begin appreciating women, according to my father, Alfredo Cosimo Benza.

And so the centerfolds stayed up. And as I learned to walk and talk, my most visceral memories included the wondrous layouts of Stella Stevens, Christa Speck, Connie Mason and the famous 1964 Playmate of the Year cover featuring Donna Michelle contorting her body into the shape of the Rabbit Head.

But almost thirty years later, me and Hugh Hefner were at odds. Well, me and his publicity staff anyway.

Early on in my gossiping days at New York *Newsday* I had made phone friends with the Barbi Twins—the curiously beautiful, bouncy and bulimic twin sisters who skyrocketed to success and riches because of their *Playboy* layouts, sexy calendars and videos. One day, the more vocal of the pair, Shane, phoned me up because she was upset with an item we ran in the column dealing with the sisters eating Gerber baby food all day long to maintain their weights. After a long-winded argument and a clarification a few days later, Shane and Sia continued to ring my line and chat me up. In time, because of the laughs we had and the information we shared and the flirting we enjoyed, the girls became a protected pair within our column. They also enjoyed similar protection later on at my tenure at the *News*. To be frank—they were brilliant at supplying me with gossip, and I couldn't lose my grip climbing the ladder.

One of the things the girls were especially clairvoyant at was "predicting" the Playmate of the Year many months before Hef and his team would make the special and secret announcement in his great backyard party every May. Because the twins knew so many makeup artists and photographers and employees within the Mansion, they were always privy to the news way ahead of the general public. To make a long story short, I went ahead and made a habit every single year from 1993 thru 1997 of printing the POY before the supposed readers' phoned-in "votes" were tabulated. And so with each year I confounded *Playboy*'s publicity staff and some of its top executives by prematurely naming Anna Nicole Smith, Jenny McCarthy, Julie Lynn Cialini, Stacy Sanches and Victoria Silvstedt before Hef made the "official" announcement. And as the story ran in my column, *Playboy*'s flunkies would deny it until the Rabbit was blue in the face. It seems inconsequential, but I'm telling you it was a big deal. They'd hate it when the big news would be let out in my column a good three months before it was time and all the tabloid television producers would call *Playboy* to put together segments on the winner. It meant I was letting the world in on The Best Kept Yearly Secret in town and there was nothing they could do to stop me. That's why the mag's publicity honcho Cindy Rackowitz finally gave in to screaming at me on more than one occasion.

"What the *fuck* is your problem?"

"Nothing," I'd say. "But if you're always going to deny my reports, then I'll continue to print what I know. All I want is for you to be honest with me when I ask you a question."

Truthfully, there was a deeper problem. I was pissed that *Playboy*'s publicity whizzes would always break their big scoops with Liz Smith or Jeannie Williams in that ugly puzzle of graphs and pie charts that is *USA Today*—which nobody reads unless they're early for a flight. Back then my battle cry was "Why are you breaking sexy news like this in columns written by old women? Why don't you break this news with me?" I just happened to believe that more *Playboy* afficionados would rather hear the news—in print or on TV—from a guy like me. A guy who would get lucky once in a while and actually date the girls in those pages.

But this Rackowitz wasn't going to budge so easily. It's a good thing the Playmates aren't as staunch as Cindy or else none of them would ever take off their tops for a spread in the first place. Anyhow, it was killing me, watching all these sexy scoops ending up in the old hands of Liz and Jeannie. So I ended up flat-out telling Cindy that I was prepared to print what I really know is going on inside the Mansion.

And back then I knew a lot. For example, I knew that Hef's marriage to Kimberly Conrad-Hefner was not quite working out and that the knockout and mother of two of his children had asked him to purchase an additional house behind the Mansion where she could reside on her own. When Rackowitz knew I knew this, she finally softened her stance with me. After a lunch or two with *Playboy*'s Chicago muscle Bill Farley and Elizabeth Norris, we all reached an agreement: I would not print information I knew to be true about *Playboy* if they, in turn, gave me first choice on all their scoops. And that meant I also wanted to be the first journalist to sit down with a girl whenever the publicity for her layout took her to New York City—my playground. And to their credit, they never broke their promise. And that's why I enjoyed private chats and watched a friendship between me and Nancy Sinatra grow right at her father's favorite table at Patsy's. That's why I got Victoria Silvstedt way too tipsy at Spy, why I bought Carmen Electra her first table dance at Scores and begged her to leave her boyfriend B-Real of Cypress Hill. That's how I watched a Saturday dinner turn into a Sunday breakfast with Gillian Bonner, how I consoled a tearful and homesick Traci

Adell—in the privacy of her little West Hollywood bungalow—after the press exploited her as the girl O. J. phoned the night before the murders. That's how I took that turn with Patti Davis. And it's the reason why Karin Taylor baked me a pie and delivered it to my home—while I was recuperating from painful spinal surgery—and we lay in bed and watched her video collection of *Absolutely Fabulous* and I remember thinking what an apropos title. Talk about bliss. A Percocet, a Playmate and peach pie.

It doesn't get any better than that.

So it was with great anxiety that I made my first trip to the Mansion in January of 1996 to finally speak to Hef—hero to the libido, king of all noncommittal men and ruler of a world virtually unknown to so many married guys. On that particular day I brought with me the heartache of a recent break-up with my steady Rebecca Soto—the stormy and steamy Puerto Rican girl who had been my girlfriend for more than a year at the time. Back at that time, Becky and I had run aground. It was a painful lesson I learned in using the "c" word during an argument with her. Yes, I was actually stupid enough to say "commitment" and Becky was holding to that like a cat on a rat's ass. So, I decided to seek consolation and comfort in Hef. Was I doing the right thing, committing to Becky, when there were so many girls and so little time? I looked to Hef as raw prudence in red pajamas.

I took Michael Lewittes along for the trip. On many occasions, Michael had to suffer through loud phone arguments between me and Becky that would only add to the tense atmosphere of our office. So, I decided to throw him a bone, pick up his airfare and drag him along for the fun. Besides, he was shopping a television pilot and needed to meet with some William Morris big shot. Anyhow, our first stop was the Mansion and Michael enjoyed a salad with Rackowitz while Hef and I chatted near his infamous grotto.

"There will come a time in your life when everything will add up to the right equation and you will simply know that commitment is not a scary proposition," Hef said, sipping a Diet Coke. "This will not be a scary day at all, but instead, a rather natural progression."

I felt like Grasshopper with a hard-on. Mind you, we were speaking on the pool deck of his great home on Charing Cross Road, while flamingos and peacocks strutted beyond the pool's waterfall and the sound of seventeen chimpanzees could be heard from distant trees. And ghosts of Jimmy Caan naked in the grotto still haunted the place.

"This all seems easy for you to say," I told him. "You just finally settled down and married again in your sixties. You finally didn't have children again until six years ago. Your wife allows you to have the most desirable women traipse around the grounds at all hours. I bet you still stay in touch with Barbi Benton."

"Actually, Barbi was up here just several days ago," Hef calmly said, not at all worried about the repercussions of an ex-lover dropping by unannounced. "We remain close friends.

"Listen, nobody had more fun than I did," he continued. "And there just came a time when I reinvented myself. It was natural. It also helped that Kimberly [Conrad, his wife and greatest *Playmate* of all time] accepted me for who I am."

So how do I do it, oh great Hef?

"The woman who loves you will understand that so long as you're honest and true to her," he said. "Grieve if you must, but stay true to your conviction. If you're not ready for a lifelong commitment right this very moment, you would have ended up hurting her anyway.

"Stay friends with her. Sometimes the Earth spins and puts you right back with the same woman down the road a bit. Believe in fate."

I left the table enlightened. Sure, I could've gotten second opinions from my new pals Jack, Warren or Bob Evans, but what Hef imparted left a profound effect on me.

"One more thing, Hef," I asked him. "Do you mind if I swim bare-ass in the grotto?"

"Knock yourself out," he said, before retreating through the back door. Then he turned and watched me, half-naked, walking toward the pool. "Now there's a man who shares the dream."

The sight of a half-naked me got Michael's attention.

"You're not doing what I think you're going to do, are you?" he asked me.

"Hell yeah, I am."

"And you're going to go in there naked?"

"Yep," I said, pulling my shirt over my head.

"Oh, Jesus . . ."

"And you know what else, Michael?"

"I'm afraid . . ."

"You're coming with me."

"I'd like to but I should really wait a good half-hour after eating or else I'll cramp up . . ."

"Now or never, Mikey. Come on, ya pussy."

Michael is hardly a thrill-seeker, and he sometimes goes about things with the same gusto as Woody Allen at Carnivale. Reluctantly, he began taking off his clothes while murmuring, "Oh, God. Oh, Jesus. Oh God and baby Jesus . . ."

With that, I handed Cindy my camera and asked if she would snap some photos of us for our wall back at the office. She had no problem with it. And within minutes there we were—the boys from Hot Copy and the girl who used to detest our column, all getting along so swell inside the heated grotto within the *Playboy* Mansion. Cindy snapped shots of us drinking champagne—*CLICK!*—reclining on rocks—*CLICK!*—and holding my cellphone to my ear while sipping the bubbly—*CLICK!*

And suddenly my phone goes off. It was Larry Hackett, our editor at the *News*.

"A.J.? Larry. What are you doing?"

"Ah, hey, Larry," I said, making huge eyes at Michael. "Just you know, nothing much, just knocking around. What's up?"

"Okay. Big news just broke and we *neeeeeed* you guys to get on this right away."

"What happened?"

"Lisa Marie filed for divorce from Michael Jackson."

"Lisa Marie is leaving Michael Jackson," I said, grimacing in Michael's direction.

Remember I'm standing there with my dick out. Just in case you forgot

"Now listen, I need you to get ahold of Michael Jackson's sister-in-law—that Margaret Maldonado—and see if she knows anything. She's out there, right?"

"Yeah. Um-hmm."

"And I really need you to get to Lisa Marie's house and see if you can get something from anyone there. I think she's somewhere in Calabasas or Camarillo. Where's Michael?"

"Probably Neverland."

"Not Jackson. Lewittes. Where's Lewittes?"

"Lewittes? He's hanging around somewhere with his dick in his hands. I'll find him and pull him along."

"Okay, no fuckin' around. This is tomorrow's wood."

"Gotcha."

"Where *are* you? I hear an echo."

"It's the fuckin' ozone out here or something. All right, I'll get on it and keep in touch with you."

And then I did what any sensible gossip columnist would do. I turned off my phone, finished the bottle of champagne and continued splashing around in the grotto in the nude for another hour or so. Michael and I never made it to Lisa Marie's hideaway, though we did make an attempt before getting terribly lost and having some LA friends steer us back while we spoke to them on the cellphone. And I never bothered Margaret with the mess, either, for fear it might have spoiled the mood for our date later that evening. Instead, I burned the phones and rode a few of my Jackson sources real hard and ended up dictating a story over the cellphone to a news editor concerning Lisa Marie seeking solace in the arms of her ex-boyfriend Danny Keough the night before she filed papers. It ended up getting nice placement on Page 3 the following day and was covered extensively on the tabloid shows. I even ended up picking up some cash from *Hard Copy* after taping something for them in their LA office.

I looked at it this way: In my opinion, the Jackson/Presley marriage was a farce anyway and I wasn't going to drop everything—especially my cock and a cocktail—just to report the end to a union that was about as real as their phony kiss at the MTV Awards.

Besides, I was staying in the guest house of legendary producer Bob Evans and there was going to be a real swanky party at his magnificent home that night and there was no way I was going to be late for that. There was no way I was going to miss one crazy second.

Emotional Rescue

Some people call it Shangri-la. Some people call it Eden. Some people call it Heaven. Some people call it and never get a call back. Ever since 1996, I've called Bob Evans's Beverly Hills estate my home away from home. Ever since meeting *The Godfather* producer and former head of Paramount Studios at a book signing for his showbiz bible *The Kid Stays in the Picture*, the two of us hit it off and his guest house door has always remained open for me whenever I flew into LA and needed a spot to crash. The only times I was denied was when Bob had a "lady-friend" in town and he had already offered her the bed with the red satin sheets. And on those occasions, I completely understood.

"You understand, don't you, kid?" Evans would purr.

"Of course, pal."

"If it were *any* other time . . ."

"Absolutely."

"But come on over anyhow. I want you to meet her. She's fantastic."

All of them were "fantastic," "terrific," "amazing" or "wonderful." Some of them he even called "the next Mrs. Evans." At any rate, I met a lot of them—and in most cases he was never exaggerating their good qualities. And what normally happens on some visits is this: You meet the "ladyfriend" in question, everyone is handed a cocktail and eventually Evans retreats to his bedroom and you are left to chat with the said "ladyfriend" by the backyard pool, amid the illuminated vanilla candles and the lemon trees, the jasmine and the rose bushes and the 100-foot mighty eucalyptus, above the sweet sound of the pool's dueling fountains. So, even when I wasn't sleeping there, it was a helluva nice way to spend an evening.

Anyhow, on this particular trip, the guest house was mine and Evans had told me to come out to the main house around nine P.M. "I'm having a few people over," he said. "It'll be a good time."

Not quite knowing how I'd mix with his pals, I asked Evans if I could invite a few of my friends over. "One is my cowriter on the column, one is my producer on *The Gossip Show* and the other is this girl I been hanging around with a little."

"How's their spirit, kid? Are they rebels?"

"Yeah, you could say that. In their own way, sure."

"Then tell them to swing by. My house is your house."

That's the way he is.

The odd thing about an Evans party is that it truly doesn't matter what boldfaced name is on the property at the time. All façades and prejudices seem to fade away, at least for the sake of the night's festivities if nothing else. I guess that's why the big names who were there that evening—Beatty, Robert Shapiro, Sean Connery, Anjelica Huston, Joan Severance, Christian Slater, Jon Peters, Beverly D'Angelo, Michael DesBarres, Geraldo Rivera, Jackie Bisset, Jack Valenti, Beverly Johnson and Chazz Palminteri—let down their guard in the face of a couple of gossip columnists and a gossip producer. Their thinking—and actually what Evans preaches—is that if we're good enough to swing by, we're good enough to mix in. Invitations like this came at a time in my tenure when I began to develop a feeling of distinctly *not* wanting to write about scenes like this. They came at a time in my life when I was having dreams of developing friendships and maybe work relationships with these people and exposing their lives in a tabloid or on television was getting tiresome. Either way, forget about reporting Hollywood gossip. That night was one of those nights where you put the job away and enjoy the beauty and irony of your surreal surroundings.

But through all the velvet, vetiver and vanilla, Evans was keeper of the gate and lead blocker for every introduction of the evening. Though, as the Great Gatsby himself might have done, Evans only circles the bash three times. The rest of the night he spent on the phone, on his bed, crushing the crushed velvet to the limit.

"You know what's great about this party?" he suggested. "There are no suits here, no bimbos, no corporate guys, no agents. Everyone is a rebel in their own right. It's the greatest example of the celebration of the human individual."

Sure, I thought, but a few bimbos wouldn't have hurt.

Either way, it was cool watching Valenti (President of the Motion Picture Association of America) take his tie off and tell me he skipped his Harvard alumni dinner to make the bash. "I feel twenty years younger just walking in these doors," he told me.

Shapiro wasn't quite as chatty, but did manage to speak to me about the O. J. Simpson trial after I told him it was a pleasure watching him work, despite the outcome of the trial.

"What trial? You call that a trial? That was no trial," Shapiro told me. I didn't get the joke, still don't. But it was obvious that Shapiro wanted nothing more to do with that guy.

What I'm getting at here is that I was having a gas just being there. Spotting Joan Severance at a stoplight gets me hard, can you imagine what sitting down with her and drowning in her big blue eyes did to me? Point is, I wouldn't have reported a *murder* had there been one committed on the scene that night. And there almost was.

I first met Margaret Maldonado—ex-wife of Jermaine Jackson— when she was publicizing her book *Jackson Family Values* for Dove Publishing. Her ghost-written tome was, more or less, a tell-all on her life and times as Jermaine's common-law wife and mother of his two sons, Jeremy and Jordyn. In the midst of our first phone call several months prior to the night at Evans's party, Margaret announced, "You sound just like a guy I dated a hundred years ago."

"I do?"

"Yes. Do you know John Calvani?"

"Let me tell you something—Calvani is my best friend."

"OhmyGod!"

Fast forward a few months later: Margaret is a guest on *Geraldo* alongside the usual gossiping suspects including myself, Cindy Adams, Mike Walker, etc., and we simply strengthened our friendship later that evening over dinner. By the time I flew in to stay at Evans's, Margaret and I were casually dating. Aside from her Latino beauty and spirited ways, Margaret was and is *extremely* plugged in to everything that goes on in Los Angeles. She is one of those little engines that help power the City of Angels and having her as a friend was and is very valuable. Only once was I careless with it and I'll deal with that later on.

At the time of Evans's bash, Margaret was working as an assistant to Dove Books owner Michael Viner. Several days before Margaret had shown me the galleys to a scathing book Viner was set to publish that was sure to have most of Hollywood's lustful men looking to take his head off at the neck. The book, *You'll Never Make Love in This Town Again*, detailed the supposed sexual exploits and alleged deviant preferences of some of the biggest names in town. It was written by those pillars of literature: Robin, Liza, Linda and Tiffany. Otherwise known as four prostitutes in search of a publisher.

The book was a quick read and an admitted guilty pleasure, but whenever a prostitute exposes her john's ways and means, I always wonder exactly where she thinks she fits in with society. What's the point of mentioning that a big-shot Hollywood director shot his load in thirty seconds? Sometimes that's twenty seconds longer than you want to spend inside a whore anyway. So their rationale confuses me and their desire for sympathy confounds me. But most of all, their ability to get a book deal infuriates me. But don't get me wrong: I respect their choices in life and wish them well. And I thank God that the beautiful black prostitute named Shante was patient with me in the back of my buddy's TransAm in the summer of '77.

Anyhow, as Margaret and I were making the rounds, she spots her boss from across the room. "There's Michael. Hi, Michael!"

I was a little confused. "Wait a minute," I said. "That's the guy who's publishing the book that fucks with a few of the men at this party?"

"Yeah."

"You don't see anything wrong with this picture?"

"A.J., calm down," Margaret said. "This is Hollywood. This kind of stuff happens all the time. Everyone will forget about it in a day or so."

I'm thinking, "Chico is right. This town *is* full of cocksuckers."

"Yeah, well, that don't wash with me. Evans and Jack and Warren are my friends and I have to tell him who just walked in."

"Please, don't!"

"Fuck that. How could you allow a weasel to do that?"

"A.J., *please*! Michael knows I'm with you, he knows we're close. He could fire me."

"He ain't firing you."

"A.J., I'm telling you. This town hates the messenger. All these guys will be talking in a few weeks and no one will talk to you anymore."

"I don't care. I feel like less than a friend not telling Kid. This Viner deserves a punch in the mouth tonight."

And with that, I hunted down Evans in his room and found him sitting on his fur bedspread. I hit him with the news. "Hey, Kid, you heard about this book coming out—*You'll Never Make Love in This Town Again*?"

"No. What is it?"

At this point, Margaret has her hand up the back of my shirt, sticking her fingernails into my back.

"It's this book where they got four call girls to talk about some of the famous men they fucked around with."

"Am I in it?"

"Hell yeah," I said. "A whole chapter and I don't want to tell you what it is they say you like doing to them."

Now Margaret is drawing blood. I was going to be spending the night alone, that was certain.

"Ah, fuck 'em, kid. Fuck 'em all," Evans said. That's his battle cry. "It's all lies anyway."

"Maybe so, Kid. But why would the publisher have the balls to come to your house tonight?"

"Who's the publisher," Evans demanded.

"Michael Viner."

"Viner! He published the audio version of *my* book. I'll break his ass. That weasel!"

When Evans stormed out of his room to look for Viner, Margaret just put her hands to her forehead and said, "You just got me fired."

I felt badly, but I asked her, "Why would you want to work for a guy like that anyhow?"

I washed down my Percocet and Valium with a gin and tonic and readied to face the upcoming drama. And then I lay down next to

Margaret on Evans's bed and waited for the pills to take effect. When I finally emerged, I spotted Evans and Warren cornering Viner in an animated meeting. About a half-hour later—with only a few stragglers left—Evans was in his bedroom speaking in hushed tones to Warren. He called me in. "You did me a solid, kid. A real solid. Can you imagine the gall of that cocksucker?"

"I just hope I didn't make a mess of the party."

"Let me tell you something—you stuck up for a friend. And there aren't enough people like that." He was really close now, with his hand on my shoulder and his face three inches away. He does that when he wants to make a point, Evans.

"This guy is one of us, Warren. He's one of the guys."

And Warren Beatty just stood there with his hand on his chin, nodding in agreement. "I see that. I see."

Fuckin' *Warren Beatty*, man!

And then the controversy was gone as quickly as it arose. "Do you like my pants?" Evans asked me. "Aren't these great pants?"

They were green crushed velvet pants specially designed by a woman whose son, Rio, acts as Evans's assistant. He didn't say, but I'm pretty sure Rio's mom was a former ladyfriend of Evans's from bygone days.

"Yeah, they look comfortable."

"Here," he said, letting them drop to his feet. "They're yours. Have them."

"No, Kid. I couldn't . . ."

"Hey. Take them. They're great to wear when you fly."

And it's hard to say "no" to a man wearing just a white turtleneck sweater and black bolo tie. So I took them and retreated back to the guest house, alone, without Margaret. Some guys give you the shirt off their backs when they're grateful. Evans gave me his pants.

Let's Spend the
Night Together

European supermodels like to end their phone calls with the very superficial yet highly sexual send-off, "I send you big kiss." That's usually followed by the sound of their beautiful lips smacking together into the receiver and the image of them stepping into their Manolo Blahniks and jumping on the next Concorde to Paris. In the beginning you think you're special and that "I send you big kiss" stuff is solely for you and that with each phone call you are actually getting closer to bedding these beautiful freaks of nature. But you're not.

The first time I laid eyes on Tasha Mota e Cunha, a supermodel of Portuguese and South African descent, I had a hard time seeing straight the rest of the day. And that's because we went straight to lunch and I stared directly into her eyes while she sipped tea and honey and I slipped on every word my tied tongue tried to say. Maybe an hour before we sat for lunch, I spotted Tasha while attending my very first runway show during Fashion Week—the very hectic time in New York City when more whistles are intended for Eastern Bloc models than Pakistani cabbies. I was sitting second row at Bryant Park for a Todd Oldham show when a group called Staxx kicked in a song called "Joy" and the lights went down and the show went up.

Tasha was the fifth girl down the runway behind Cindy, Claudia,

Kate and Linda and, no doubt, there were a dozen other beauties who followed her. (And forgive me if I forgot your name or even forgot you were in the show.) But the bottom line is, I didn't care. I had seen enough to know I had seen too much. It wasn't that Tasha had the strut skills of Naomi or the blank beauty of Kate or the awesome proportion of Elle. Here it is in a nutshell: I'm a face man and Tasha simply possessed the gorgeous face of a long-dead childhood fantasy of mine: Sharon Tate. You could've even mixed in a little Jennifer O'Neill in there. Grace Kelly too. And from certain angles, Ursula Andress. Put it all together and that splendor sent me straight backstage as the show ended and directly into the throng of admirers already assembled in front of her. Tasha was stubbing out an American Spirit cigarette by the time the cameras and reporters were walking away. And at that point, I made my introduction and tried to form the most difficult word a man must if he is to take a step toward knowing a woman he absolutely must have.

"Hi," I said.

After some awkward pleasantries were exchanged, I told Tasha I was a fashion show virgin and that I was amazed at what I saw—and that I particularly liked the way she handled herself—and I asked her if she would like to get some lunch sometime. You know, no rush. Just one day when she had time. Whenever.

And here's where it gets cool.

She said, "I'm free for a bit now."

And suddenly I was walking out into the misty rain that was falling on Sixth Avenue and this great big Portuguese beauty—a stranger less than an hour ago—was bending her long legs so she could share my umbrella.

Moments like this are why John Lennon wore the fuckin' T-shirt.

And so a relationship began and roots were planted for a friendship that still exists to this day. And it's a small miracle we ever meshed to begin with. Tasha was a privileged child who was reared in South Africa by wealthy parents who owned acres and acres of eucalyptus trees, which would be cut down to help build the railroad system. I was raised by a mother who doled out food in the cafeteria of my elementary school and a father who worked in the exciting field of carpet remnants and linoleum. Tasha and her parents summered in the French Riviera. We dug for clams with our feet in the Great South Bay. Tasha's family were millionaires. We weren't, but we did have an emergency stash of $1,500 in cash should anything go wrong and an uncle Larry who always came through with a few hundred bucks in a crisis. Like the time our dog Pippin needed a hysterectomy.

Strange as it sounds, when different worlds like that collide it can sometimes make for a fun time. And it was. Tasha and I didn't have ordinary dates. I took her to the Vegas Diner in Bensonhurst to meet a guy named Carmine. She took me to the Frick Museum to see Gainsborough. I taught her the best mozzarella in the city was at Joe's Dairy on Sullivan Street. She showed me bedsheets I couldn't afford at Frette on Madison Avenue. I let her in on the beauty of a Jimi Hendrix riff. She taught me the words to Yves Montand's "Rue St. Vincent." When she spoke, she giggled her way through most of her stories and almost always seemed to inject the names of immensely wealthy men whom she called friends. It was always the prince of this, the king of that, the count of whatever—every man she knew seemed to be seconds away from inheriting a huge fortune or blowing the one he was given at birth. And I was counting my money—sixty bucks at a clip—every time I visited an ATM. It was enough to turn the strongest of men into an insecure pussy. But I hung in.

I hung in despite the fact that guys like Rofredo Gaetani—who's now Ivana Trump's stud—would get up in Tasha's grill every time we ran into him at a party. I hung in despite the fact that legendary ladies' man George Hamilton wooed her in Europe and sent her a private jet to go to Los Angeles for acting lessons. And I hung in despite the fact that Ranger star Mark Messier invited Tasha to sit with his parents for Game 6 at Madison Square Garden the year the Rangers won the Stanley Cup. And I'm glad I did because what was cool about Tasha—as opposed to other supermodels I've known—is that she wasn't too affected by the blur of playboys before her. In fact, on the night she could've accepted Messier's invitation, she was with me dancing on tables at Boom and then afterward she giggled the night away when I tried to coerce her to steal a candy bar from a Korean deli on Spring Street. Despite teaching her all sorts of diversionary tactics, the stunner's conscience wouldn't allow her to lift a Snickers bar.

At any rate, we were a cute pair, and most of our nights consisted of dinner and funny conversations followed by me driving her home to her Central Park West apartment in my Nissan 240SX. And sometimes she'd ask if I could stop at my apartment and bring along my Yorkshire terrier puppy, Cesare, so she could pet him along the way. He must have made a strong impression because about a year later, she bought one herself.

Well, time went on and Tasha and I saw less and less of each other. It got to a point that more and more of her modeling gigs were in Europe, so she'd forever be flying away at the drop of a hat and calling me on her cellphone from airports around the world.

"Hello, A.J.? It's me—Tash. I'm in Egypt, it must be 115 degrees in the shade. I did a horrible pack. I don't know what motivated me to pack my Gucci duster, but I did and now I have to lug it around."

Most of the calls went a lot like that. I let my friends listen to them, playfully holding up a beautiful photo of her all the while. And I'd laugh like hell. I don't know, there is something undeniably cool about a beautiful girl phoning you up from across the world with the great Pyramids in the background.

It's easy to see I was unreasonably obsessing over models back in those days. In fact, I was always taking hits because the column was jam-packed with supermodel news. But it ain't like I was in love with every single one of them, either. I dished out plenty of jabs back then, too, and I recall Naomi Campbell and Kate Moss were two of my favorite targets. Matter of fact, when Naomi split with Robert De Niro and took up with U2's Adam Clayton, I was scared she might bust up my favorite group à la Yoko Ono. And, in one column, I swore if that ever occurred, "I'd hunt her down like a dog in the streets and run her over."

Even Michael got in on the act. And sometimes we'd have a few nips in the afternoon before writing the column and we'd laugh our asses off looking for an inventive way of referring to Kate's skin-and-bones appearance.

"Come on," he said, "let's come up with something nobody will ever forget. It's always the 'anorexic mannequin' or the 'rail-thin runway girl' or the 'skinny supermodel.' "

"How about this," I said as I began pounding out a lead paragraph: "If Kate Moss gets any thinner, she's going to fall through her ass and hang herself."

Right at that monent, I was interrupted by a phone call from Tasha at midday.

"My God, baby, you sound like you're right around the corner."

"I'm at the Essex House," she said. "It's urgent I see you."

Despite her upbringing, standing and beauty, I didn't know Tasha to be a drama queen, so I left the column in Michael's hands and booked it over to Central Park South to see what was eating her. I sat on an ottoman and sipped a whiskey sour as she paced her beautiful suite and told me of her dilemma. It wasn't even lunchtime and I was a little loaded already.

"I've been asked to move to the Principality," she said.

It was obvious this was a serious quandary for Tasha, yet I had absolutely no idea what that meant.

At all.

"The Principality, huh?" I said.

"Yes. The Principality. I've been asked to move to the Principality."

"Wow," I said, hoping she'd give me a little more to work with.

"Yes. He has asked me to move there because he wants me to be quite close to him."

I was still a mile off from understanding anything. But I knew it was some fancy-pants bullshit she was sometimes getting mixed up with. I swear, sometimes the more beautiful the girl, the worse her choice in men.

"So this guy's pretty serious about you, huh?"

"I guess so."

"And . . . is that something you feel comfortable with?"

"Well, I don't know. I mean, he's normally very private but lately he doesn't seem to mind people seeing us together. There was that photo of us in *Hello!* magazine and I've met his father, which, I understand, never happens."

I was getting warmer, but still far off. "Well, any time a guy has a girl meet his dad . . . that is kind of a serious thing, I think."

"Well, the prince is a private person, as well. A man of very few words."

And then it hit me. Prince Albert was making moves on Tasha and the phony playboy was offering to move her to the Principality of Monaco.

Apparently, Albert and Tasha were supposed to go on some date later that evening and he was hiding her out at the Essex House until it was time to dine and pose for phony photographs. Her phone call to me at midday was, more or less, a "what do I do" sort of thing.

In my opinion, Tasha was born to be a princess and a fine princess she'd make. But the notion of that guy marrying her for the purpose of siring an heir to his throne didn't sit right with me. And though I didn't want to rain on her parade, it did need some misting to tell you the truth.

"Tasha," I said. "You're a big girl, so you do what you want. But this guy has ulterior motives, you know that, right? I mean, yes, you're a beautiful girl. Yes, you're perfect to have a child with. And yes, you're classy and intelligent and just the kind of woman a prince would want . . ."

"But . . ." she said.

"But I don't think this guy is doing this for love and I don't think you are either, otherwise you wouldn't have asked to see me."

I left Tasha to her date that evening—I think it was the Red Cross Ball or some shit. In the weeks that followed she did, in fact, move to the Principality and when rumors reached me through my modeling contacts that Tasha and Albert might actually be headed for the aisle, I made up my mind to do something about it. I mean, I can't tell you how many times I had read in other gossip columns the countless women Albert had squired around and had hinted about marriage plans to, but never had his antics hit so close to home.

I had heard through a booker I knew that Tasha was in Paris on a job. So, with absolutely no knowledge of the country or the language, I called my pal Rocco and booked a flight to Paris.

"Come on, buddy," I said. "For nothing else but a good story to tell one day."

"Only you, baby. Only you."

And off to Paris we went, with the only nonstalking event scheduled being a luncheon with exiled director Roman Polanski arranged through my pal Bob Evans. At least that way, I would be able to come home with a story for my column.

· · ·

My game plan was sad. We left several days before Super Bowl XXX. We flew in and found out where we could rent an apartment for a few days for cheap. We literally found the place we selected on a corkboard in some smokey luncheonette where we guzzled red wine and ate steak au poivre at the ungodly hour of 9:45 A.M. East Coast time. After renting a yellow Renault, we found a supermarket and stocked up on essentials for our four-day stay—cheese, wine and bread. We also bought ten rolls of toilet paper figuring the French cuisine wouldn't be so kind to our unsuspecting American bowels. And we were right. And then we holed up in our Parisian abode somewhere in the 7th District on Boulevard du Montparnasse.

Anyhow, there is a reason why Doris Day sang "April in Paris." In April, Paris is beautiful. The trees that line the Champs-Elysées are in full bloom. Little boys in high-waisted short pants shuck fresh oysters in St.-Germain-des-Prés. Beautiful women, wrapped in obscenely expensive Christian Lacroix, walk their perfumed Yorkies along the Avenue Montaigne. Lovers walk hand-in-hand beneath the Eiffel Tower, then stroll the banks of the Seine and pitch francs into its fast currents, hoping to ensure their return.

Paris in *January*, however, is a different story. On our trip, temperatures dropped to an unromantic 0 degrees Celsius. Berets were replaced by hoodies. Cab drivers (who own their own BMW cabs, by the way) whooshed right past us along the city's impossible maze of zigzaggy streets. The town's too-cute-to-believe elevators get jammed between floors. The city is damp, icy snow blankets the cobblestone streets, traffic snarls are worse than midtown Manhattan during a Papal visit. The town's stores and flashy nightlife slows to a crawl and—just between me, you, the lamppost and my pal Pierre—it's cold and flu season in the worst way. So, as cool as Paris may sound to you, my trip had all the charm of a Peace Corps mission.

All I was armed with was the name of a woman—Eileen—who my booker friend said was handling Tasha's Paris modeling job. It was my insane intention to find this woman, explain who I was, have her let Tasha know I was in town and that I desperately wanted to speak to her and then wait for my phone to ring. That was all well and good, except I didn't know anything about the woman and, should I meet her and

Here's my father supporting me in 1962. Twenty-two years later, I would be the one supporting him. But that's what happens in life: The son becomes the father and the father becomes the son. I never met a funnier, tougher man.

Hairs to Eternity. It was the eighties, so the high hair, long gown and *Good-Fellas* wedding was permissible. Jenny got remarried and has a couple of kids now. I still remember crying the first day I saw her walk up my driveway, wearing a lavender jumpsuit. She was sweet sixteen.

Sometimes I tell people my nephews, Joey and Jake, are really my brothers. And other times I feel like they're my sons. Either way, I never laugh more than when we're back home, ragging on one another.

Me and my famous wall at the *Daily News*. Back in the day, if I was in love with you or obsessed with you, I found a spot for you on the wall. Thanks to my appearances on *The Gossip Show*, I had out-of-work actors asking me to slap their headshots on the wall.

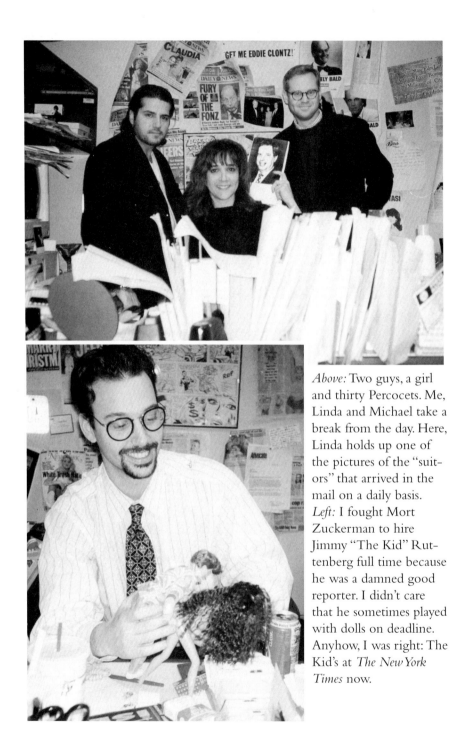

Above: Two guys, a girl and thirty Percocets. Me, Linda and Michael take a break from the day. Here, Linda holds up one of the pictures of the "suitors" that arrived in the mail on a daily basis.
Left: I fought Mort Zuckerman to hire Jimmy "The Kid" Ruttenberg full time because he was a damned good reporter. I didn't care that he sometimes played with dolls on deadline. Anyhow, I was right: The Kid's at *The New York Times* now.

Richard Bey, *Playboy* Playmate Stephanie Adams, me and Lisa Gastineau. One time John Gotti handed Lisa all the money he had in his pocket and told her to buy something nice for herself.

"But that's all the money in your pocket," Lisa said.

"I got two pockets," John shot back.

Me and Margaret Maldonado at Indochine. As much as the column helped Margaret, there came a day when it hurt her, and our fizz went flat. And that sucked, because . . . well, because look at her.

Mickey Rourke, Chuck Zito and me, clowning around after dinner at Nello. Too bad action hero Jean-Claude Van Damme wasn't in the photo that night. Then every guy Chuck ever punched out at Scores would be present.

Here's me and Rocco with exiled director Roman Polanski in Paris. As soon as we walked into the director's favorite café, the maître d' held up a baby bottle and said, "Mr. Polanski, you forgot this." And I thought *Oh my God, Roman's dating again.*

"One more wass of gline, tarbender." As me and Rocco head off to Paris, it looks as though the bottle of wine, two Valium, two Dramamine and four Percocet are beginning to take effect.

Me and Chico—Mafia wanna-bes.

Looks to kill and guess who's dying. Me and Tasha Mota e Cunha in Paris. I knew flying off to France on a whim was going to be worth it. And it was. That was the last night I ever saw her.

Ballbusters on parade. Here, me and T.K. share a moment with Ashley Richardson, Kathy Ireland, Angie Everhart and Vendela at the first *Sports Illustrated* Swimsuit Issue dinner. Security had us removed several moments later.

Walk This Way. I met Aerosmith's Steven Tyler in South Beach to hip him to his ex-wife's proposed tell-all on their hellish married days. "That's cool," he said. "As long as she admits to being just as fucked up as I was." Tyler ate salad and drank water all night, but we laughed our balls off anyway.

Me and Kara, present day, being silly at Boom. War wounds and all, there isn't a person I connect with better.

At my buddy Tico Torres' extravagant wedding to supermodel Eva Herzigova on the Jersey Shore. "Marriage is just like a long, hot bath," I told Tico. "After a while it's not that hot anymore." The couple divorced a couple years later.

Bob Evans wouldn't let me stay at a hotel or rent a car whenever I was in L.A. So I slept on his satin sheets and drove his Jaguar. One night, as I was sulking around the house because Kara "needed some space," Kid walked into my room with Jack Nicholson and Warren Beatty by his side. "You got dumped, my boy. Nobody knows more about it than I do. But don't feel too bad. I got dumped by Lana Turner and Ava Gardner before I turned twenty-three." That put things in perspective for me forever.

Sometimes Kato Kaelin and I went to Scores to check out the girls. And sometimes he was inclined to give me a free lap dance. Say what you want about the guy, but I found him honest, smart and sincere. I like him a lot.

JohnnyBoy, a guy who only missed five nights in Studio 54's thirty-three-month reign, taught me to stay home some nights. "Buddy," he'd say, "once in a while it's good that people say 'Where's A.J.?' than always saying '*There's* A.J.'"

I loved Becky like a wife, a daughter and a mother. And leaving her was the hardest thing I ever had to do. I don't know where she is today, and I miss her like hell. Looking back . . . maybe she was "the one."

Downtown Julie Brown and me at the party E! tossed after they signed her to host *The Gossip Show.* Julie met me in the middle of a punch-up in South Beach and we have been close friends ever since. Trust me on this: She is one of the funniest, toughest, sexiest women you will ever meet.

Me and actor John Enos in South Beach. He once had a beef with me because I referred to him in a column as "Madonna's boy toy." Enos called me, fuming. "I ain't nobody's fuckin' boy toy." And he isn't. John has already had and forgotten about more beauties than you long for.

Rocco Ancarola, JohnnyBoy Calvani, "The World's Greatest Attorney" Frankie Giantomasi and me. Every night, no matter where we went or what we did, Frankie would ask, "Can it get any better than this?" And it always did.

Not long after Paula Barbieri found God, she found me. Here we are at some phony film premiere dinner party at Tavern on the Green. I knew Paula reached out to me for a dose of good press, but I didn't care. I was sky high and didn't mind feeling scandalous for a night.

give her the number to the apartment I was staying in, there was no guaranteeing Tasha would reach me because we had no answering machine. So, after the first night of fishing, I was basically going to stay by the phone and wait for it to ring. It didn't take long for the story to unfold.

Rocco and I went out the first afternoon to meet Polanski for some oysters and wine. That went well. It went so well, Polanski insisted we take his table at a premier spot in Paris called Chez L'Ami Louis later that week in the fancy Marais District. Apparently, this spot is like the Rao's of Paris with something like ten tables, an adorable maître d' and—quite simply put—the best fuckin' food and wine list in town. Later that night, Rocco and I went to a spot called Barfly and—as God is my witness—I stumbled on this Eileen woman and let her in on my desire to speak to Tasha as soon as she could arrange it.

"I'm her friend from New York," I said. "Just tell her to call me where I'm staying and I'll explain everything."

Eileen, her French attitude intact, said she couldn't guarantee anything. I wanted to say, "Hey, bitch, I introduced this girl to Carmine at the Vegas Diner on 86th Street. She *owes* me." But I figured it was wiser to keep my mouth shut and hope for the best.

Two days and nights went by and when I wasn't incessantly watching MTV Europe or ordering in pizza from some outfit called Speedy Rabbit, I was playing with one of those red-laser pens—the first I had seen of its kind. I was getting cabin fever and I was content pointing the laser at people speaking in a glass phone booth a block away. It sounds sad and it was. I did this for two days and nights. And then the phone rang. It was Tasha, very surprised to hear from me in the City of Lights.

"What *are* you doing in town," she said.

"Came here to talk to you."

"You have?"

"Yeah."

"How *ever* did you find me?"

"I got my ways."

I asked Tasha to dinner that evening at Chez L'Ami Louis. Told her I'd pick her up around eight. She was anxious to see me and chat but was doubtful I could get a table at the hot restaurant.

"Tasha, you think I'm just the King of New York?"

"I'm just saying, A.J., you cannot just come to Paris and simply get a table at Chez L'Ami Louis just like that. Do you have a reservation?"

"I don't need one. Just be ready at eight, baby."

Before picking up Tasha, I told Rocco I needed a drink to take the edge off. We drove off to some local dive bar on a hooker-lined street and right there in the middle of my drinking a goblet of red wine, I spotted a Card Bleu—France's version of our Visa cards—on the floor at my feet. I chugged the wine, stepped on the card and dragged my leg out the door until I could pick it up and put it in my pocket without anyone seeing me. I will not reveal the man to whom the card belonged because I had every intention of ringing up a huge, fancy dinner bill with Tasha and Rocco and make the poor sap pay for it.

"Not only do you fly across the world to find a woman and have dinner with her, but then you find a lost credit card and have someone else pay for the dinner," Rocco said.

"I know. I know. My life."

"Only you. Only you."

I don't know how, but we found Tasha's beautiful apartment on Rue de l'Université and I remember leaving Rocco in the car and calling up Tasha's name to a maze of balcony apartments. There was a huge gurgling fountain in front of me and a playful chocolate Labrador snapping at the falling snowflakes.

"Tasha!"

"I'll be right down," she called out to me, before summoning for the dog to come inside. "Chocolat!" And the dog disappeared from my view. A moment later Tasha appeared and gave me the hug and kiss that motivated me to book the crazy-ass flight in the first place. I mean, at this point in my life, this girl hung the moon as far as I was concerned. "I can't believe you're actually here."

"Never mind that," I said. "I'm freezing. Just direct us to this restaurant."

With that, we hopped in the yellow Renault and made off through the maze of tiny, twisting streets. And suddenly, my harebrain plan didn't seem so stupid.

I felt like James Bond when I walked in, gave my name to the maître d' and was escorted to the best table in the joint—red-checkered tablecloth and a window view to watch the snow blanket the cobblestoned street. A moment later a bottle of red wine arrived "compliments of Mr. Polanski" and we began ordering the finest food I have ever had: foie gras, steak au poivre, a broiled chicken so fresh we found a shotgun pellet in it. Not to mention several dozen oysters, unimaginable desserts and three more bottles of red wine, each with price tags well over $100 apiece. And then cigars were ordered and fine cognac and espresso and Sambuca. I was not worried about the $700 bill because I wasn't the poor schmuck paying for all of it.

However, when our stomachs were bursting and we called for the bill, I reached for the stolen Visa and Rocco and I prayed for heavens that the scam would work. Everything was fine until the waiter came back to our table with a small card-swiping mechanism unlike anything we have ever seen here in the States—where paying for an expensive meal with someone else's credit card is simple, for God's sake. The waiter swiped the card through and asked me for my pin code.

"My what?" I said.

"Yur code, sir. I cannot use zis card wissout ze pin code."

"Yeah, well, who remembers," I said. "It's a new card. I honest to God don't remember. Just run it through, no problem."

"No, I cannot do zat, sir." My waiter was Inspector Clouseau. "I need ze pin code."

"All right, uh, 3-8-5-7-8," I said.

As he was punching the phony numbers through, I leaned into Rocco and asked how much money he had on him. "About $200," he said. "You?"

"I got $1,000," I said. "We're covered, but let's just see if we can get away with this."

Well, after several tries it was obvious Clouseau wasn't going to budge, so I reluctantly pulled out my dough and left $850 on the table—more than twice the airfare it cost to fly to the fuckin' country.

After dinner, Rocco dropped me off at Tasha's apartment and left the two of us alone to talk. We sat on her bed and ate chocolate truffles and played with the chocolate Lab she was baby-sitting.

Anyway, it didn't take me long to tell Tasha that I thought the whole Prince Albert thing was bullshit. "Tasha, I don't like this Prince Albert for you. Do you understand what I'm saying?"

"Yes. But tell me what you think it's all about."

"Look, unless there is a male heir, Monaco will cease to exist and it will be absorbed by France and everyone there—all those lucky bastards who don't pay any taxes—will have to start digging into their tight pockets. That's what all his 'dating' is all about. It's not about love, baby. It's about a forty-year-old guy looking to have a son and save the Principality."

"Is that what you think?"

"Hell yeah. It's what I know. And I'm not saying me and some other members of the media are not guilty of perpetuating the myth along the way. The guy is a Prince. He's loaded. He's always got some beautiful European woman accompanying him to the Red Cross Ball or the World Cup or World Music Awards. And we're always printing who he's with. But out of all the knockouts he's been linked with—from Naomi Campbell to Isabelle Adjani to Claudia Schiffer to Sharon Stone—he can't find one and make a baby?"

"So what are you saying?"

"I'm saying add all that up, baby. I don't think the guy is, you know, girl crazy."

I think Tasha got the gist of my plea. She just played with her hair and patted Chocolat on the head. There was more on her mind, I could tell.

"Anyhow, that's not the guy you're in love with. I know the guy you're in love with," I said.

"Oh you do, do you?"

"Yeah, I do."

"Who," she asked curiously and coyly. She liked this game.

"The guy you love is the guy who owns this dog," I said.

"Why do you say that?"

"I own three dogs of my own and I know I would never leave my dogs with anyone unless I loved them very much. This guy who owns the dog is your guy. Fuck Prince Albert."

"Oh my God," she said. "How could you know that?"

"Listen to me . . . get with this guy with the dog. I get the feeling he's not getting your full attention because all this heady Prince bullshit was sidetracking you."

"You're probably right," she said. "He's a good friend. But we're just getting to know each other."

"Let me ask you something: Is he the last guy you talk to at night?"

"Ummm, yes."

"First guy you speak to in the morning?"

"Yes."

"Then he's your guy. Period."

I'm not going to lie to you. I would have much rather pushed Tasha down on her satin sheets, tied her to the wrought-iron bedpost and made love to her until the gargoyles on the side of the building turned red with shame. I would have even accepted jerking off on her tear sheets. But facing two A.M. and an empty box of truffles, she offered to drive me back and I accepted. I stroked her hand as her shifter-car jolted me closer to home and back to reality.

"So when will I see you again?" she said.

"I get the feeling it ain't gonna be for a while."

"Well, what I didn't tell you is—you're right. The man who owns Chocolat is in love with me and has asked me to marry him. But I have to wait and see how things work out."

"It'll work out," I said. "Everything always works out in the end."

"Well, if it does work out and we do get married, you'll have to come to my wedding."

"Nah. Don't even tell the guy you know me, Tash. Guys never like to know their girl is friends with me."

"Nonsense. You're my friend from America. You're *Pope.*"

"Tash," I said, kissing her face good-bye. "Don't tell him nothing. I'll see you around. You'll turn up in all the magazines and I'll say, 'Hey, I know that girl. I stopped her from being a princess.'"

And with that, she was gone. The little red car made a U-turn that sent the chocolate Labrador from one side of the car to the other. I stood in the snow until I could no longer hear his barking.

Fast forward a year. I am reading some fancy European magazine at a Times Square newsstand and it says Portuguese model Tasha Mota e Cunha is engaged to be married to Jean Charles de Castelbajac—a guy who designs robes for Pope John Paul. There is also a picture accompanying the article and next to the happy couple, I see Chocolat, my old pal who knows our little secret.

Gimme Shelter

Toward the beginning of 1996, I could hear the faint cry of New York City's star-making mechanism spitting out my name. Magazines were calling to interview me, television shows were mentioning me, neophyte Manhattan publicists were aching to have me at their parties while the ancient ones—most of whom shilled their items in the days of the Stork Club—were mentioning my style in the same breath as Walter Winchell's. And more than once, rumors about Hollywood that I would normally run through my screen of sources began to have my name attached.

"Hey is it true E!'s plans to give you your own talk show were scrapped because the pilot you shot wasn't well-received?" one gossip columnist asked me one day on the phone.

"We never shot a pilot. We just had a couple of meetings and we couldn't agree on money," I'd say. And I was telling the truth.

"Well, is it true the producers of *The Naked Truth* want you to play yourself on the sitcom?" another asked me.

"Jesus, where are you getting these things from?" I was beginning to sound like a celebrity—or worse, a publicist for God's sake. And I didn't like it. And I swear, I had no idea where the rumors were born. But I know where they died—at my desk, usually with me hollering into the phone at another columnist.

But still, it was the kind of attention that doesn't come around too often in life and I was romanced by it a bit. Call me shallow, but one of the biggest perks I had always aspired to were front-row tickets to the annual Victoria's Secret fashion show. I remember *giving* away my Game 7 tickets to the Rangers championship at the Garden *and* a locker room credential to Chico, but I would've crawled across cut glass to sit front row at The Plaza for the smoky lingerie show. So when my pouty and pretty publicist pal Desiree Gruber handed me the tix, I felt like one of the big dogs, sitting right alongside fellow dogs like Richard Johnson, Russell Simmons, Andre Harrell, Tony Shifrazi, Michael Bolton, Marcus Schenkenberg and old man Trump. Felt like I had made it. And once again the chorus of the Beatles' "Baby, You're a Rich Man" rattled around my head.

I can't lay any major kind of importance on attending the event, other than to say it's both beautiful and frightening to see eighteen women make seventy-two turns down a catwalk as nothing more than two ounces of fabric stand between you and your first rape. I'm here to tell you I got a bout of Bell's palsy while keeping one eyeball on Rebecca Romjin walking toward me in a waist-cincher brief and the other eyeball on Veronica Webb walking away from me in a sheer floral kimono. Bell's palsy, swear to God. Left side of my face went and got paralyzed on me. Still acts up to this day.

Anyhow, the point is, all the perks for me and all the phone calls and the inquiries and the flat-out interest in me was what I had always wanted. Why, then, was I nervous as all hell? I'll tell you why: In any other city, in any other country, on any other continent and on any other planet, when the star-making machine calls out your name, you prepare to be propelled toward fame—whether it's fifteen minutes' or fifteen years' worth—with the happy anxiety of a kid watching the Good Humor man turning the corner. But in New York City, sometimes the Good Humor man gets a little sloppy and jumps the curb before he can stop the truck and hand you your toasted almond bar. In other words, New York City is a city very willing to make you a star, but it doesn't promise you a smooth ride to the top. At the start of 1996, the Good Humor man ran my ass over.

When writers from the *New York Observer* and *New York* magazine were both calling me and mentioning me as candidates for lengthy profiles, I made what I thought was an easy decision. I decided to cooperate with *New York* magazine because of its prestige and the possibility—according to the editors—of using me on the cover. Let's face it—that would've been a big smile for a long time. Further, I thought I liked the *New York* magazine writer—Nancy Jo Sales—because she was a Yale pal of Michael's and sometimes contributed to our column with bits of gossip. In the meantime, I basically told the *New York Observer* writer, Nick Paumgarten, to go fuck himself after he asked one of my colleagues, "What do you know about Peter Gatien throwing A.J. out of Club USA because his girlfriend was caught peeing in an ice bucket behind the bar?"

(What had actually happened was my cousin Barbara—and an entire group of Staten Island girls out on a bachelorette party—got past Gatien's door by dropping my name. As the night wore on, and one of the high-haired lovelies got blind drunk, she chose to pee in a bucket in a back room somewhere rather than wait on the long line for the ladies' room. When my cousin saw what had occurred, she chewed out the girl, put her back in the limo and instructed the driver to take her sorry ass back over the Verazzano. Somewhere along the line, a doorman thought the drunk was my girlfriend and believed Gatien had had me removed from the club. All of it is untrue, but that's the way the gossip game works sometimes.) Anyhow, in retrospect, the lying snitch was probably Gatien himself. That guy always had a hard-on for me after I hinted in a column back in 1992 that he had doormen at his clubs taking $2,500 from Ecstasy dealers before they allowed them inside to do their business.

Anyhow, I wasn't going to fall victim to all that untrue bullshit. When I got wind of the line of Paumgarten's questioning, I called and ripped into him.

"Listen to me," I said. "I'm not some pussy from the Columbia School of Journalism. I'm a fighter who can write. You print lies like that and I'll break your fuckin' hands so you can't peck out a story for years. You'll be looking over your shoulder for the rest of your life."

"But, A.J.," he stammered. "I am just checking to see if the rumor is true or . . ."

"The rumor is wrong and so is your approach," I said. "I swear on my mother, I will wait in front of your fancy brownstone and break your ass one night."

Long story short. I didn't cooperate with the salmon-colored weekly the rest of the way. I turned all my attention to *New York* magazine's marquee appeal—its bulky readership, color spreads, eye-grabbing headlines and fancy photo shoots where snotty stylists would bathe me in all the Gucci and Prada I ever dreamed of.

Nancy Jo told me her editors suggested she follow me on my rounds for a week or so. I thought that was fine, except, not every night is as exciting as everybody outside the world of gossip seems to think. To add to that, the possibilities of a wild New York night are somewhat dulled when everyone around you knows their every move may be written about by a writer who's writing how a writer writes his column. See what I'm saying? More often than not, that type of coverage doesn't fly. It's too inside. It's "inside inside" as my friend JohnnyBoy Calvani would explain it, and that explains it all.

But wherever I went for an entire week, Nancy Jo followed. And basically, whatever she asked of me, I was open and honest with all my replies. I took her to my office and had her watch me work the phones. I let her watch me tape my E! segments. I took her to my courtside seats at a Knicks game. Pulled her backstage at a Victoria's Secret fashion show while I chatted up Naomi Campbell, Karen Mulder, Rebecca Romjin-Stamos and Stephanie Seymour. I introduced her to the gang at Rao's. Bought her lap dances at Scores. Sat her down with my best friends. Gave her my ex-wife's home number. I even went way beyond what a person being profiled is apt to do when I told her extremely intimate stuff about my relationship with my girlfriend at the time. I took her behind the curtain. Let her in the locker room. I just felt like Teflon back then and I truly believed that unabashed honesty was the best approach. Like my lawyer and pal Frankie Giant always says, "With truth as my shield, I am impervious to attack."

Overall, we got along just fine outside of a couple of tense moments.

Like the time she watched me work the supermodels at the Victoria's Secret show at The Plaza.

"Well, you call yourself a journalist and true journalists don't work that way."

And that's when I felt I had to put her in her place a bit. "And how many columns do you write for a major daily again? I'm sorry, I forget. I have two columns. Two. And you write as a *freelancer*. So keep reminding me what I'm doing wrong."

I was probably a little hard on the girl, but I didn't need her critiquing me on the way I gathered information, gossip and quotes. If I wasn't good at what I was doing, her editors wouldn't have suggested a profile on me in the first place.

Later that evening, I apologized to her and we retreated to a dark corner of Cafe Tabac (or what remained of the once-great gossip battlefield) and I told her of the insecurities that sometimes afflict me—i.e., people confusing my whimsy for lack of journalistic know-how. And at some point, Nancy Jo let me in on what my competitors had to say about me after she called them for comments. And apparently my speech worked because it compelled her to do something a reporter never does. She turned her notebook over to me and showed me what other gossips had said to her. And among the praise and interest that she stirred up with her queries, there were some disturbing—but not surprising—tidbits from George Rush, my competitor within the *News* building.

"A.J., I have never seen a more catty and jealous bunch of people in my life as I have while I've been working on this story about you," she told me. "There are a lot of insecure, resentful and envious people in your field. I swear this is worse than working on an article about a movie star."

I swigged back my second espresso and Sambuca and said, "Now you know why I don't need you to dis me in public like you did at the fashion show. Some prick in the back room hears you say that shit about me not being a real journalist and he's on the phone to Richard Johnson telling him how the *New York* magazine writer and I are fighting in the middle of my profile."

"Yeah . . . I see what you're saying. I didn't mean anything bad by it," she said.

"Yeah, but let me tell you how it goes," I said. "Two days from now, I open the paper and Page Six has—*New York* magazine's proposed profile on *Daily Snooze* gossip columnist A.J. Benza is not off to a good start. Onlookers backstage at the Victoria's Secret fashion show were *thisclose* to the tirade that Benza launched at writer Nancy Jo Sales after Sales wondered why Benza chose to store his quotes in his head and not use a pen and pad—like real writers do . . .' "

Nancy Jo was giggling now and it was obvious she knew where I was headed.

"Wait . . . it gets worse," I said.

"No, no," she laughed. "I see. I see what you're saying. I didn't mean what I said about you. I think you're a great writer, A.J. I really do. You definitely have a style no one else has in the business. You're original at what you do. And I'm going to show that."

And, I'll tell you the truth right now, I never claimed to be the best gossip columnist in the business. I can tell you right now how Richard, Liz and Cindy had it over me. I only laid claim to telling it like it is and like it was—while I was given the platform—and having the most fun while I was filing away the memories and wringing out the words. And hearing Nancy Jo tell me I was an original and that no one else in the business did it like I did, well, that was enough for me. At that moment, it was better than sex. She went home to write her story and I went home with a hard-on.

Fast forward four weeks later. The *New York Observer* is due to hit the stands in the morning and I am too afraid to walk to the news-stand to fetch it. All my friends and colleagues knew it was being published that day, and I could've called any of them, but I chose not to. I didn't want an objective take. I wanted someone to look at it, swirl it around and give me the good, the bad and the ugly. So I rang crotchety press agent Sy Presten and asked him to read it to me because I knew he was at the friggin' newsstand at sunrise. Besides, on two hours' sleep and a handful of Percocets, I was in no mood to rustle out of bed and read.

"How bad is it?" I asked him.

"Let me tell you something, baby. You listening?"

Sy always asked you if you were listening because over the years he had gotten used to people paying less and less attention to him and his clients, most of which had dwindled down to the Parkinson's Disease Foundation, former Yankee Phil Mintz, Page Morton Black, Da Tommaso restaurant and Dr. Marc Lowenberg—"dentist to the stars." And that's always kind of sad because I know there were days when Sy worked with the best gossips of all time. I know because he'd tell me like an aging father reminds a son how he used to throw a perfect spiral. "I used to bend elbows with Winchell at the Stork Club before your parents even had the lousy thought of making you," Sy would often say. Still and all, I liked working with old Sy a lot. And he truly did get me some very juicy stuff over the years just for giving an old steak house a pop now and then.

"Tell me," I said. "I can't get out of bed until I know what it says."

"Well, you better get your ass out of bed because it's a pretty goddamn good day to be you."

"Why. What's it say?"

"It's a blow job, baby. A complete blow job."

How much of a blow job? The story, complete with a drawing of me, ran on page 1 with the headline, "Sneer at His Column, If You Like; A.J. Benza Is Ready for Stardom." Jesus Christ, it was embarrassing as all hell.

It went on from there and I will spare you the details. But, as you can imagine, Paumgarten got an apology phone call from me and he was a man about it. "Listen, A.J.," he said. "No hard feelings. I was just checking into rumors about you and I found they weren't true."

And I, of course, attempted to give him the necessary hat-in-hand blow job in return. "Nick . . . if there's ever *anything* I can help you with . . . absolutely *anything* . . . do not hesitate to call me . . ." Blah, blah, blah. He never has. Cool guy.

At any rate, I was thinking, "How bad could the *New York* magazine profile be if the *Observer* piece was so sweet?"

I'll tell you real quick. After it was printed I was banned from Rao's, my car was set on fire, a stalker stole my Calvin Klein briefs from my dryer, I had to change my address and I was knocked bloody and un-conscious by Hell's Angel Chuck Zito. All in the same week.

I knew I had a beating coming to me the minute Larry Hackett dropped the issue on my desk and my eyes swam all over the pages.

"How is it?" I asked, without even looking at him.

"It's a bad day to be you, my friend."

"Fuck."

And then I saw it. And I can't explain why some phrases and words JUMP out at you in some stories, but they just do. And in this case the words "HELL'S ANGEL" and "EVERYBODY'S A RAT" were too close for comfort, thus making it seem like I was calling Chuck Zito a rat. And that's a no-no where I come from. And I come from the streets.

What had happened was—the first night of her following me around Nancy Jo asked me the same tired old question everyone used to ask me: "How do you get all your gossip?" And my stock answer was always, "Everybody's a rat. Everybody tells on everybody." Three or four nights later Nancy and I bumped into Zito at Scores where the Hell's Angel told me, "You should've been here last night. I had Sean [Penn] here. We had a nice time."

As I turned to walk away, Nancy Jo asked me who I was talking to. "That's Chuck Zito," I said. "Hell's Angel, actor, stuntman, bodyguard. Everybody knows Chuck. Nobody fucks with Chuck."

"What was he telling you?"

"He just said he and Sean Penn were here last night and they had a good time."

"Is that an item for you?" Nancy Jo asked.

"Nah. Sean's got a girl. I like him. I'll leave him his privacy."

Now when Sales put her article together she casually slapped together our meeting Chuck with my "everybody's a rat" comment from four days earlier. I'm not gonna say that sort of thing isn't done in a profile— and I've been guilty of connecting the dots in a similar fashion. But I don't think Nancy Jo knew the exact danger she was placing me in.

I remember reading it and punching out her number immediately.

"Hey, you're gonna get me killed with this 'rat' shit."

"But that's what you said."

"Yeah . . . but I didn't say it about Chuck. I said that four nights earlier."

"Oh, come on, A.J. What's the big deal?"

"The big deal is I'm gonna get my ass kicked. Do you know anyone who calls a Hell's Angel a rat and lives to talk about it?"

"You really believe in all this *street* code stuff?" And she said "street" with a lot of disdain, like it was from a fairy tale world.

"Jesus Christ, Nancy Jo. You're a Jewish girl who narrowly got into Yale. I'm an Italian kid who narrowly avoided jail. You'll never have any idea what kind of shit you placed me in."

And with that I went on with my harrowing week. And as each day went on, something more perverse or painful awaited me—including my car being set afire in front of my apartment on Madison Avenue to my girlfriend, Becky, telling me to fuck myself and disconnecting her number—until it reached a climax with Chuck one-timing me in a tight storage room and me seeing stars. And not the kind I was used to seeing.

I had enjoyed a Spanish dinner with my nephew Jack and my pal Jose Zuniga, an actor who worked with me on *Ransom*. We were headed to the back of the room at Scores when the club's publicist Lonnie Hanover walked up and looked me in the eye.

"A.J., it's always a pleasure to see you but I have some news: Chuck's here and he's looking for you."

"All right. Shit."

"I'm sorry, A.J.," Lonnie said.

"Fuck. Here we go."

And with that, Jose and Jack asked why I was alarmed.

"Well, guys," I said, "Chuck is going to kick my ass over the article."

"What can we do about it?" Jose asked me, clutching his dessert in a doggy bag.

"Nothing. You just take your little tiramisu back to your girl and call me tomorrow."

My nephew grew concerned. "And what should I do?"

"Nothing. Just watch where they take me and stay close by. After he's done with me, come help me up. But don't interrupt him. Understand? Let him do what he has to do."

And within seconds, Chuck appeared in his leather pants and vest. And I knew that walk. I'd seen it before.

FLASHBACK: One year earlier. I am sitting in Scores watching a Roy Jones, Jr., fight with Mickey Rourke, and Lonnie comes by our table and tells the actor, "Chuck is looking to talk to you." With that, Chuck walks out of the President's Club and says to Mickey, "You don't answer my beeps no more?"

"What do you want to talk about," Mick offers.

"Let's do this in the back room."

And with that, the two men walked to the empty President's Club and Mickey emerges ten minutes later with a fat lip and a bloody nose.

"What happened?" I ask Mickey, after he sits back down to his Coca-Cola.

"It was an old beef. What happened was bound to happen," Mick says.

END OF FLASHBACK.

Back to present day. Chuck was now making the same walk directly at me. He was holding a copy of the magazine. Following him was a guy named Johnny C. and then Steve Sergio, a Gambino crime family associate who saw that John Gotti, Jr., got his envelope from the topless mecca every week. And Steve, a guy who had comped me hundreds of drinks and dinners over the years, was now looking for an empty room to let Chuck go to work on my face. He found it in a cramped storage room, right off the men's bathroom.

We stepped inside and Johnny C. leaned against the door. Chuck cracked his knuckles and handed me the magazine and said, "Read it out loud."

"The whole thing?"

"You'll know when I don't wanna hear no more."

"Chuck, listen . . ." I began. "I know how this looks, but I didn't call you a rat. It's the way the writer juxtaposed the words . . ." And let me just tell you right now—when you're trying to save your ass by explaining "juxtaposition" to a Hell's Angel, you can smell the punch coming.

"Just read." He was breathing real heavy now.

"I mean, come on, you know how these articles turn out," I offered. "Half the stuff you read is . . ."

"A.J." He cracked his knuckles. *"Read!"*

And so I read. And Johnny leaned on the door and Chuck let out wicked little breaths from his nostrils like a bull looking to run for the red. And when I got to the word *rat*, I heard the slight grunt of a man unleashing a punch and that's all I remember. Next thing I knew I was on my knees, my mouth was bleeding and I don't know how long I was out cold. Probably ten seconds, but it felt like an hour. Chuck's a very strong man. You've seen HBO's *Oz*.

"You wanna hit me back?"

"Not particularly," I slurred.

"I'm supposed to hurt you tonight, A.J. There are guys who want to see you in the hospital tonight," Chuck said. And then, as God is my witness, Chuck's beeper went off.

He looked down at the number. "That's R.C. I gotta go, but I'll be back and we'll settle this. Wait here for me."

"Is there going to be any more punching when you get back? Because if there is, I'd rather go now."

"No," Chuck said. "That's done. Now we have to correct it."

I want to act like I sat in the club unfazed while Chuck was off at his immediate meeting with R.C., but I can't lie. In the twenty minutes Chuck was away, I needed to fly to the men's room twice. He literally knocked the shit out of me. But I remember my nephew making a much-needed trip, too. So, in retrospect, it could've been the Spanish food.

When he returned, I popped three Percocet to deaden the pain and I watched Chuck wolf down an order of penne ala vodka. Correcting the "rat" comment meant writing the clarification in my column the next week. It also meant *New York* magazine running some sort of clarification in their magazine, which they never did. But Chuck took mercy on me.

"I gotta admit," I said, with a swollen jaw. "Now that it's all said and done, it's kind of an honor to have gotten punched out by Chuck Zito."

"Ah . . . come on," Chuck was almost blushing with pride.

"Nah, really. First Mickey and now me. Both of us punched out at Scores."

"Yeah, but there's a difference. Mickey got two smacks. I *punched* you."

A year later, Chuck punched out *Jean-Claude Van Damme* in the Champagne Room, completing the trifecta and placing me in some sort of elite group of beaten men. I'm not quite sure how I feel about the company or the cause, but it comes up a lot in conversation—especially whenever I sit and chat with Howard Stern—so it must mean something.

And the profile must have meant something, too, because I did receive calls from editors at Random House and Simon & Schuster saying they'd be very interested in reading the proposal for my book. Problem was, those folks wanted a "tell-all," something along the lines of a gossip confessional, and I wasn't about to do that. After all, I told them, I had Hollywood on my mind.

As for Nancy Jo—she went on to become a damned good writer in her own right. We never did get along too well after all the shit and glitter settled. But then again, there is nothing written that says writers and the writers who profile them are supposed to get along. Maybe that's why painters don't pose for other painters.

Honky Tonk Woman

tell people my sciatica is the result of an old football injury. I say that *all* the time.

"How'd you hurt your back?"

"Who remembers? Halfbacks take a lotta hits over the years."

Or sometimes I attribute it to something equally as manly.

"What was the start of your back hurting you?"

"Lots of squats with no spotter."

Lies. Big lies. And I have to stop the bullshit right now. I threw my back out over a supermodel. And not the way you're thinking, either. She had a little too much to drink and I carried her home. But I'm getting ahead of myself.

I fell in love with Kara Young long before I ever knew her name. She used to stare at me on the subway all the time and I wouldn't dare turn away until the ride was over. I might have talked to her, except it wasn't her on the train with me. It was her startling image, shot by Albert Watson, that the MTA was using on posters as part of a beautification campaign. I can't tell you how many times I missed my stop because I couldn't pull myself away. I had never seen a face like hers.

And so, I eventually found out her name and went searching for her everywhere. I found her in Revlon ads, Victoria's Secret catalogues,

Sports Illustrated swimsuit issues, L'Oreal hair boxes and in a hundred fashion layouts. I even spotted her in Prince's "Kiss" video and the rarely seen Guns n' Roses video "Since I Don't Have You." At any rate, I was hooked, despite the fact that she was married and she was pregnant when I finally saw her in the flesh for the first time. And when I did finally lay eyes on her, it was at the same fashion show I had first spotted Tasha. Only Kara was sitting across the runway from me, with big black sunglasses on, leaning on her pals Jaye Davidson and Christian Slater. They had front row seats and she was in a completely different league than I was and I couldn't even find it within me to introduce myself. I only caught glimpses of her through the parade of ridiculous beauty that separated us.

From that day forward I loved her from afar. I even successfully begged Watson to give me a print of the photo that hung in the subway and stuck it on my bathroom wall. But, like I said, Kara was married. To a good-looking and successful fashion photograper, no less. And the chances I had of making her mine were slim and none. Why, then, did I possess the balls to feel like she was destined to be mine? I'll tell you why. Because I've always believed in destiny like people believe in God. And the funny thing about destiny is, it either grabs you by your collar or gently guides you by your arm. But either way, it gets you there.

When word spread that New York City jet-setter Johnny Chappoulis had brain cancer, I approached Kara's husband, Sante D'Orazio, and told him I wanted to write a nice column about his ill buddy.

"Not that cancer's anything nice to write about," I told Sante. "But I lost both my parents to it and I think I'd like to write something about Johnny. And since he's your pal, I'm coming to you for some quotes and stories."

Sante explained that while Johnny epitomized what "downtown" was all about, he wouldn't have enjoyed a column about him laid up in a hospital with a deadly disease. When the time is right, Sante said, you can call me and I'll help you put something together.

We both knew what he was saying. I wouldn't write anything until Johnny was gone. And with the rate his cancer was spreading, that wouldn't be too much longer. Sante gave me his number and when the unfortunate time came I called. And at that time, it was Kara who supplied me with Johnny stories and Johnny ironies and Johnny pictures so that I could eventually write the column that bid him farewell. We spoke in the wake of her good friend's unexpected death and our conversations were awkward, but I knew a friendship between us was born.

Around the same time, hip-hop impresario Russell Simmons approached me and asked if I'd be profiled in his magazine, *One World*. I said, "Fine. As long as I can choose the writer." He said, "Who do you want?"

"Kara Young," I said.

"Done," Russell said. "Kara is one of my best friends."

I knew that. I also knew we'd get along just fine. That's why I chose her.

During our "date," Kara clicked on her microcassette recorder the second I picked her up at her monstrous loft on Crosby Street and only shut it off several times during the interview. But by the time we left, I learned more about her than she could ever know about me. In the three hours we spent at Arte, a little out-of-the-way joint on 9th Street, I learned that Kara was not in a happy home and that the horse was running away from the carriage. She didn't have to say it out loud, I could just feel it. And I remember thinking, "I have a shot at this woman." But then that thought was immediately followed by a more realistic take on the situation: "Where did I get the balls big enough to believe I have a shot at this woman?" And, of course, my final thought as I drove home was "Not on your fuckin' life, pal."

But then destiny stepped in when Kara called to say she needed one more dinner to really nail down the interview. That didn't go over big with my girlfriend, Becky—who was sick and tired of hardly seeing me at all due to my running around every night. Cancelling on her at the last minute was something I had to do, but something I knew was going to bring her Puerto Rican temper to a boil.

FLASHBACK: I have just hung up with Kara, made the reservation at Arte and I am calling Becky behind the closed door of my office at the *News*.

"Hey, baby, I got a little bad news . . ."

"What's the matter, Pie?"

"I think I have to cancel tonight."

"What a surprise. Why now?"

"Well, it's that *One World* interview. The writer, Kara Young, needs to see me one more time. And she can only do it tonight."

"What is it with you and this girl?"

"What? Nothing. She just needs more time with me."

"Great. You go see your supermodel friend and don't expect me to sit home and wait for it to be over."

"Come on, baby. Don't be that way. You think I want to sit down again and rehash all that same shit people ask me during interviews?"

"With her? Yes!"

"Well, I don't. I'd rather be with you."

"You're a bad liar. Good-bye, A.J."

Simply hanging up on me was never good enough for Becky. She liked to unplug her phone for hours, sometimes the entire night. But the truth is—she was right. I did want to see Kara that night more than I wanted to see Becky. And that was a truth that I would eventually own up to one teary day on my bed with Becky. But for that night, lying—even poor lying—had to do. And as hard as it is to come out and say—I was drowning in the shallow end of the pretension pool and I thought a supermodel would make for a better lifeboat.

Despite Becky's pain, I went to eat with Kara and it was apparent from the get go, the night was headed for a spot I had only dreamed of. We were midway through discussing our personal pains and troubled relationships—and nearly through with our meals—when the waiter approached.

"How about another wine for signora?"

"Um," Kara stuttered, "if I have one more wine, I'm not going to be able to walk out of here."

And then there was a very pregnant pause that would have made Harold Pinter nervous. And then Kara spoke again.

"Okay . . . I'll have one more wine."

And that wine—a glass of red Sancerre—changed everything.

Within a couple of months, Kara and Sante had separated and she moved out of the loft and found a cozy apartment on the edge of SoHo. And almost every day, we'd meet at out-of-the-way spots in the West Village for secret dinners and quiet conversation where promise and passion were born. And then we'd say our good-byes and I'd run all the way home in celebration of us. But because of the delicacy of her marital state (her divorce would not be settled for two years) and my occupation (Kara was plugged into almost everyone I wrote about) we made like we didn't know each other in public but made mad dashes for the loft I had just leased in the Meat District.

We called it loving each other "on the creep" and it was never easy. In fact, it downright hurt when Kara would tell me her friends wouldn't understand her being associated with me because they would assume she was supplying me with tidbits on their personal lives. But that was not the case. I never asked Kara for a word on anyone. And she never offered. Never. Nobody will believe that, but it's true. In fact, in the long run, it was a big reason why I wanted out of the business. In so many words, it got increasingly difficult writing about Madonna, let's say, when I knew she and Kara had dinner at Mister Chow's the night before.

But I'd be lying if I said "the creep" didn't have its cute side. I remember hundreds of cellphone calls to each other. My beeper, heavy with her number, dancing across the dresser of another girl's bedroom and me pulling the phone into a strange bathroom to call her back in hushed tones. The catch in my heart when all ten messages on my answering machine were hers. The hundreds of e-mails. I also remember following her home from Spy one night and the both of us flirting from opposite sides of the street, as I made sure she was fine every step of the way home. But one of my favorite memories of us turned me into a liar. Until now. It was Kara who threw my back out. And not in the sexual throes this chapter would have you think. It was a manly gesture that some people confused for a sexual overture. But either way, it slipped a disk in my back real bad.

I walked into Bowery Bar for Annabella Sciorra's birthday party one night and was met by Kara's tear-filled eyes. Apparently, she had just gotten wind of a *Star* magazine story that was hitting the stands with photos of Sante kissing Sharon Stone on a California beach during a photo shoot. By the time I had gotten to the joint, Kara was three past her limit of one Cosmopolitan per party, and I was not about to let her walk home. I offered to drive and she accepted and we walked out of the hotspot with all eyes upon us. And I remember Tupac Shakur was singing "Skandalouz." The Thursday night regulars at Bowery Bar had heard rumblings of her and Sante's marriage coming to an end, but they never expected to see me walking alongside her.

I dropped Kara in the passenger seat of the Nissan and drove her to Crosby Street. With her unable to walk, I hoisted her over my shoulder and walked her up to the door of her second-story loft and fished in her purse for the keys.

"Which key gets me in the door, Kara?"

"The round one," she said with her eyes closed and her teeth clenched.

That would've been fine except they were all round.

Once I got us inside the door and made the long climb up the first set of thirty steps, I then reached another door leading us to the back of the loft.

"Which key opens this door, Kara?"

"The round one."

"Again with the round one."

I eventually figured it out. But there was one more flight awaiting me. And those were the twelve steps or so to her bedroom—a spot I had dreamed of being in when I first set my eyes on her at the fashion show. But when I finally dropped the 117-pound beauty on her bed, I kissed her on the forehead good-bye and headed back to Bowery Bar just to show the nosey troops my intention was true. I then headed to Boom to lay it all out for Rocco. It wasn't until I made it home at the usual hour of four A.M. that I first felt the undeniable pain of sciatica that hadn't plagued me in years. The unmistakable tingle and slow burn that showed its teeth on the right side of my ass and radiated down my leg until I'd have to rub my calf with tears in my eyes. In the weeks to come, the pain would intensify to the point where I was swallowing handfuls of Percocets and Valium every day and night. And whenever my supply would run out at inopportune times, I would simply rummage through the medicine cabinets of unsuspecting friends. One time I found five Dilaudids belonging to a friend's grandfather who had just come off major surgery. It was like hitting the lottery.

And falling in love with Kara was like hitting the lottery, too: a beautiful loot that came with its problems. My heroic climb would eventually lead to another delicate spinal operation and our clandestine meetings would eventually turn to true love—but not the kind that was truly carried out in the public arena too many times. Nonetheless, it remains the strongest love I've known. But thirty months later—with ferocious on-again/off-again fever—it would die when she couldn't keep her affair with New York's most pompous billionaire "on the creep." Our once sweet, private love affair was now a public and ugly breakup splashed across the top of Page Six. But more on that fuckin' story later.

Start Me Up

What I began to love and hate most about the *psst!* business came at me like shrapnel in a lonely foxhole toward the end of 1996—which, up until then, had been my favorite year of all time. Matter of fact, I'd have to go back sixteen years earlier to pinpoint a year in which I had more fun. And that was my senior year in high school, hotdogging my way through my varsity basketball season. I wore Chuck Taylor white canvas high-tops and I'd write the phone numbers of cheerleaders from opposing teams on my sneaks as often as I could get them. I thought I was real hot shit driving my father's hand-me-down '72 Impala home from my games on Tuesday and Friday nights, sometimes stopping at the strip clubs along Sunrise Highway in Bay Shore, Long Island—LaLa's, Lemon Tree and the Dollhouse. Oh yeah. I was real hot shit. Maybe nobody told you.

Anyhow, I'm not gonna lie to you. I still live in those high school memories. I think it has something to do with the immense significance we all placed on being popular among our peers. Well, this is just a long way of saying, here I was sixteen years out of high school and suddenly I felt like the most popular guy in the hall again. But popularity comes with a price.

I remember I hit 1996 with my feet running. The money and the perks were very good. Between my *News* job, my E! gig, various TV appearances, half-assed nightclub promoting and some freelance maga- zine work, I was zeroing in at $250,000 a year. Things got even crazier when I met a Mercedes-Benz executive at a dinner and he offered me a 1996 300SL convertible Benz for $400 a month just because it would be "good for business."

"I was supposed to save it for [New York Jet] Keyshawn Johnson," the car guy said. "But he's dropping the goddamn ball so much I'm not so sure I want him to drive the car."

I'm a fan of Keyshawn's as much as the next guy, but you can bet your ass I didn't ask any questions and I put my ass in the black beauty within days. Sure, the car payment and the insurance money and the garage fees amounted to $1,600 a month, but I wasn't going to say no to a beautiful black Benz when I had just gotten me a beautiful black supermodel.

It was dreamy, I'm not gonna lie to you. But it didn't come without its price. I wasn't saving a penny and I was paying other people's bills, stupidly falling victim to sob stories dripping from the pretty lips of girls I was dating now and then. One lovely Cuban girl even got a small down payment for a truck one drunken night at Spy and I have the cancelled check to prove it. On top of that, there wasn't a dinner bill or drink tab I didn't pick up. I was sending my nephew to acting school and still paying Becky's medical insurance. I even paid actress Shari Headley's cable bill for two years because I couldn't stand the fact that her child's deadbeat dad, Kid 'N Play star Christopher Martin, wasn't paying child support and that meant Shari couldn't afford cable. And when Barney's owner Gene Pressman decided to give me a 40 percent discount on anything I wanted, I started stepping in $600 Prada shoes and walking off in $500 Gucci shirts and $2,000 Armani jackets. So the money was leaving me as quickly as I made it. I was also developing a deeper relationship with pain pills, thanks to my second laminectomy in eight years. This surgery was performed by superneurosurgeon Dr. Mi- chael Lavyne several hours after he successfully removed a blood clot from the brain of a Central Park rape victim. My surgery was a success, but the residual pain would last for many months to come. And part of that was my fault. Yes, the doctor did tell me my sciatic nerve had been pinched so long it looked fire-engine red, but most of my nagging pain stemmed from being insubordinate to his aftercare demands.

"Okay," Lavyne told me in my hospital room, a day after surgery, "I don't want you to drive your car or have sex for at least three weeks. And don't get on your feet too soon either."

"Doc," I said, the morphine drip taking me into the cold fadeaway. "I just got me a new Mercedes and a supermodel girlfriend. And the first chance I get, I'm gonna drive that car to her house and make love to her."

And I did. And there was nothing any man was going to say that would've changed my plans. Of course, that meant many more months of fighting that inexplicable burning pain that shot from my hip to my heel—virtually all day long—with a daily mixture of thirty pills—with my pals Percocet, Percodan, Vicodin and Valium heading the list. God knows little fellas like Flexeril and Diflusinal and Elavil and Klonopin made appearances, too. I was taking about 1,000 pills a month. But for the most part it was my buddies Vitamins P and V who were with me every ginger step of the way. And here's the way those steps went.

Waking up for work at nine A.M. was impossible without setting my alarm for eight A.M. and gulping down five Percocet. The "starting five" as I called them were strictly for allowing me to begin my ten-minute crawl to the bathroom and starting my day with a twenty-minute Epsom salts bath and a gentle five-minute shower. The remaining twenty-five minutes was reserved for limping down to the corner to hail a cab. Minutes later I'd be crouched in the back eating my bacon, egg and cheese sandwich and keeled over in the backseat.

By the time I arrived at work it was ten A.M. and the first order of business was to pull my phone on the floor and begin to return as many as thirty-five calls each morning while I lay flat out on my back and stared at the ceiling. That usually took me to high noon. And I do mean *high*. Around that time the "second unit" would come into play and I'd wash down five more Percs with my second 16-ounce cup of coffee. I'd then drag myself to my desk and begin writing the column while simultaneously getting ready for the various TV appearances I had sched-uled for the day. Five more Percs slammed into my system at three o'clock, but because of the stress of the column deadline—as well as feeding stories upfront that I preferred not having my name on—I'd need another five at five P.M. So, while all the paper's editors were ready for the six o'clock crunch for the starter edition, I was twenty pain pills into the wind and setting my sights on another wild night.

And it's funny when you're on a path to destruction in an arena that pits anxiety with notoriety and fame with stress—few people intervene to help you. It's almost as if they want to watch the show drag on just for the entertainment value. It was a car crash everyone slowed down to watch—even me—only now I was seeing me in the car.

Perhaps that's why I felt slightly akin to Mickey Rourke back in those days. I had practically been Mickey's self-appointed policeman of the press. If a bad word was printed about Mickey anywhere, the troubled actor wouldn't even have to pick up the phone to ask for my help. I was already on top of it. I admit, it wasn't the best example to set in terms of being a good journalist, but I was ecstatic that I was in the position to help an idol of mine. And eventually any gossip columnist with a heart—or a dream to work alongside the stars he covered— develops that protective layer. And it takes true genius to wrap that protective layer around journalistic objectivity and continue your career for many years. (See: Smith, Liz—gossip legend.)

At any rate, I couldn't do that. I got too close to some of the people I covered and there were times I flat-out knew I was lying to protect them. Risking my job to snuff out a budding scandal. Putting the paper at risk to strengthen a friendship. Tossing objectivity aside to keep the good times rolling. I did that more than a few times for Mickey Rourke.

Mickey was obsessed with getting Carré back, but he was not obsessed with following her or finding her. He especially was not guilty of "stalking" her, which is exactly what the model said to my *News* contemporaries Joanna Molloy and George Rush. For the record, Mickey would call me each afternoon and specifically ask me what Fashion Week parties Carré would be attending and we would purposefully go to the other side of town to avoid her. Though we did this numerous times, there were still times when the *Post* would print an item about Mickey spitting at a photographer at an uptown party while me and his crew had partied downtown all night long. Or Mickey scouring every club in town looking to find Carré on nights when we all went to Pastel's in Brooklyn. It was ridiculous and it's that car-crash mentality I talked about earlier.

There came a time when the public perception was way off and every tabloid producer and news reporter wanted to see the guy fall.

One particular day I was alerted by my editor-in-chief, Martin Dunn, that the next day's wood would be a story on Otis claiming Mickey was "stalking" her and that she was "begging" fashion designers to disallow him from attending any of the shows she was walking in. I sat down with Martin at a bar and told him Rush and Molloy's story was bullshit and that the *News* would look like one great, big, uninformed, giant asshole when Mickey and Carré reconcile in a matter of days.

"This is a publicity ploy," I told Dunn. "This is Carré Otis trying to get herself a big hit of publicity to restart her career during an otherwise dull Fashion Week in Manhattan."

"George and Joanna stand by it," Dunn said. "They spoke directly to Otis."

"It's all crap. She just bullshitted her way to the most influential front page in America. And George and Joanna want that wood so bad they can taste it."

Dunn ran the story and I ran for South Beach two days later to recharge and get away from the bullshit. I did that from time to time. There was something about reading on the beach and watching the lovelies on Rollerblades on Ocean Drive that calmed me. But before I went, I recorded a *Gossip Show* segment in which I held up Rush and Molloy's front-page story—with the giant photo of Otis on a Bryant Park runway—and essentially told America that their scoop was a load of crap. I then went into my side of things and how I predicted a reconciliation, before I tossed the paper over my shoulder and onto the floor to end the segment. I firmly believed my take on things, but I'm sure a lot of the flair with which I told the story was the drugs talking.

When E! ran the segment, Rush and Molloy ran to Dunn's office and demanded to know how I could be allowed to do something that denounced a front-page story for the paper that employed me. That's when Dunn watched a tape of the show and angrily tracked me down at Bang, my pal Rocco's restaurant on Washington Street, smack-dab in the middle of the South Beach strip.

A wonderful and drunken dance on a table to "Djobi Djoba" by the Gipsy Kings with a pretty Cuban girl named Yoandra was interrupted by Dunn's call to my cell.

"What the fuck did I just see?" he shouted over the noise.

"But, boss, I know their story is wrong. I got a strong hunch . . ."

"A hunch?"

"All right, not a hunch . . . but my intuition tells me . . ."

"Intuition? What are you, a fucking woman?"

"Listen . . ."

"No, you listen. You get home tomorrow. *Tomorrow.* And come straight to my office."

"But, boss . . . I swear."

"You know what? If you want your job back, you better leave right fucking now and see me as I walk into my office!"

Click.

Tone.

I bid farewell to Yoandra, grabbed a ride to the airport and went straight to Dunn's office and basically told him if Mickey and Carré didn't reconcile he could fire me on the spot.

"I bloody well might have to," he said. "This is the kind of shit Mort will have your ass for. And mine."

Mickey was aware how far I had stuck my neck out and was appreciative as hell. Which meant more to me than the job, to tell you the truth. Before I headed back to South Beach, Mickey invited me to join him and Tupac and the rest of the guys for dinner at Nello and an excursion to club Expo.

"You're gonna like it," he said. "It's payback time."

I didn't know what he meant, but I went just for fun's sake. After all, how often does a guy get to hang out with his favorite actor and favorite poet? Spirits were "high" at dinner. I remember Mickey rising from his seat and stepping on the tops of occupied tables just to greet me. He could do no wrong at Nello.

"Hey, here's my man . . ."

He sat me next to Tupac and I remember being amazed how much the maligned rapper knew about literature and acting and how he could literally recite the top ten books on the *New York Times* bestseller list.

"But don't write that," he told me. "I don't need niggahs thinking I'm a faggot or some shit."

(Needless to say, that dinner solidified my decision to protect Tupac in the press, too. And that's probably the reason why I was the only reporter who gained access to his room at Bellevue the first time he was shot. Tupac's mom knew through Mickey that I "was cool" and she gave security the nod. The visit wasn't professional and I never let the *News* know I was going, despite the fact that it was *the* story in town. I just wanted to go see how a friend was doing. That's the kind of shit that gets a columnist an immense dose of credibility that goes a long way.)

At any rate, after dinner we all hit Club Expo—fighting through the throng of paparazzi and gossip reporters all hungry for a scoop during an otherwise dull Fashion Week—and tucked ourselves into the VIP area. Within seconds, Mickey spotted Carré across a room of hundreds.

"Go ahead," Mickey said, motioning for Tupac to go on his mission. And with that, Tupac got up and the sea of people parted for him as he made his way to Carré. While Tupac was chatting her up, Mickey had a bottle of champagne sent over. A few minutes after the cork was popped, Carré was smiling at Mickey from across the room. And the paparazzi had their picture. A day or so later, Mickey and Carré were back together again and the model was on record with her comments regarding her love for him.

Mickey called me the next day. "Thanks for everything, man. And hey . . . they can't fire you no more now."

I headed back to South Beach the next morning and was reading Bukowski on the beach by noon. Later that night, I practically found Yoandra where I left her a few nights earlier. And it was the last time the paper's hierarchy would ever question me again regarding my crazy hunches and an intuition that's more often housed in a woman's soul.

She Smiled Sweetly

Nothing is as soothing as feeling all those layers of separation melt away from your body. I'm talking about the famous six degrees of separation that playwright John Guare hipped us to. By the end of 1996, I was capable of calling anyone I desired to speak with. I was capable of getting a return phone call from just about anyone I hoped to know. But more important, I was growing very accustomed to fielding phone calls from people I secretly dreamed of meeting and meeting people I always dreamed of knowing.

And that's why I chose a private backyard barbeque with Warren Beatty and four beautiful models in JohnnyBoy Calvani's backyard ahead of a dinner at Rao's with a table of tough guys. That's also why I elected to have dinner and share a joint with Jack Nicholson rather than feeding details of John Kennedy's secret wedding to my news desk the night before the nuptials no one knew about. And it's essentially why I usually dropped a blockbuster story now and then for the sake of a budding friendship. And I'm glad I did that sort of thing to this day—placing the brotherhood ahead of the byline. Four years out the *Daily News* door, I don't give a damn about stories I broke. But I do care about the friendships I built.

Anyhow, it was all done for the inexplicable bliss of feeling the degrees of separation slide away.

I can't say I ever wanted to be near the circus atmosphere of the O. J. Simpson Courthouse Gang, but in a weird way I had dealings with just about every damned name associated with the accused murderer. Now that all the DNA has cleared, I believe the only one I can't lay claim to knowing or dealing with is Juror No. 5. God knows I had my dealings with O. J.—both on TV and, once, in an LA hotel lobby. I tailed Fred Goldman and family. Had a face-to-face chat with Al Cowlings. Did *Geraldo* with Denise Brown. Knocked back a drink with Robert Shapiro. Enjoyed a Scores romp with Kato Kaelin and a private dinner with Faye Resnick. But the most enjoyable night was the out-of-the-blue meeting with O. J.'s God-fearing former girlfriend, Paula Barbieri.

It all happened when I had elected to take a week off from work to rest my blistering backache. I remember the end of October '96 being a slow news week and leaving the column in the capable hands of Michael and Jimmy "The Kid" Ruttenberg, an intern who still had the balls to ask the tough questions we no longer wanted to. I was home, screening phone calls from my bed and deep into a twenty Percocet swoon, when It Models owner Paul Fischer chimed in.

"Hey, Benza . . . who you taking to tonight's VH-1 Fashion Awards?"

"No one, pal. I'm passing on it. I'm just laying in bed with a bad back waiting to watch the Yankees and Braves World Series game."

"Well, someone wants to go with you," Paul said.

I figured this was Paul's way of engineering good press for his agency, an agency that more than a dozen models had always called me to complain about. Usually a call like this one suggested Paul was looking to lay a girl on me to thwart a bit of bad press he could smell coming a mile away. And sometimes that worked: Lend me a twenty-year-old for the night and—*voila!*—you could wash that bad press right out of your hair.

"You pimping a girl out to me," I said.

"No way, my man. I know who wants to go with you. No bullshit."

I sat up in bed and listened.

"Paula Barbieri wants you to take her to the event. She has no one to go with and she asked if you could take her."

Okay, I knew Fischer was lying from the jump. I knew he was handling Barbieri's attempt at a modeling comeback and her being seen
with me meant a week of good press in my column. But I didn't give
a shit. The notion of taking Barbieri on my arm was a sweet daydream
that was about to become a reality in two hours. And I'm not ashamed
to admit, I held up her *Playboy* layout with one hand as much as the
next guy.

I stood up now, trying to cough the high away, walk off the cobwebs.
"I didn't call for credentials, Paulie. I been in bed all day."

"Don't worry. Paula has everything. Meet her outside the Paramount
Theater in two hours."

And so I did. Showering and eventually putting on—get this!—a purple velvet jacket Donna Karan had given me the week before. I cabbed
to the Paramount like who the hell I thought I was and waited for Paula
to arrive. When she appeared, in an ankle-length black backless dress, I
almost shit. She bounced right toward me, oblivious to the throng of
press that was stalking her and looking quite comfortable amid the crowd
of civilians who brushed shoulders with her and had no idea who she
was. No matter how high I was, or how taken I was by the sight of her
beauty, I remember wondering, "If this chick doesn't spend a weekend
in Vegas with Michael Bolton maybe the murders don't ever happen."

"Hi, A.J.," Paula chirped, breaking me from my spell. "I'm Paula."

No shit, sweetie.

"I'm so happy you could make it. Paul told me you've been suffering
from a bad back."

"Yeah, it's an old football injury."

"Ouch. You know my ex-boyfriend still has bad knees from football."

I swear she said that.

With virtually no chance of following up that dooz, I took Paula by
the hand and made the walk through the army of paparazzi and reporters
who were all positioned outside the velvet ropes. I had been on the
vanity side of the velvet before—and admittedly made those trips more
times than my gossip contemporaries—but never before had I accompanied a star whose tail was still white-hot in the press.

By the time Paula and I sat down, we were a little more comfortable
with each other and able to enjoy the show despite everyone sneaking
peeks at us. And by the time the BeeGees sang, "You Should Be Danc-

ing," Paula was holding my hand the entire time. "I had such a crush on these guys when I was young!" she screamed in my ear.

And right around this time I remember thinking, "There's no telling what I'd do if she were mine and she decided to go to Vegas with Michael Bolton."

Paula was sweet the entire time we were there and, truth be known, Fischer did—in fact—buy himself some good press with his eleventh-hour setup. And technically, once the show was over, Paula didn't have to stick around with me. But she did.

"All right, girl, I better get you home," I said as we walked to my Benz parked in an outdoor garage on Eighth Avenue. It was cold enough that I draped my ugly-ass purple velvet jacket around Paula's shoulders. "Come on, I'll give you a ride." It was a stance I had to make since I had Kara waiting for me at Spy.

But Paula had designs on other plans. About a hundred feet from the garage, Paula pulled me into a Blarney Stone pub and bet me her Braves would be beating my Yankees in the series game, which was still on. When she lost the bet, she asked how I'd like to be paid.

It took everything I had not to come back with a payment every man would love to receive. Instead I just asked her to dinner. She accepted and off we went to Tavern on the Green, unwittingly crashing the private premiere party for the Miramax film *Unhook the Stars*. And it was there where the beginning of a friendship between myself and Harvey Weinstein began.

It was somewhere between the asparagus spears and the prime rib that Harvey approached me on line and asked what I thought of the film.

"Didn't see it, Harvey," I said, holding Paula's hand. "I just got here. Do you know Paula?"

And then it was Harvey's time to almost shit. Not that he hasn't seen his share of beautiful women, but nobody expected to see Paula out and the sight of her was quite grabbing.

"No, I haven't had the pleasure. How do you do?" Harvey said, before moving away and keeping an eye on us from a neighboring table.

Several minutes later, Harvey ambled by to bust balls. "Okay, what the hell's going on? What don't I know here?"

Paula laughed. "Nothing, Harvey. Just a guy having dinner with a girl."

"But why," Harvey demanded. "Why A.J., Paula?"

"He's a gentleman," she said. "And women like gentlemen."

Despite the fact that that statement made her relationship with O.J. almost impossible to understand, I *was* a gentleman that night. I only brought up O.J. a few times and each time I did, I did so off the record. On top of that, I promised Paula nothing we spoke about or anything we did would end up in the column. And on that night, Paula was candid enough to talk to me about her relationship with O.J., her *Playboy* pictures, her six-figure book deal and her new lease on life. And, of course, her finding God. In the end, she was just another in a long line of the O.J. Courthouse Gang who put her mouth where the money was. But despite all that—and despite the fact that the media was dying to get to her—I didn't print a word of it. I traded in the blockbuster for a few innings of baseball and tap beer with a beautiful BeeGees fan. I was more interested, perhaps foolishly, in making her my friend.

I say "foolishly" because Paula and I never spoke again.

Dandelion

Some columnists hate it when their publisher knocks on their door with a favor. It usually means the columnist has to scrap the column he has spent time building and compose another column to fill the agenda of the boss. And when your publishers are Fred Drasner and Mort Zuckerman, the agenda could be anything from loosening gun control laws to the Artists vs. Actors Hamptons softball classic.

At any rate, I liked it when Fred or Mort came rappin' at my door. Partly because I could never believe that I had ascended to a place where millionaires and billionaires relied on me to make their lives easier. But mainly because I liked having powerful men indebted to me without having to do anything too fucked up or compromising.

One day Fred walked in and tossed *Vanity Fair* on my desk.

"You read this yet?"

"No," I said. "These fuckin' articles are so long, I'd rather wait for the movie."

"Read the piece on Tommy Mottola and call me."

And with that, Fred was gone. On to his next agenda.

Fred and Mottola are hunting buddies, drinking pals and Rao's regulars. And on one of those occasions—maybe even the previous night—Mottola let Fred know that Robert Sam Anson's *VF* profile on him was a hatchet job. Fred then took it the next step by dropping it on my desk and asking me if I'd correct it in my own way. In other words, the orders came down for me to do a hatchet job on Anson. I answered the order without knowing Mottola or Anson from Adam. And it was easy. Principally, Anson just rehashed the usual shit mostly associated with the Sony bigwig—alleged mob ties, hot Guinea temper, controlling husband, etc.—and went about it in a lazy, stereotypical way. I can say that because all writers have done that now and then and I'm just as guilty as any of them. I can also say "Guinea" because I'm damn proud to be one.

Anyhow, a week later I ripped Anson a new ass and pledged my allegiance to Mottola—without having ever met the guy, mind you. And Fred was happy. And that made me happy because all I ever wanted was a pocketful of favors when I left the business.

A day after the column ran, Mottola was kissing my ass over the phone.

"Hey, man . . . you did me a real solid. A real solid," Mottola said. "Let me know if I can do anything for you. *Anything*."

I thanked Tommy and let that sit for a few days. And in the time I pondered what I might enjoy as a payback, my mind wandered to a rainy day in June several years earlier, when I was looking to make a splash in the gossip business. Just dying to make my bones as the new guy in town.

FLASHBACK: The newspapers and tabloid TV shows are abuzz with the impending nuptials of Tommy Mottola and Mariah Carey. The ceremony will take place at the fancy Metropolitan Club in Manhattan. The guest list includes Robert De Niro, Tony Bennett, Michael Bolton, Dick Clark, Barbra Streisand and more. I am sitting at my sister's kitchen table spooning Cap'n Crunch into my mouth when I decide to sneak into the wedding. Just crash the fuckin' thing and bring in this giant scoop for my newspaper. To go from "Who's the new guy?" to "Hey, you're the guy who sneaked into Mariah Carey's wedding!"

The wedding is starting in six hours, so I have to work fast. I rent a tux at RSVP in Bay Shore. With no time for tailoring, I use staples to keep the hemline at the back of my heel. I kiss my sister good-bye—"Good luck, you're crazy" she shouts as I drive off in her old Buick—and head into Manhattan. As soon as I put the car in the garage, I stick some kind of official-looking pin in my lapel (it was my ex-wife's high school honor roll pin), run the wire from my Sony Walkman into my ear and calmly walk up to the Metropolitan Club, smack-dab in the middle of the entire security team Mottola has assembled to keep out assholes exactly like me.

I look one mook in the eye and say, "Hey there, is Jimmy working the back detail or the front detail?"

The guy shrugs his shoulders and says, "I guess the back detail."

And with that, I had penetrated the first and only wall of defense and I remember thinking, "Is this the kind of security big money buys you?" It was tougher to get into my niece's spring recital for God's sake.

Once inside, I marched straight to the bridal suite to get me a peek at the new Mrs. Mottola and, man, she looked gorgeous.

"Mariah," I said, knocking on the door and peeking in. "Hi, my name is Al Romano and I just want to let you know I'll be right outside if you need me. Just holler."

"Oh, thank you, Al."

And then I heard all the girls in her bridal party giggle.

Meanwhile, I spent the better part of the night just walking around with my hands folded behind my back and looking very "official." I directed De Niro to the men's room, helped Dick Clark off with his jacket, showed Barbra Streisand to the registry book and, basically, eavesdropped to my heart's content. Every fifteen minutes or so I was running off to an old-fashioned phone booth and scribbling notes on cocktail napkins. And the following day, my tidbits got heavy play in the paper. But I heard through the grapevine that my crashing his wedding brought Mottola's temper to a boil. I didn't care much. To me, Tommy Mottola wasn't much more than a name I had heard in that "Cherchez la Femme" song.

But suddenly he was willing to let bygones be bygones and now he was on the phone with me thanking me for watching his back and offering me the world in return. The friggin' guy even sent me a Sony television set. I decided to handle the payback in a professional manner.

I had heard Mottola and Mariah were having their difficulties and that the songbird was looking to fly the coop. So I asked Mottola if I could speak with Mariah from time to time with regard to her career.

"I think she gets a bad rap," I said. "And I just want my column to be the column she runs to whenever she has to clear shit up. Can you do that for me?"

"Done," Mottola said.

A few days later Tommy arranged it so I could meet Mariah—and a few of the bodyguards he employed for her—at Spy. Basically, Mariah's little bit of independence was a new label she was starting called Crave— a place that would later become the home from which she carved her new sexy image. Tommy wanted to see to it that I gave her new venture a little play in the paper. "And while you're at it," he said, "let's see if you can set a few people straight who say we're having trouble in our marriage."

"Done," I said.

Not that this is anything new, but by the time Mariah arrived at Spy, me and my pal JohnnyBoy were feeling pretty loaded sitting atop the club's piano—the perch that was reserved nightly for us by Spy owner Jeff Gossett. Rather than waltzing right up to her, I decided to spy on her from twenty feet away just to get a feel for where her head was at. You can tell a lot about someone when they don't know you're looking at them. To be honest, I thoroughly believed every report I had read about the couple's marriage headed for the toilet, and on that particular occasion Mariah was huddled with New York Yankees shortstop Derek Jeter on what turned out to be the first night the future lovers had ever hung out. But on this night, and because my new pal was the almighty Tommy Mottola, I didn't let that interfere with my mission. I threw back my fifth gin and tonic and headed over to the velvet couch she and her girly friends were sitting on.

"Okay," I said, "I got direct orders from your husband to talk to you. You okay with that?"

"Oh great, another one who takes *orders* from my husband," Mariah shot back.

"Listen, I'm my own man," I said. "I just want to talk to you a little bit and clear up some of the bad press you get."

"And how do I know you're just not going to give me more bad press?"

"Because I already arranged it with your husband what we're going to talk about and all," I said. "It's gonna be fine."

"So, let me get this straight, you and *him* decided what you and *I* are going to talk about?"

Jesus, this one was a tough nut to crack. But I have to be honest—forget the crazy lion's mane of hair she sometimes weaves in and forget the slightly tacky dresses she's sometimes busting out of and forget the fact that she likes to be swimming in spiked heels in almost all of her videos—you can fall in love with this woman after a five-minute chat. Not real love, mind you. But at least the kind of love where you feel—crazy as it might sound—that you might actually have a shot at this woman. I don't know, maybe it was the gin talking, but I was falling for her and I didn't give a shit who her husband was. Or that the Yankees captain was sweating her as I leaned over him to get some quotes. Anyhow, it wasn't the first time I fell in love at Spy.

"I have to ask you about your marriage," I said.

"We on the record or off?"

"We're off. Way off."

"We're fine," Mariah said. "People want to spread rumors and cause trouble. But we're fine."

I knew she was lying like a rug, but I was going to write that their marriage was fine just so I could placate my new best friend Tommy. And with the weight my column carried around that time, a confirmation like that was doing a tremendous service to the little big guy. So there I was and there was Mariah and there was way too much fun taking place between us and I didn't want that night at Spy to be the last time I got to speak with her and flirt with her—even if I was the one doing most of the flirting. And I just said "fuck it" and dove right in.

"Listen, I want to call you sometime, but I don't want to have to go through the Pentagon to do it. You ever come down from that Ivory Tower? You're twenty-six years old for God's sake."

She laughed.

"Do you expect me to trust you after you sneaked into my wedding?"

she asked. "What if you were a murderer? Half of Hollywood could've been dead."

"Would that be so bad a thing? Anyhow, listen," I said. "I don't know how to say this but I don't want to go home and never talk to you again. I want to be friends with you."

Then there was a huge moment of silence.

"Wait, that sounded gay as hell. What I mean to say is . . ."

"I know what you mean to say. But it's hard for me to trust a lot of people. And how do I know you aren't gonna fuck me? Are you gonna fuck me?"

"I can't believe I'm saying this, but *no*, I'm not gonna fuck you."

There was another awkward pause between us.

"I might *say* I did one day . . ." I said.

"Okay, here," Mariah said. "Call me at this number if you want to talk. It's my machine and only I check it."

"Cool," I said. "Gimme a kiss. You're a cool girl."

"You're all right yourself," she said.

And then I walked out of Spy with JohnnyBoy hanging on my arm and Mariah Carey's phone number in my back pocket. I jumped into my Benz, popped the top down and listened to Sly Stone sing "M'Lady." Who was cooler than me?

A week or two goes by and I decide to give Mariah a jingle, but when I dial the number she scribbled on the napkin the answering machine pops on with a routine from a Jerky Boys CD. I dial again and get the same thing. Stupidly, I then dial Mottola to find out what's what.

"Tommy, I'm trying to get ahold of Mariah to ask her a question about an item I'm writing and the number I'm dialing . . ."

Mottola cut me off real fast. "What's the number she gave you?"

I read it to him.

"Listen to me," he said. "That ain't the number. Throw it out. If you want to get to Mariah, you call me and I'll get her for you. Understand?"

"Sure," I said. "No problem."

At that moment it dawned on me: Mariah had given me a number, a private number, that her husband wasn't hip to. A few minutes later Mariah calls me.

"You told Tommy I gave you that number?"

"Yeah, what the fuck did I know? I just thought it was a service or some shit and then I heard that Jerky Boys stuff and I didn't know what was going on."

"Listen," Mariah said. "That is my number. He just hates when I get calls that he doesn't clear first."

Jesus Christ, I thought to myself, that's a hell of a way to keep a woman happy.

"A.J., if you ever want to call me again, just call that number and I'll call you back."

And that's the way it went for a few months. I would routinely dial Mariah's number—giggle at her outgoing Jerky Boys message—and she'd usually phone back within a few hours. And our conversations were sweet. I learned that she is one of the funniest chicks I have ever met and I also learned that she was once convinced that I was gay—and that the macho image I'd project on TV was a big con. At any rate, I was happy I had a new friend and happier than hell that it was a sexy international pop star. That sort of thing kills me. It was like Beatty giving me his number and asking me to call him as I left Evans's house that night. Or sharing a joint with Jack.

It didn't take long to figure out that the great Mottola-Carey marriage was all but over and that her husband was using his friends in the press to deny the reports. There was one particular day where Mariah and I were about to hang up and she said, "Tommy is a good man. I know he wants the best for me. But it's hard. There is a big age difference between us and sometimes that works against us."

I half-jokingly said, "Well, whatever you do, if you ever get around to having an affair with someone, don't do the guy who cleans the pool or the limo driver or another old millionaire. Make it with somebody cool. Writers are cool, you know . . ."

"Shut up, you idiot." She laughed, and hung up.

Now here's where it gets creepy.

Bad marriage or not, I know I was being awfully flirty with another man's wife and I knew that meant I was in line for some kind of reper-cussion. So when my phone rang with a calm but irate Mottola on the other end, I was half-expecting the date with destiny.

"Hey, man, listen," he purred. "I want you to come to my office tonight after work. We need to talk. I'll see you at seven."

Truth is, I know I was being half a scumbag with the guy's wife, so

I dutifully hopped in a cab and visited him in his grand office. Strange as it sounds, I was okay with anything he was going to do to me—whether it was threaten me or warn me or simply tell me to go fuck myself and never call his wife again.

I walked into his office and he was on the phone with his buddy and my publisher, Fred Drasner, at the time. They were setting up a hunting trip and the talk was guns and ammo.

"Sit down, man," Tommy said. Before him was a tray of shrimp, some hot and cold antipasto, nice Italian bread and a bottle of Riserva Ducale breathing on his giant desk. "Help yourself."

My instant take on the situation was that my name had come up one too many times in the Mottola mansion and the king of the Bedford castle wanted to put an end to it.

"Tommy, am I breaking up your marriage," I joked.

"Listen to me, man. Mariah is young and she sometimes feels like she is missing out on things. It doesn't help me any when I got you telling her she needs to go out more and she needs to have fun and let loose and all that shit."

"I'm just trying to change the public's perception that you're controlling the poor little rich girl . . ."

"You know what, fuck that," he said. "There's nothing out there. You know better than I do. You go out every night and you see the same assholes and night after night it's the same shit all over again. Everyone is swimming around the fishbowl and everybody not inside the fishbowl is dying to get in. But once you're in it a while, you realize there's just a bunch of shit in the fishbowl."

"So what are you telling me."

"I'm telling you, man to man—and this is not some tough guy meeting—that me and Mariah *are* having a tough time and marriage is not always easy, but I don't need you speaking in her other ear. You understand what I'm saying?"

I absolutely did. It was the kind of shit I went through with my ex-wife and the Special Ed teacher who was always sabotaging me in the fuckin' teacher's conference room every morning. Instant fantasy by the instant coffee.

"I mean, why would you want her on your side more than me anyhow," Mottola said. "Do you realize what I can do for you? I can make any call you want me to and get you what you want."

"I know . . ."

"Don't you want to be an actor?"

"Yeah."

"Bobby De Niro's my best friend. I can call Jane Rosenthal at TriBeCa and have her see you in a second. Do you understand that?"

"I know, I know. I'm not trying to sabotage anything between . . ."

Before I could finish, he had already rung up Rosenthal and was asking her—no, *telling* her—that he'd like her to see me at her earliest convenience. And a date was set on the spot.

"What else do you want? You want more money from Drasner? I'm going hunting with him this weekend and I'll bust his balls about it."

"Jeez, Tommy . . ."

"You need me. You don't need her."

It was going to be hard letting go of the fun and whimsy and sex appeal of chatting up Mariah from time to time, but this was her husband talking and her husband was right. It's just a thing some guys suffer from that has to do with needing the high of getting close to a piece of ass, even though you already have one at home. And, in my opinion, my piece at home was hotter. But that's guys for you and don't ever let anybody fool you and tell you otherwise. I'm telling you right now, if there had been another woman in addition to Eve in the Garden, Adam would've tried to fuck her like crazy.

As I got up to go, I swigged back my wine and reached out to hug Mottola good-bye. "Listen, Tommy, I'm sorry," I said. "It won't happen anymore."

Everything would've been fine except I spotted something in the way Mottola embraced me that gave him away—in my mind anyway—as a complete phony who could never be trusted. He shook my right hand firmly and reached around me with his left hand and rubbed my back. Might sound nice and civil to you, but my Sicilian father always taught me to never trust a man who greets you in that fashion.

"Those are the men who are looking for a soft spot to stick the knife in your back," he always said.

Poppa was right.

. . .

Fast forward several months later. Tommy—who's now publicly separated from Mariah—sees me at Boom Bistro in Sag Harbor and asks me
and my nephew Joey to pull up a couple chairs. "What are you guys
drinking? Lemme buy you a drink." He was crazy with kissing our asses.
The talk was light and generally entertaining, aside from the times he
would send a friend over to surrounding tables and ask girls to join "us"
for drinks. I wouldn't have minded except all the girls he was trying to
hit on were girls who rode in on the Jitney. And, I'm sorry, but that's
a long way away from rolling off Mariah Carey in the morning. Anyhow, I was feeling kind of ridiculous, so I pulled my nephew Joey from
some pretty young thing and split.

The next day, I told Kara what had happened with my meeting Mottola in Sag Harbor and she innocently told me he had sat at her table at
another restaurant an hour before he ran into me. And that didn't sit
right in my book: You don't sit at my girlfriend's table and chat her up
for an hour—no doubt flirting to your heart's content—and then neglect
to tell me you saw her when you run into me an hour later.

"Was he flirty with you?"

"Come on," Kara said. "He was, you know, the way guys are."

"What the fuck does that mean?"

"He was like all men," she said.

"Bottom line," I said. "Did he act like he was looking to fuck you."
Kara stuttered a little bit.

"Did he make me look like an asshole," I said.

"I don't think he's your friend, let's put it that way."

Kara always said more with the space between the sentences than she
did with the actual sentences, but this time it was good enough for me
to want to punch that fucker out.

I never went at Mottola or called him or anything like that, but I did
run to my phone a few hours later and ring up the private number of
Mariah's I had promised Tommy I'd never dial again. And this is basically
what I said.

"Hey, baby, it's A.J. Hey, I just want to say I just saw your new video.
And you look so fuckin' good. You look black for a change, your tits
looked great, you're in that little bikini and you're smooching it up with

that good-looking guy on the beach. Good for you, baby. I'm glad you got rid of the old man. I'm glad you're happy, sweetie. I'll talk to you later. Take care."

I never got a call back from Mariah, but I did run into Tommy two nights later at the premiere party for *Cop Land*. I was sitting at a table with Sly Stallone and Frank Vincent at the Supper Club when Mottola walked over and started to chat up my pal Frank.

"Tommy, how are you," Frank said. "You know my friend, A.J., right?"

And Mottola just looked at me and said, "No, I don't."

I just sat there and said, "No you *don't?*"

Mottola looked away and kept right on chatting with Frank.

"Tommy, you don't *know* me?" I said.

Again, Mottola kept on talking but Frank knew shit was starting to brew between us.

"You got a problem with me, Tommy? Something you want to talk about?"

Finally, he looked at me all innocentlike and said, "No."

". . . Because we can go outside and talk about it any time you want?"

The table grew quiet. And Tommy said good-bye to Frank and walked away.

The only reason why he would've adopted that attitude with me is if he had heard what I said to Mariah on her private phone machine. And the only way he could've heard what I said on that machine was if he was somehow listening in. I'm not accusing him of it, I'm just talking out loud. Either way it's a creepy thought.

Sympathy for the Devil

There are three definitive stages of a beef, sometimes four, when you square to fight an Italian guy. First, you have to find out if he is, in fact, talking to you. And that's why "You talkin' to me?" is usually a good little icebreaker. Once you establish that he is talking to you, it's a good idea to analyze the trouble at hand. And that's why a good follow-up question is usually, "What's your fuckin' problem?" The third step in the beefing process is nothing more than qualifying if the guy is sane. So, a strong closer that usually works is, "Are you outta your fuckin' mind?"

Still, there are those times when a stalemate occurs with both men hauling the accusations and neither man throwing a punch. They stand there measuring each other, like two fight weary boxers who had their stools kicked out from under them to answer the bell for the tenth round. And usually one of the guys lofts the inquiry, "Who you with?" And depending on the weight of the name heaved back in whispered tones, the beef is usually settled without one single punch thrown.

"Who you with" is another way of asking someone, "Who do I have to answer to if we throw down right now?" And I was always fortunate enough to have some heavy names in my corner. Stemming back to the days when John Gotti was an acquaintance of mine and throughout my tenure as a *Daily News* gossip, I always seemed to have big, important men take me to the side and—in no uncertain terms—tell me, "Anybody asks you, you're with me now. You say you're around me. *Capeesh*?"

Yeah, I understood what it meant. I always did. And that's why I ate it up in that moment during the film *Donnie Brasco* when Michael Madsen cuts right through Al Pacino's jealousy over what crew was responsible for Johnny Depp. For a *nonpaisan* Madsen was brilliant when he stopped Depp in midsentence and uttered, "Yeah, well, you're with me now. That's it. It's settled."

And that's the way it is. I don't care if it's out of the movies or not, when a powerful man lays that sentence on you, you bristle with pride and you shake with fear. But you walk away knowing no one can fuck with you. It's your ace.

I'm not stupid. I know why Gambino Family associate Joe Watts extended that privilege to me. I was somewhat of a passing friend, a guy who would drift by him at the nightclub Rouge and pay my respects whenever he was tucked in his tight banquette—third from the bar. Guys like Joe dig that kind of respect and it really doesn't cost anything to extend it, when you think about it. It's just an unconscious decision you make when you're raised around men like that.

But for a year or so, the friendship had meaning because of the club Rouge and because my mentions of the club in my column kept the place packed and kept the money coming in. And because it was a haven for guys like Joe and other gangsters from competing families and crime factions. They liked that they could converge on the nightly fun and not have to worry about their forays being mentioned in the press. I can only imagine the conversations that took place within those booths—the diagrams for murder, extortion, loan-sharking and gambling—while a close-knit group of us would sit and talk or dance with some of the high-haired lovelies who would wander in. And through it all, Joe would make sure my girlfriend, Becky, would get the crisp $100 tip just for walking his scotch and soda to his table. And he'd also see that my roommate Chico would distribute the $1,500 in dough to the rest of the security crew on duty that night. And he did this on a *nightly* basis. Joe was out as much as I was and he didn't have a gossip column to fill. His gigantic samaritanism was the kind of thing that affected your livelihood—when he stopped going to a particular club, that nightspot's crew of bartenders, bouncers and barbacks had to look for other work. If Joe liked your bar and he was extended his privacy, nobody had to look for a moonlighting gig.

Like I said, Joe bopped in every night, but he particularly liked Wednesday nights the best. Hump Day had been a slow night for the club's secret owner—Genovese captain Ralphie Coppola—but that was about to change. One night R.C.—or "That Guy" as we referred to him—approached me and asked if I could make it my point to throw parties on Wednesday nights. "I figure with all the people you know downtown, you could put a lot of ass in the joint," That Guy said. "And then you could give it a pop in your column that morning and make it a weekly thing."

It was really a simple request. Round up a few friends—in my case it was Chico, Rocco and Jimmy Christmas—and put the word out that Rouge was a happening spot on Wednesday nights. That Guy told me he would be willing to let us keep the entire door money, but that the entire bar take would go in his pocket. Everything sounded jake to us. With everyone paying $20 at the door—and usually 200 partiers expected—the take amounted to a clean $1,000 in my pocket each week. Cash. Meantime, the bar take would go from a measly $2,000 to maybe $15,000 if we managed to lure those champagne-drinking phonies from downtown. So, just like that, I was a party promoter.

All that cash and gash would make us happy, keep Joe in the joint and make things a lot easier on That Guy. The only problem was mentioning the parties in my column—hardly the objective view most journalists are supposed to take. Anyhow, the Serious People inside Rouge knew the chance I was taking and they were very appreciative. After several weeks of knockout parties, I was called into Joe's booth and poured a snifter of Paradis cognac as I sat down.

"We want you to know you've done very well for yourself and very well for us," That Guy told me.

"Nah . . . it's nothing, R.C.," I said.

"No, no, no. We're very appreciative of what you do. The parties, the pops in the column, the mentions on television. All that stuff adds up."

Joe just nodded.

"Well, thanks."

"And that's why we're thinking of giving you a little piece here. Giving you a nickel or so a night—in addition to what you make on Wednesdays—just to have you around and make some calls and bring people in on other nights as well."

"Jeez . . . R.C., I don't know . . ."

"Just an idea. You don't have to give me an answer now."

"Just think about it. It's on the table," Joe said.

Yes, the generous offer was on the table but my balls would've been on the block had I accepted. No publisher or editor would stand for that sort of double-dipping and my newspaper guys would've had my ass sacked in a second if they found out. So, I profusely thanked R.C. and Joe that night but I politely turned down what amounted to a $100,000 a year offer.

Despite turning down the offer, I was still getting extremely close to the guys inside Rouge and they were letting down all sorts of guards allowing me to stick around them so much. There was even a time they invited me to their giant Christmas party at Mulino's in Westchester County and another time when I needed a message sent to Becky's jealous ex-boyfriend after he broke into her apartment one night, sat on her chest and held her at knifepoint. And they were happy to deliver. But the topper came when I was asked to play on the club's Central Park League flag football team.

It seemed simple enough, and what could the harm be? I thought. It was just a bunch of guys getting together on some weeknights and Sunday mornings to let off a little steam, toss the pigskin around and brag a little. What I didn't know was that I was being selected for a team that was filled with several mafiosi and many others who were being followed by the Feds or were seconds away from a major indictment.

At quarterback we had Ralphie Coppola, Genovese capo and right-hand man to crime boss Barney Bellomo. Our quick-footed halfback was Barney's brother-in-law, Anthony Fiorino, a chief steward of the Carpenters' Union who would be thrown out of the Jacob Javits Center for his alleged mob ties a year or so later. Ralphie's nephew James Simon, a receiver, would also lose his job at Javits after an investigation revealed his was a no-show job handed to him by his uncle. We also had Joe's righthand man, Johnny DeLuca (aka Johnny Handsome) and mob lawyer Pat Stiso, who eventually had his license revoked after setting up a fake Bronx heroin den so his drug-dealer client could get a good plea deal exposing the bogus operation. On the sidelines rooting us on was our pal Allie Salerno (nephew to former mob capo Anthony "Fat Tony" Salerno). It's amazing we ever won a game with all the outside interference going on in the lives of my teammates. I remember games when the guys would point out Feds and their cars, which would sometimes line the outside of the field.

"That's a Fed and that's a Fed . . . and that's a Fed," some guys would proudly point out.

"How can you tell?" I'd ask.

"They wear sunglasses on overcast days. And their car tires got no whitewalls."

It usually took the opposition about fifteen minutes to figure out who they were playing and when that sunk in, most judgment calls went our way. No one wanted to beef with Team Rouge, especially when we were wearing $200 red official NFL jerseys and our bench was lined with enough cellphones and beepers to fill a Radio Shack. Not to mention the stone faces of the men who sometimes came to watch us play and smoke cigars on the sidelines. I don't care what type of athlete you are, you don't know pressure until Ralphie Coppola is tossing you a bullet in the back of the end zone for the game-winning touchdown and all those eyes are upon you.

But not all of it was scary. Truth be told, I was never more comfortable around a crew of guys in my life and I never felt more welcome by anyone. You could've walked a supermodel onto the middle of the field, dangling her house key for me, and I wouldn't have left the guys. It was that much fun. The best way I can describe the type of men those guys were is to take you back to a moment in a Central Park game in which Ralphie's three-year-old son Dukie escaped from his mom's hand and ran onto the field during a crucial moment. Ralphie took the snap from center, scrambled away from the rush, scooped up his son with one arm and tossed a touchdown pass with the other. And afterward the man with a ton of things on his mind told us why he threw the pass with his right arm with Dukie tucked in his left. "I didn't want to waste a time-out," he said. "You guys would've given me a lot of shit if I did."

I'd love to round up the guys once again and play. Not so much to run up and down the field, but more just to see everyone again, maybe knock back a few cognacs at the club after the game. But that's kind of impossible now with Rouge shuttered down, Joe locked up on RICO charges, Pat out of business and Ralphie whacked for pocketing money that should have been passed on to his mob superiors.

Funny, I never knew him to be a stingy man.

In Ralphie's case, he simply disappeared one day and probably ended up in an oil drum somewhere. In the case of another mob figure, Lou "Louie Domes" Pacella, his slow and agonizing death from bone cancer was a better alternative.

Lou didn't have to help me when I reached out to him so I could attend his buddy Frank Sinatra's eightieth birthday bash at LA's Shrine Auditorium. But he was more than happy to. See, Lou and Frank went way back, back as far as the Rat Pack days. And once upon a time, Lou's name was one that Frank used to drop from time to time. So, when "Domes" gave me the same privilege as Frank, you could imagine my pride.

Nah, on second thought, you can't imagine. See, I was raised in a house in which Sinatra was bigger than God. My father didn't rush me to go to church on Sundays. But he made damn sure I was awake to listen to Sinatra on Goombadah Joe Rottolo's Sunday morning AM radio program. And forget my mother altogether. She was a Brooklyn bobby-soxer who used to cut school just so she could see "Bones" at the Paramount Theater. One of my most vivid memories as a kid was being in Madison Square Garden for Sinatra's Main Event concert and watching my mother literally paralyzed as Sinatra drowned out Howard Cosell's thrilling introduction with the first few words to "The Lady Is a Tramp."

My mother was standing up for, "She gets hungry for dinner at eight" and had already collapsed in her chair for "adores the theater, never comes late."

Anyhow, twenty-three years later, when the entire entertainment world was looking for a ticket to attend Frank's birthday gala, I was given a stern "no" from Frank's longtime publicist and mouthpiece Susan Reynolds. I didn't ask her why because I already had an idea. See, several months earlier, I had gotten wind of the boldfaced names who were invited to attend the televised event—which would turn out to be Old Blue Eyes' last public appearance, as fate would have it. And, frankly, I didn't like the list. Actually, to be honest, I don't think Frank had any idea who some of the people were. In one particular column, I wondered why the brains behind the show—Frank's wife Barbara, Susan Reynolds and *Laugh-In* producer George Schlatter—would ask Hootie and the Blowfish to play. I also had a hard time wondering why Eric Clapton was signed on. Or even Bob Dylan for that matter. That's not to say Clapton and Dylan are not gods, but I just didn't think they fit the mold for the type of entertainer Frank would've wanted to see looking up from his front-row seat. Anyhow, like usual, I aired my feelings. And I really let the bullets fly once Frank's daughters, Tina and Nancy, called me to say they were unhappy with the invite list and flat-out disappointed with the list of entertainers the above-mentioned triumvirate compiled.

Long story short. That sort of story kept me off the press list the second it ran. So, thanks to a mutual friend and some words of encouragement from Ralphie Coppola, I took my beef over to the old timer Domes.

It was arranged I'd meet him at Caterina's, a little hole-in-the-wall Italian joint in Murray Hill. Far as I knew, somebody else briefed the frail but unforgettable man before I had gotten there. Once I got there, I was met by an older gofer, who was cleaning off his week-old manicure with cotton balls and a bottle of Cutex. "Yeah, how you doin'? You're the reporter, right? Sit down at the bar, he'll be with you in a few seconds."

A few seconds turned into an hour and when the first hour started to bend to the second and the blind piano player started his fourth set, I shuffled in my seat a little and started to get up.

"Kid . . . he'll be here. Lou wouldn't like it if you leave."

"Leave? I ain't leaving," I lied. His Cutex fumes were killing me. "I just need a little fresh air." Outside on the sidewalk, I bumped into Lou.

"You Benza?"

"Yeah. Listen, thanks for seeing me. I know you're a busy man and all . . ."

"Come on in. Sit down. Eat. Gimme a minute, though."

And with that we walked inside and before Lou did anything, he walked directly to the blind piano player and squeezed $100 into his tip glass. Then he sat me down in a chair at a table and ordered a bunch of beautiful food. The topic of Frank Sinatra was not raised at all. After my fifth hour in the joint, and about an hour after I drained my third espresso, I started to get antsy again. And that's when Lou finally spoke up.

"So this Susan Reynolds is breaking your balls?"

"Well, she's a little mad at me for a column I wrote."

"What did you write?" Lou asked.

"Well, I wrote about Susan and Barbara and George Schlatter inviting a bunch of people Frank couldn't care less about to his eightieth birthday party. I mean, do you think Frank knows who the hell Hootie is?"

And with that Lou raised his hand in disgust. "That Hootie and the *Blue*fish?"

"Hootie and the *Blow*fish," his gofer interjected.

"That's what I said," Lou shot back.

And then there was a beat.

"Sounded like you said *blue*fish," the gofer said.

"Bluefish, blowfish . . . who the hell cares," Lou said. "Frank doesn't give a fuck for either one of those guys."

It went on and on. But before the inadvertent comedy routine was through, Lou got down to business.

"Listen to me now . . . this Susan Reynolds don't mean any harm, but I know she can be a real ball-breaker when she wants to be. Let me ask you a question and it's a very important question."

"Go ahead," I said.

"Do you love Frank?"

"Like crazy. Do you know I got more pictures of Frank hanging in my apartment than I do of my own father. Matter of fact, I got a framed picture of him that my mother used to hang above the sink in the kitchen. I remember every time she'd pour the macaroni into the *sculabasta*, the steam would rise and cloud Frank's face for a little while. Now the picture hangs over my sink."

"If you go to California and see the show, you're gonna write nice things?"

"Yes."

"I know you don't care for Susan and you might not care for who's appearing, but how about we put an end to that and from now on you write what a tremendous night it's gonna be?"

"You got it, Lou."

And then Lou turned to his phone and dialed Susan Reynolds's number and told her that she needed to save two seats and a pair of credentials for me and a guest. When he hung up a few minutes later, he turned to me and said, "Okay, Susan knows what she has to do. Give her a call tomorrow and it'll all be straightened out."

We kissed good-bye and I left.

Unfortunately, the next morning when I phoned Reynolds, it was as if Lou didn't exist.

"Hey, Susan, it's A.J. I'm just calling to see what I've got to do to have my credentials and all that jazz."

"I'm sorry, A.J.," she said. "I have absolutely no more room. We are booked solid."

Rather than say anything to her, I just hung up the phone and dialed Lou, who was hanging out at his other joint, Veniero's Bakery on East 11th Street and 2nd Avenue.

"What's what, kid?"

"It's this Reynolds, Lou. She says she has no more room for me."

"Hold on," Lou said firmly. "Can you get down to the bakery? I want you to see how I deal with this woman."

I hopped in a cab and got downtown fast and watched Lou punch out Reynolds's digits. "Susan, it's Uncle Lou here. What the hell are you doing to this kid? I didn't ask if he could go, I told you he's going. There's a difference."

I couldn't hear what Reynolds was saying back to Lou, but it was a short phone call and as soon as I got back to my office, she had already called and left me a message. It went a little something like this: "Hey, A.J., it's Susan. Okay, I spoke to Uncle Lou. I'm sorry about the foul-up. We will have two seats for you and a guest and we will have credentials as well. Everything will be ready by the time you get into town."

Ah yes, the sounds of a publicist eating shit.

The next day, my first-class airline ticket—compliments of Louie

Domes—arrived at my office and I flew off to Los Angeles for Frank's birthday party. Not that it matters now, but I was right: Nobody wanted to see Hootie and the Blowfish there. But when the show closed and Frank took the stage to give his inaudible thanks, Nancy Sinatra waved me down front and pulled me onto the same seat she was sitting on. And with me on that seat, sat the spirit of my mother—who twenty-three years earlier was strong enough to see that her son got to watch Frank Sinatra in concert but was too weak in the knees to do anything more than swoon like a fifty-one-year-old little girl.

Heaven

"OhmyGod, he's here" came the breathy voice over my telephone.

"Who's *he?*" I shot back.

"OhmyGod, ohmyGod, I can't talk. I'll call you back."

In all the years I spent covering the biggest names in the world, no name elicited more insanity from women than John Kennedy, Jr.

On that particular day, the breathy voice belonged to my friend, a publicist named Rosemarie Terenzio. Rosemarie is a remarkably funny and extremely tough Italian girl from the Bronx. And on that very afternoon, John Kennedy had walked into the firm she was working for to lunch with her boss, Michael Berman. No one except Kennedy and Berman could have known the meeting that day was to discuss developing a political magazine together. Actually, Rosemarie might have known, but because she was a tight-lipped and true-blue employee, her lips were sealed to me.

"What's Kennedy doing in there?" I asked her when she calmed herself and phoned me back a few hours later.

"I have no fuckin' idea. But he said 'hi' to me."

"Wow, sounds like true love to me, Ro."

"Just because it's sunny over by you, doesn't give you the right to piss on my parade."

It went like that a lot between me and Ro.

Remarkably, over the years—before *George* magazine was started and during its run—Rosemarie rose in the ranks within the organization until she finally settled in as John's assistant and, to be honest, somewhat of a voice of reason amid all the ass-kissers.

Once Ro was firmly planted in the seat outside John's office and was enjoying all the perks of being around him and under his employ, I'd have to call her to get a comment on any number of stories we were running on John. I never wanted to, but my editors knew I was tight with Ro and I was pretty much the only journalist who'd get a return call during crunch time.

"Ro, it's A.J."

"Yes, what can I do for you, A.J."

"I need a comment, baby. Don't make me beg. Is he going to marry this girl, Carolyn Bessette?"

"No comment. I'm sorry."

A few seconds later the phone would ring and it was Ro.

"Are we off the record?" she'd ask.

"Yeah."

"I hope he does marry her. You would love this girl. She doesn't take any shit and she seems like the only real girl who has ever phoned here. And, believe me, I know. I field every call for him."

"Ro, I can't write *any* of that?"

"Not if you ever want to talk to me again."

Before long I knew everything I wanted to know—everything anyone wanted to know about John Kennedy—but my desire to print any juicy details waned with each passing year. I had heard too many good-hearted stories from Ro, too many humorous moments that seemed uncommon for a man as big as JFK, Jr., to care about passing the word to my readers. I didn't want to be another nudge with a notepad or pain in the ass behind the paparazzi. And I'll tell you why. I just didn't want to seem uncool in John's eyes. And that's a power I don't think I can lay on a whole helluva lot of people I ever covered.

I used to measure John and all things John stood for in a way I measure all men. And that is to say, I always measure all men with this question:

Would I accept it if my girlfriend dumped me for John?

And the answer was always *yes*. A resounding *yes*. In my field I was always coming upon men with riches and nobility and great influence and power and fame and sexuality, but very few of them got the quick *yes* I always reserved for John. I'm telling you, it wouldn't have mattered to me if I was feeding my young son his bottle of milk at four A.M. and my wife walked up to me with her bags packed and mascara streaking down her cheeks. "I'm leaving you for John Kennedy, Jr.," she'd say. "We are madly in love and I want to have a life with him."

"Of course," I'd say. "I *completely* understand."

And then I would burp my son and spend the next several years telling him his mother made the right decision. That's about as much as I can tell you about my awe for John John's charm and beauty and poise. He was James Bond with a backpack.

On the day before John and Carolyn's wedding, I phoned Rosemarie on a hunch.

"Ro, I got a gut feeling something is going on this weekend."

"Like what?"

"Like a wedding."

"Nothing is going on. I can assure you John and Carolyn will not be in Hyannis Port or Martha's Vineyard this weekend for a wedding," Ro said.

"Who said anything about Hyannis Port or Martha's Vineyard," I said. "Is that the only place people can get married? Ro . . . I know all about it."

Ro was battle weary.

"Come on, A.J., leave me alone."

And I did. I did because I loved Ro too much, and I didn't want to subject her to the bullshit that gossip columnists sometimes dish out to the important people behind the Very Important People. The bottom line was I knew about the secret wedding somewhere on an island off the coast of Georgia and I was telling Ro that I wasn't going to do anything about it. What was most important to me was that word of my classy treatment of Kennedy's privacy get back to John and Carolyn someday after the dust settled and Carolyn's bouquet was caught and all the Minute Rice was plucked out of John's thick hair.

"Ro, I swear on my mother's eyes, I won't print a single detail about the wedding nor will I tell anyone about them. I just want him to know I knew and didn't do anything about it."

"Whatever, A.J. There's no wedding."

Ro was loyal to a fault.

I hung up the phone and walked out of my apartment, thick with the secret of the year and calmly attended an NAACP function in Battery Park and then had a quiet dinner in the village with JohnnyBoy, Jack Nicholson and Ashley Judd. While every newspaper in the country would have killed for the scoop, I was more content to give John and Carolyn their privacy. I didn't want to beat anybody to the punch. If, indeed, the couple was ever going to have one day of peace, let it be the night before they were to wed in privacy and secrecy. Besides, I was having a ball picking off Jack's plate and, later, doing my Chris Walken impression for him as his limo took us to Spy. While my memory of that night could've been me bringing the blockbuster story to my *News* editor, I am much happier I made Jack's drink come through his nose with laughter.

Eventually, as the months passed, I would call Rosemarie to shoot the breeze—making fun of our Italian families and stuff like that—and sometimes John would talk to me through Ro in the background. "Tell him he made me laugh on *The Gossip Show* last night," John would say. Small shit like that, but it would make me feel like a million bucks, nonetheless.

Toward the end of my tenure at the *News*, I had written a freelance piece for *George* magazine on the whole paparazzi dilemma. That went well enough that barely a month after I was fired in May of 1997, John asked me if I'd like to write for *George* magazine on a regular basis. I was thrilled. "I'm on severance right now and times ain't so good. A regular gig would be perfect."

"Come on in and we'll talk about it," he said.

"Before I do that," I hesitated. "Can you guys pay me for the paparazzi piece I wrote months ago?"

John was incredulous. "We haven't paid you yet? Shit, do me a favor, fax me over an invoice for payment and I'll get on it right away."

I sat at my computer and I banged out a letter. I was still in awe of John, but something told me I could get away with writing something smirky.

John,
Please remit payment of $800 for services rendered on A.J. Benza's pa-
parazzi freelance article. Please hurry payment. Times are tough around

here. I didn't sell all my mother's shoes in a garage sale and make 20 million bucks.

Sincerely,
A.J. Benza.

I was referring to the estate sale John and his sister Caroline had on the wishes of their deceased mother Jackie Onassis.

An hour later John called me laughing like crazy, his sense of humor intact. "You're a sick bastard."

On the day I walked into his office, shoes were once again the subject of conversation. I was wearing a pair of sky-blue leather loafers and John went crazy for them. "Cool shoes, man. Where'd you get them?"

"Somewhere on Spring Street," I told him.

"I should get them," he said. I wanted to give him my pair. They were only two days old. "Yeah, I should. But I know I never will. Anyhow, those are some pretty cool shoes."

During the meeting—which was also attended by the magazine's editor Biz Mitchell—John and I went back and forth on what I thought I could bring to the magazine. "Don't look at me for political insight or political knowledge," I said. "I would just like to write insightful, irreverent stuff. I want to make people laugh."

John was hip to my take on things and even more willing to listen to where I thought the mag needed bolstering up.

"You can do whatever you want," I said. "I don't know if you know this from where you sit, but I think the days of making fun of John Kennedy, Jr., are over. I don't think people expect to see you fail or even want to see you fail. This ain't about you flunking the bar anymore."

John sat there amused.

"You're JFK—John Fuckin' Kennedy, Jr., man. Just do whatever it is you want with the magazine. You can totally afford to let your nuts hang. No one's gonna cut them off anymore."

"As long as you think so, A.J." He was amused.

"I'm telling you. I'm telling you as a former member of the press. It's over. Do whatever you want. Everyone's swords are down. You're untouchable."

I'm not trying to make this sound like "John Kennedy, Jr., Owes It All to Me," but there was something cool about having an audience with a guy like that. And John let you talk. And I was going to tell him what I wanted. How many times do you get chances like that in life?

Anyhow, the meeting went great, even though I don't think Biz Mitchell understood a word of it. But before I left, we agreed I'd write a piece on the gross changes around the world in the wake of Princess Di's tragic death. Some of those changes would have me railing at the fact that the price of roses ironically went up all around England just in time for all the mourners to pay their respects. "Italians go through the same thing with seafood around Christmastime," I told John. "And now the rest of the world knows the true horrors of that sort of thing."

You get the idea of the article. My usual take on things, only this time for a highbrow political magazine.

I was so happy with the deal, and the fact that Kennedy was going to pay me $1,000 for the piece—let alone listen to any other ideas I had—that I walked to the same Spring Street boutique where I bought my shoes and I purchased a pair for John. I had them sent over by messenger the next day. John called my office to thank me and suggested dinner one night soon.

We never did do dinner, though I would always bump into him at Knicks games up in Suite 200, where all the celebrities eat before the game and at halftime. And John was gracious to invite me to *George* dinners after I was gone from the *News*. And I'd sometimes see him on line with the rest of the regular folks at Bubby's in TriBeCa.

The last time I spoke to him was a cold and rainy day in late September 1998. Kara and I wandered into the Moondance Diner on a Sunday morning. And sitting at the cramped counter were John and Carolyn. They called us over and made room for the two of us to eat alongside them.

"Let me see your *Post*," John said to me.

"Why? You ain't in it. I already checked."

John and Carolyn had just returned from the island of Dominica the same day they arrived to find natives and shopkeepers hammering plywood to all their windows. A hurricane, ironically Hurricane George, was headed their way. Carolyn said the couple boarded another plane a few hours later and flew straight home.

"We literally spent a whole day in the air," she said. "So much for our second-year honeymoon," she said, laughing.

It was a pleasant breakfast sitting there with America's Most Beautiful Couple. Eventually, John and Carolyn said good-bye and walked out into the cold, holding hands, to hail a cab.

"I love that kid," I said. "What a cool guy."

"Yeah, he's great," Kara said.

There was a beat between us.

"See, that's a helluva man," I said. "If it were him you dated, I'd understand."

Kara just silently pushed her food around and I went back to reading the *Post*.

But that moment's another story. And more on that later.

Fortune Teller

I am guilty of dancing on tables to the first strains of Prince's "You Sexy Motherfucka." I am also guilty of lusting for all of the women Prince has either: A) Put in his videos; B) Put in his band; C) Employed as dancers; D) Dated; E) Married.

I have always been a devoted Prince follower, seeing him in concert at the beautiful surroundings of Radio City Music Hall as well as the cramped, smoky confines of the Palladium. I've also been known to wait as long as three hours after a concert to see him just to get a measly quote from the publicity-shy musician. And, for the most part, I respected his privacy and bolstered his reputation—as best as I could—from in front of my keyboard or in front of the camera. And this is the thanks I get: One night the purple-panted rocker—equipped with a goon on each arm—thought it was okay to verbally attack me for one of my TV reports. I wanted to crush him on the spot, and have my boys deal with his boys. But I didn't. The little guy had a point.

In my tenure as a gossip—through all the stories I broke and scandals I followed—I do recall dealing with some subjects calling me or approaching me and basically asking me, "What's your fuckin' problem?" I can also remember the thousands of letters that flooded my mail bin with similar sentiments. There are even some stars—Michael Jackson is one—who have an army of insane fans fire off dozens of letters in their defense. These are usually the people who scribble "666" on your re-cycled articles and remind you that Satan has a special purpose for your ass once you arrive in Hell. I can even remember some psycho-delicate stars like Roddy McDowall, who ranted and raved because we always listed him as "*Planet of the Apes* sensation Roddy McDowall."

"I have an impressive body of work," he once screamed at me. "Must you include that film!"

"But, Roddy . . . it's a classic," I calmly asssured him.

"Ohforcryingoutloud," he said, and hung up.

And that's exactly what I became expert at dealing with—the hang-ups of stars.

Prince's hang-up, apparently, was the way my report included the name of his beautiful wife, Mayte, along with his when my *Gossip Show* producers asked me to mention who I thought exemplified the "Strang-est Couple of the Year."

I certainly believe in stars letting civilians in on some of their lives' most special moments. But I think allowing computer nerds to down-load your wedding—like Prince and Mayte did—went a little too far. I just think the madness has to stop somewhere and if we're not too careful there will come a day when a female celebrity accepts a hefty sum to have a baby on the air and everyone can watch it—afterbirth and all—through the wonders of Pay-Per-View.

"Is the popcorn almost done? The contractions are one minute apart!!!"

At any rate, Prince didn't see it that way. Obviously he saw the thirty-second spot on *The Gossip Show* in which I aired my feelings and he had been waiting a while to let me have it.

A vision: You pull your Benz up to the curb at Chaos as the doormen scatter the orange cones to give you the ultimate spot out front. You and your boys hop out, toss your keys to the pretty little lady with the list and ride the elevator to the second floor. At this point in the night, 'round three A.M., you're usually riding the daily max of thirty percs, two vallies and seven or eight gin and tonics. For some reason, you end up at Chaos either because Spy was dead or Wax was too druggy or some girl is camped there that you've been following around for weeks and it's only a matter of time before you hit it. But tonight is different. Tonight you're at Chaos because one of the club's trio of owners, Tony

Theodore, rang your cell and tipped you off to a nice possible lead for the next day's paper.

"Prince is up in the club," Tony told you. "He just got here and it looks like he's gonna be here awhile. Where you at? I could use the shot in the column."

Tony knows the drill. He has already cleared a table right beside Prince and has a bottle of Dom bathing in an ice bucket before you even fire up the Benz. A couple of cuties from Company Models keep your booth warm. Tony is like that—the ultimate in pimp, pomp and circumstance.

Everyone is happy when you arrive at the club. Tony gets his publicity. The models get their champagne. And you get your fun on. Prince—who sips his Earl Grey tea and always looks as delicate as one of those gazelles on the Discovery Channel the moment before a tiger mauls its ass—is a bit different tonight. Tonight it looks as though he's ready for the ambush, but he ain't going down without a fight. And that angers you a little. Talking to a rock star at Chaos after three A.M. with a little liquor in you and a handful of pills is a home game for you. And you haven't lost at home in years. But tonight the streak comes to an abrupt end.

You realize one of Prince's goons is about to tap you on the shoulder at any moment and request that you slide over so his boss can talk to you. And you're already figuring out how to shape it for tomorrow's column. Sometimes the column rings more true and is funnier when you let a celebrity rip you a new ass for a paragraph or two. It gives you and the column more credibility with your readers and other celebrities who wish to do the same. And maybe tonight's that sort of night. Prince looks pissed in his purple pantsuit and, honestly, you're tired as hell and kind of just want to take that model home with you. But tonight the model will have to wait. Tonight the rocker's words rip loud and clear within your conscience like a guitar riff from "Let's Go Crazy." Tonight Prince makes you stop and think about how you make a living, why you do it and how much longer you ought to be doing it. And, more important, what price you would have to pay in the long run.

"You need to go home and look up the phrases 'karmic debt' and 'speculate' and 'strange' and figure out what you're doing wrong with the way you talk about me and my wife. Now, I'm through talking to you. Go get to work."

There's no way Prince just spoke that way to you and calmly went back to sipping his cup of tea. But he did. And the looks on the girls' faces say so.

"First of all, you don't even know my wife and you're calling her strange," Prince continues. "Second, have you even looked up the word 'strange?' And third, we didn't put our marriage on the Internet. The people at Paisley Park did that."

You got some face-saving to do, so you lean into his space so close you can see the dark blue eyeliner he's wearing.

"Prince, since you never talk to the press and your people never talk to the press, a columnist is left to speculate about a lot of things that you do and a lot of things you stand for."

But then the motherfucka interrupts you. Nobody interrupts you.

"Have you even looked up the word 'speculate?' "

"I don't have to, man. I know what the fuckin' word means," you shoot back.

"The last time you and I spoke, I thought we straightened things out," he says, referring to a chat the two of you had at Spy. "Then I turn on the TV and you're talking shit about me and my woman. You don't even know my woman and you're talking about her. I wouldn't talk about *your* woman because I don't know *her*."

He does know your woman. She was in his "Kiss" video, the one where he had to stand on an apple box just so he could be tall enough for her to plant a kiss on his cheek at the end of the song. As a matter of fact, you have had three of the same women he's had. But you don't tell him this.

"Listen," you say, "now that Prince has become TV friendly, it will certainly be easier to understand what you stand for and who you are. But up until now, up until that song you sang on *The Today Show* the other day, you were an enigma."

By now the models are squirming in their seats. They want to sit near Prince. They don't want you to argue him right out of the tight banquette he's in and back to his limo. But you're in a game with this guy. And you're always ready for a game.

"But why is that important," he says, leaning away from you. "Why is any of that important?"

"Come on," you say. "You're only one of the biggest stars in the world. You do know that, don't you?"

Prince just sits there wearing a smirk and sipping from his little teacup. His two goons are ready for shit.

"Look," you finally offer, "I just think that you could clear up a lot of things about yourself if you'd only talk. Put it this way: You'd be helping me a lot."

Then it was time for another pop quiz.

"Do you know what 'karmic debt' means?" he asks. "Look that up, would you? You might learn a lot more about yourself."

And with that, Prince is up, pulling on his lavender hood and leaning on his walking stick and headed out from the booth. And you turn back to your table of cuties and your boys, but none of it looks as cool anymore. You don't want to admit it but the little guy got to you. As you leave the club and drop the top on the Benz, you think about what your mother always told you: Never climb a mountain leaning toward you and never kiss a woman or talk to a man leaning away from you. But tonight you did and you fell on your ass. And everyone saw.

End of vision.

There is an immense high that accompanies the duties of being one of New York City's voices. It's almost worse than heroin because—once you lose the voice—you simply can't go to a corner to cop. It's as if you're still addicted but all the dealers have been cleaned off the streets. I knew that would be the case once I left the industry and that's why I embraced the job and the duties as long as the privilege was mine. And, along with the daily rituals of putting a column together, I embraced the nightly ceremonies of partying and building contacts and sharpening my wit and opinions and sarcasms to a sword's point. I knew someone was going to get cut once every so often, but you get so caught up with the fact that you're the one holding the weapon that you sometimes sacrifice people's feelings for the sake of a stranger's handshake on the street or the sight of a straphanger devouring the column within the flickering light of a downtown subway car. You forget that you are holding both the pen and the sword.

The basic rule I always tried to follow in placing an item in the paper, was to always make sure all parties mentioned in the report were notified that they were going to be in the next day's paper. Unfortunately, the time restraints of a daily deadline make that duty impossible, but a reporter always has to try. Even if you make the call and leave it on someone's machine. For some reason—and I learned this years later—one of the scariest things is to open the paper and see your name highlighted in bold in a gossip column. It makes you look at the page over and over and over again. You feel like you've undressed in front of your window with the shade up and the neighbor's kid wheeled his telescope out of the closet and had it aimed right up your ass. A television report is different, at least in the sense that you never take the same responsible precautions before making your report public. When my E! producers asked me on the spot who I thought was the strangest couple of the year, I blurted out Prince's name and made my thirty-second opinion known. What was I supposed to do—make a call to Paisley Park and ask permission?

I think Prince was trying to tell me that my reports or my style were strong enough. And that I didn't have to muddy the water with my "speculation" on why things were the way they were. In other words, Prince would've been fine with me breaking the story about his wedding being splashed across the Internet, he just didn't want to read that I thought it was strange. While I respect his feelings, I have to say Prince isn't up-to-date on a columnist's duties. And, for that matter, he isn't up-to-date on what makes New York City's tabloids a better read than any other papers in the country. We speculate. We indicate. We predict. We convict. We ascertain. We entertain. And, above all, we inform. We simply don't just regurgitate facts. You want that, go read *People*.

But the truth of the matter is, Prince was right to warn me of the perils of the *psst!* business. This was not a missive with a million misspellings fired off from a crazed fan of Michael Jackson. Nor was it the time a legion of religious fanatics wished me an eternity in Hell for making fun of the Vatican opening a tacky gift shop. It wasn't a Nation of Islam follower threatening to shoot me from a Midtown rooftop after I had the nerve to uncover an old recording of Louis Farrakhan singing a song about a transvestite. Hell, it wasn't even soldiers from GLAAD—the Gay and Lesbian Alliance Against Defamation—demanding a reason why I would raise the question "Who Will Make a Better Father—Michael Jackson or Melissa Etheridge?" It was just a guy looking me in the eye telling me I ought to watch what I print, and the way I print it, because I was going to have to answer to all of it one day.

That particular night I remember not letting Prince's advice get to me too much, particularly when I told people about it in public.

"What did Prince want?" JohnnyBoy asked me.

"I don't know. Some shit about 'karmic debt.' "

"Fuuuuuuck hiiiiiim and his purple pantsuit."

But in private, especially in the silence of my lonely room—when my head hit the pillow and I wrestled with the demons of what I wrote—I thought about it a lot. And if you really want to know the truth, I got the feeling I was starting to pay for some of the stuff I had written already.

A bunch of things had begun to happen. For starters, the entire crew of wiseguys I had grown close to during the Rouge days suddenly had me on the tips of their noses. It was all over a beef concerning which direction the club had to take in order to stay in business. It didn't take long for the government to find out who were the real guys pulling the strings behind Rouge and once they did, everyone was on alert to be careful. We were literally sat down one afternoon and told that the chances were very good that there were recording devices and surveillance cameras planted within the club that were marking our every move. We were also warned that some Feds might be making personal visits to some of us.

"Smile, you're on *Candid Camera*," we'd whisper to each other as we passed through the club. It got to the point where we couldn't even mention Ralphie by name anymore. In fact, it was best we didn't even say R.C. or "That Guy" either. Instead we used to touch our chests when we mentioned R.C., brush our hands through our hair when we spoke of Barney Bellomo, point to our noses when we dropped Gambino boss Jack "The Nose" D'Amico's name and tap our chins when we needed to invoke the name of the Genovese crime boss, Vincent Gigante. We didn't look like people anymore. We looked more like crazy baseball coaches sending signals for the batter to lay down a suicide squeeze and get the man home from third.

The tough times hit a crescendo when R.C. asked me and Chico our opinions on what direction he should take the club in an effort to save it from going belly-up. And over dinner at Sorvino's, on the Upper East Side, we gave him our opinion. Frankly, it was mostly cosmetic changes, but they were important. We told him to eliminate the booths, get rid of the carousel, knock down the back room for a bigger dance floor and hire a completely new staff. We told him downtown denizens are never fooled by a new name on a marquis. If they see the same waitress or bartender—not to mention the same promoters throwing the same parties on the same nights—they simply turn their noses to the club and walk away. Ralphie and Pat thanked us for the advice but went out and changed nothing except for the club's name. Rouge became Le Zinc. And, within two weeks, the place was empty. No mobsters, no millionaires, no models and no more moolah coming in to save the joint. Le Zinc was done and the guys who ran it were being too closely watched to do anything as flashy as another nightclub.

Joey Bravo, the club's eternal greeter and manager, sounded the death knell on his way out the door after his final shift. "Fill it up with cement," he said. "This joint is over."

Rouge wasn't the only club presenting a headache to me at the time. Back in the day, I had the power to coax the managers on duty at Scores to sometimes let one of the peelers leave a little early and on that night I worked my magic and Trixie (as I'll call her) was allowed to leave with me. One thing led to another and before long there we were back at my apartment and back in the familiar position we assumed some three years earlier.

Anyhow, let me get right to the point. She got pregnant.

"I wanted to tell you in person," Trixie said crying, "but I couldn't *faaaaaaace* you. I didn't do this to trap you. Don't get mad at me but I want to have the *baaaaaaaaaaby*."

It was gut-wrenching. It was sad and extremely unfortunate. But there was no way we were going to have this baby.

"Listen, Trix," I calmly said. "We can't have this baby. We hadn't seen each other in three years. We don't love each other. We aren't dating. We don't even *like* each other very much. That is not the criteria for bringing a child into the world." Eventually, she agreed. In time, Trixie left the strip club and eventually married a broker in Brooklyn Heights. Last we spoke she had just given birth to a healthy baby boy.

My relationship with Kara wasn't clicking on all cylinders either. Although we were very happy with each other, we were constantly coming face-to-face with the slings of backstabbers and doomsayers all over the city. To put it bluntly, nobody thought it wise for Kara—a woman just stepping down from her early nineties supermodel pedestal and three *Vogue* covers—to get close to the bad boy gossip columnist. The thinking was, I would become privy to all the secrets of the stars Kara had had whispered in her ears over the years and print them the first chance I got. So, in order to save our relationship from the public's perception of it and in order to let our love grow shielded from the winds of doubt, we retreated. We ate at out-of-the-way places, never attended a public event together, walked into movies after they had begun, rarely held hands in the street. Like I said earlier, we loved each other "on the creep." And it was a big price to pay for plying the gossip trade because I loved her like crazy.

To add misery to insult, there were a number of times when Federal Agents were making visits to my apartment. Not to see me, mind you, but to repeatedly check up on Chico. None of these guys had anything solid on Chico, but because of the fact that he had been employed in managerial capacities at both Scores and Rouge—two mob hotspots—the men in black always had questions to ask him. To Chico's credit, he gave them nothing. But that only makes them keep coming back. Anyhow, it was a hectic time. And it eventually caused Chico to move out.

"You can't have this, Pope," he told me one day. "You're making a nice life for yourself and I got Feds knocking on our fuckin' door. I don't want to get you in a trick box." It was a tough decision, but the right one. So, Chico was gone and with him went a lot of fun. The kind of fun you can't duplicate when it's shared between two friends who have been best friends for more than twenty years.

But wait, it got worse. In the next year, everything came crashing down. It was as if someone had put a curse on me. But maybe it was everything Prince was trying to warn me about.

Torn and Frayed

I don't think there are any colleges offering a major in Gossip Reporting. If there are, I'm sure there is a phony professor somewhere standing in front of his class pontificating on the puissant practices of Walter Winchell or the gossip wars between old broads Louella Parsons and Dorothy Kilgallen. But that would be a great waste of time for any and all journalism students wishing to carve out a career in a niche in which very few have settled and even fewer have succeeded. No, the first lesson the phony professor would have to teach is coping with the instant pain of injuring friendships beyond repair.

The first question I always came up with—and not every gossip reporter faces the dilemma with the same delicacy—was "What do I stand to lose if I print the story?" And I didn't care if my publishers were up my ass with their desire to see the column item run. I always let the question swim around my head a while—amid the ringing phones and the foot-tapping feet of editors on deadline—before I made the call on whether or not to print something explosive. Because, usually, what's at stake is a friendship—or, at the least, a good source. Unfortunately, the longer I was in the business my good sources became my good friends—that can happen over whispers and wine—and, well, that fuckin' twain should never meet.

The first moment I saw Margaret Maldonado I knew I was going to like her. And, as soon as I learned she was Jermaine Jackson's former common-law wife and mother of his two sons, I knew I had to make her like me. And that ain't easy when you're a gossip columnist approaching anyone remotely near the Jackson clan.

The first time I saw Margaret we were sitting on the same panel on *Geraldo*. I had been a regular guest of Geraldo Rivera's weekly Friday afternoon celebrity gossip show. The usual suspects were myself, Cindy Adams, Mike Walker, Steve Dunleavy, Flo Anthony and any number of assorted gossip hounds from LA like Janet Charleton or Anita Talbert. There were more, but I forget. The names changed but the facelifts remained the same. Margaret was on the show to promote her new book, *Jackson Family Values*—one of those flimsy as-told-to jobs put together for some immediate cash flow. I remember flipping through her book and getting disgusted that everyone in Los Angeles assumes the book deal is the natural progression of things after courtship, marriage, parenthood and divorce.

At any rate, I remember making Margaret laugh a few times during the commercials and making a date to eat with her at Indochine later that evening. That was a nice change of pace. Normally, during commercial breaks, I was either making plans to go to Scores with Mike Walker or quietly remarking which stars certain audience members resembled. When I first started the silly game a year before, no one wanted to play—especially Cindy Adams. And most of them acted as if I was an immature ass. But then as the weeks rolled on, I was relentless with it, despite the pleas from the show's producers who'd use the commercial breaks to help steer the show.

"Okay, when we come back to air, we're gonna begin with Mike's story on Keanu Reeves and then we're gonna go straight to Cindy's item about Michael Kennedy," frazzled producer Kevin McMahon would say. "And that might be a good time for A.J. to give us his story on John Wayne Bobbitt's porn career."

"Yeah, that sounds good. Listen, don't look now," I'd say, "but third row from the front, second seat in. That guy in the toupee and pink shirt?"

"Yeah," Geraldo would laugh.

"That's the demon child of Dennis Franz and Peter Allen."

Cindy usually held her laugh inside, but one day she really got me good a few seconds to air—right before we were about to come out of commercial with me speaking about the death of Jackie Onassis.

"What a shame," Cindy leaned into me and whispered while she was pointing at a frail ninety-year-old lady in the front row. "Look at what all that fucking did to Angie Dickinson."

I literally howled and fell to the floor.

Anyhow, like I said, this time around I was making arrangements to eat with Margaret and it had a different level of excitement attached to it. Dinner went great even though the conversation was a little bit guarded. But a few hours and a bunch of drinks later, Margaret was well on her way to relaying some unbelievable stories about what she had endured while she was in the Jackson clan. The only one I can tell— the most innocent—is how Jermaine used to go to sleep at night with a clip on his nose in order to keep it skinny. I'm not going to say she never dropped any dirt on her common-law brother-in-law Michael Jackson, but I will say she kept that stuff to a minimum. Which was wise, since Uncle Michael was helping with the bills a bit. At any rate, I already knew she was somebody I was going to see more of. And, you know how it is—the more you see someone . . . the more they reveal.

I would let Margaret know I was in town and she'd take me every-where. Restaurants, bars, premieres, house parties in the Hollywood Hills—Margaret was plugged in. And we got close. And getting close to Margaret was a little surreal.

Like the time she had a tough time finding someone to watch the boys because I called at the last minute.

"You find a sitter?" I asked.

"No, nobody was home."

"Ah . . . I'm sorry."

"No, it's okay. I just dropped them off at Janet's house."

Let me get this straight. In other words, Janet Jackson stayed home to baby-sit so I could go off and have a good time? Talk about helping me with *my* pleasure principle.

Or like the time Margaret told me to pick up her ringing phone and a man with an Indian accent was on the other end asking to speak to the boys.

"Margaret, there's some Indian guy looking to speak to Jeremy and Jordyn," I said, cupping the receiver.

"What? Gimme that phone," she said. And suddenly her eyes doubled in size when she realized it was Michael clowning around, making sure his nephews were ready for their planned trip to Neverland that afternoon.

"OhmyGod, Michael . . . I forgot to tell them!" she screamed. "I'll tell them now. They'll be ready in a half-hour."

Can you imagine? Michael Jackson not knowing he's speaking to a gossip columnist is like a burglar not knowing he's breaking into a cop's house. Anyhow, it was really surreal stuff . . . but I loved it.

I'm not gonna lie to you, Margaret never forgot who I was. Almost every time the topic of Michael was about to come up, her big brown eyes would constrict to pinpoints and she'd look me straight in the face. "A.J., if you write anything about what I'm going to tell you . . . I'll kill you."

It went on like that for a long time. She'd make me privy to a host of things and I'd never mention them in the press. And, as a matter of fact, there were times when I knew a story about Michael was brewing and bubbling on tabloid shows and copy desks across the country and I'd call Margaret to let her know about it.

"Maggie, this is one story that's gonna be hard not to cover."

"A.J., it's not true. Just drop it. Do you *have* to write something about it? Can't you let someone else at your paper write about it?"

"But, Margaret, he's reeling. This guy is one scandal away from ruin."

"That's all the more reason why you should lay off. He's gone through enough hell. Please."

It doesn't even matter which crazy story I'm evoking. After a while, they all blended together for poor Michael, didn't they? The hair on fire, the sexual harassment lawsuit, vitiligo on his penis, flying off to Switzerland to seek treatment for a drug addiction, his cryptic, taped TV message to America, his oxygen bed, buying the Elephant Man's bones, fainting on stage, his friendships with Webster, Liz Taylor and assorted chimpanzees, marrying Lisa Marie Presley out of the blue. Christ, I know there were more, but my memory has taken mercy on him.

The point is, even I started to feel a little bad for the guy. It was like hitting someone when they were down on their belly and curled up in a ball. And that's not the way I wanted to be when I was a mere ten years removed from practicing the moonwalk in my sweatsocks on my mother's kitchen floor. Hell, I wanted to *be* Michael Jackson when I was eight years old. So, put that all together and you'll understand why I began to spare Michael's feelings. I'd drop stories that would literally fall into my lap. Or avoid huge stories that Dunn or Hackett would put me on immediately. I'd hide in my office for a few hours and at the end of the day I'd walk to their offices and tell them I couldn't reach my sources or some shit. Anything so I didn't have to have my name attached and so as not to get Margaret in hot water with her helpful in-law.

But these are things Michael didn't know. And these are the sorts of things a lot of big stars don't take the time to know when their careers are spiraling and their big security blankets get dampened with disgrace. They lose their reference. And rather than acknowledging the myriad stories a reporter doesn't print, they focus on the one thing a reporter does put in the paper. And sometimes it's a really innocuous item that brings them to the biggest boil. Like Linda Stasi always told me, "You never know where the hit is gonna come from."

On one particular day, Lewittes ran what we thought was an innocuous item about Jackson tossing a birthday party for one of his nephews at his ranch. It sounded fine when he read it to me. Not too mean an item, just some of the surreal facts surrounding a party at Neverland. Big deal. Problem was the party was for one of Margaret's kids and when the item hit the papers, Jackson believed Margaret had leaked the private info directly to me and the column. But, actually, it had all come from one of Lewittes's sources. Well, within a day or so, word came down from Neverland that Uncle Mikey was cutting off all financial support to Margaret and her boys. No more health insurance. No more schooling. No more rent on their modest Beverly Hills apartment.

Naturally, Margaret was furious at me and ripped me a new ass. When I offered to write a letter to anyone at Neverland clearing her name— or to make a phone call to someone in charge—she got even more incensed.

"I don't even want them knowing I'm your friend," she cried.

That stung like hell. I understood it, but it hurt nonetheless. And that kind of dis had a special sting to it whenever it fell from the lips of people who were dear to me. People who I believed knew that the blood in my heart was a helluva lot thicker than the ink in which my column was printed.

I don't know what happened the day the birthday item ran. Maybe it was a really slow news day and we had to fill a few inches. Maybe the Percocet kicked in too much and tact and timing took a backseat to a good, hearty laugh with my partner. Maybe I was tired and I just wanted to finish the column and get the hell home. I don't know. But I do know I didn't purposefully forsake my good relationship with a beautiful woman just so that story could see the light of day. That's not the designs I had on me and Maggie.

Things got bad for Margaret after our benign birthday party item. No one at Neverland wanted to hear that she had nothing to do with the item finding its way in the paper. And the truth is, Margaret's fingerprints were nowhere near it. Back in the day, if wealth could've been measured in the amount of Michael Jackson sources one had, I'd have had my driver taking me to work in my Bentley. Before it was all over, Jackson did hold back on paying for things and, in the long run, that just ends up hurting the boys. I'm not exactly sure what was and wasn't paid for, but it was enough to make Margaret scared shitless.

With nobody to talk to at Neverland and Margaret not returning my calls, I closed one of my Downtown columns in a manner that made me want to show Jackson he was fucking with the wrong person.

Michael Jackson should only know that his former sister-in-law's once-tight friendship with me saved his ass a number of times: in this column and on TV. He should know that one phone call from Margaret and the story used to die at my desk. While I'm at it, he should also know I've spent nights at the apartment he pays for, with his nephews by my side, and heard nothing but good things about him from their young, unlying mouths. With his army of supporters headed for the exits, Jackson should know he might have just disarmed some of his best soldiers. He's a general out of control, with the media's sights set bull's-eye on his pretty little nose. And now there is no more Margaret Maldonado to step in front of the bullet. I'm gonna miss you, baby. But Michael is gonna miss you more. Ready. Aim. Fire.

The morning after the column appeared, my phone rang. It was Margaret.

"What are you doing?"

"I'm trying to help."

"You're making it worse."

"But, I'm trying to make them see . . ."

"A.J. Keep. Me. Out. Of. Your. Fucking. Column."

Click. Tone.

Margaret and I never truly resurrected our friendship again, though it did get a little civil after I left the industry altogether. But it's never been the same since. I think since I've moved to LA, I've spoken to her twice, three times tops. There was a time when we spoke three times a day.

Wild Horses

Martin Dunn knew what my lifestyle was all about. That was part of the reason he gave birth to Downtown to begin with. He liked the Damon Runyonesque quality to it all. So he could hardly blame me on the occasions—take Michael Jackson, for instance—when I found it difficult to hit on a source on a delicate issue. But that's not to say he didn't try me.

"You ever hear of burning a source?" he asked me, half-kidding.

"Come on, you know I won't do that. And you know how close I am to Margaret."

"Too fuckin' close for *my* own good," he'd say.

Although there was nothing funny about possibly getting beat by the *Post* in the next day's paper, at this point in Dunn's tenure there was something funny about he and I having animated closed-door discussions after we had spent the better part of the previous evening bulking up at Rao's before buying each other lap dances at Scores until two A.M.

"Bloody hell, A.J., I know we're friends," Dunn would say between swallows of his draft, "but I'm your goddamn boss first. Now, go get me something on Jackson or Simpson or whoever the hell I ask you for."

Sometimes he sounded just like Dudley Moore with a little more kick.

I loved Martin, but I didn't take his diatribes too seriously or too much to heart. But there was some concern around the newsroom that the Brit was setting to bolt the paper very shortly. Word was he could no longer take Zuckerman up in his grill every hour of every damn day. And once word came down that Dunn might be done at the *News*, the rumor mill swirled like crazy. And articles about who his successor might be ran almost on a daily basis in the *Post, New York Magazine*, the *Observer*, you name it. And the sad thing is, many of the *News* staffers were piping the stories to those papers on a daily basis. It was gross.

There was one time that I asked Dunn if we could hire Jimmy "The Kid" Ruttenberg as a full-timer since he was getting nibbles from the *Post* and the *Observer*, and frankly, I couldn't afford to lose his legs. Much less have him work for the fuckin' competition.

Dunn, who at this point was so beleaguered by the rumors of his rumored resignation, closed the door to his office and told me Zuckerman was tying his hands in terms of hiring anyone.

"But that's fucked up, Martin," I said. "He's aces. We need that kid. What are we talking, $40,000?"

Dunn exploded and his words thundered through the newsroom. "There are more important things going on than making sure your assistant is hired full-time or compensated more so that you have an easier time of your job! Now, I said what I have to say. Don't bring it up again."

I did a stupid thing. I phoned up Zuckerman, not thinking that would be viewed as going behind Dunn's back, and made my plea to the publisher for The Kid to get hired.

"I can't afford to lose him on the page. And we can't afford to let someone else have him. And you can certainly afford to keep him here," I said.

Zuckerman told me he needed time to think about it. But what he did was phone Dunn and rip him a new ass, wondering aloud why one of his columnists just phoned him up in the middle of the day about hiring an underling.

Dunn called me into his office and went ape shit—this time with the door open. About thirty minutes later a reporter from the *Observer* was on the phone asking me all sorts of questions about the confrontation. I stayed calm—I knew what they were looking for—I was far from being a disgruntled employee. I admitted there had been a beef but I told the reporter I respected Dunn's decision and opinion. "And besides," I said, "I could be in the middle of deadline and Martin Dunn could ask me to go pick up his dry cleaning and I'd go. I love that guy."

Anyhow, not too long after that altercation, Dunn decided to leave the ship and head back to London. He'd been pretty tight-lipped about it to the press and the rest of the newsroom but one night we were drinking in an Atlantic City casino when he opened up about it.

"Tell you one thing," he said, at a blackjack table. "The *News* ain't gonna be nearly as fun without me to push around."

"You leaving, Skip?"

"Yeah," he said. "Time to go. I had a great time but I can't work this way."

He was referring to Zuckerman phoning him at every hour from the first hour on the job to the last. "And at home at any hour he wants," Dunn said. "It doesn't stop.

"Anyhow," Dunn continued, "no regrets. I had a good time. And any time you want to come work on Fleet Street, I'd grab you in a second. They'd love you out there."

"Nah, I'm a New Yorker, boss," I said. "It's gonna suck without you here. Who's Zuckerman bringing in?"

"Looks like Pete Hamill. A true New Yorker. You two ought to get along famously."

Yeah, I thought so, too. But I was wrong. And more on that fuckin' story later.

Whatever life was sucked out of the newsroom when Linda Stasi left, suddenly the place felt like a morgue when Dunn announced his resignation and headed for London to work for some TV station. I couldn't get mad at the guy, either. He was going back home, he was getting more money and he had himself a beautiful woman he planned on staying with once he landed across the pond. The guy had come to New York, conquered the city's newsstands, and went home a hero, all before he turned forty years old.

In terms of my all-time favorite list of Things That Are British, Martin Dunn ranks second, smack-dab in the middle of the Rolling Stones and Tracey Ullman.

Shattered

Despite my former editor-in-chief's gut feeling that Pete Hamill would be his successor, there was a weird period of time when no one was quite sure who Zuckerman was aiming to lure over. And during those times, a newsroom takes on a lurid state. Loyalties are aligned, phony friendships are born and all sorts of cliques crop up all over the place. In essence, when a popular editor-in-chief leaves, people all around the newsroom ready for the new guy to implement his team of new hires and fire the old gang who had some strong allegiances to the former editor. It's no different than a baseball manager bringing in his favorite pitching coach and batting coach, along with a few players who he's made promises to along the way.

Despite the fact that I was a staunch Dunn supporter, I remember not being too worried when I heard Hamill was, indeed, the new guy who was slated to run the paper. I had always loved Hamill's New York City attitude, his past as a fighter and a womanizer and even his bouts with alcoholism. In my mind, we were getting a man with a past. And those are my favorite kind of men. But Pete hadn't even been there more than a few weeks—and we hadn't even had one face-to-face meeting— when I heard some disturbing news.

Pete Hamill hated my column. It was becoming obvious to me and more or less obvious to some of the bigger brass around the paper. It wasn't that he was flat-out telling people, "I hate Benza's column," but something was going down with my new editor-in-chief. I remember my editor Larry Hackett and I just kicking it in his office one day.

"Pete's trying to figure out what he wants to do with Downtown," Larry said.

"What the hell does that mean?"

"He wants to do *something* with it."

"Yeah, and I want to do *something* with Elle Macpherson's ass."

"Well, let's not jump the gun. Let me see what he wants before we do anything. He probably thinks it just needs a little tweaking."

Tweaking. I hate that word, *tweak*. Matter of fact, I hate its partner *twinge*, too. I hate *twist* and *twat* and *twixt*. There aren't a whole lot of words that begin with a "tw" and I hate them all. I even hate TWA mostly because their LA to Newark flight continues on to Tel Aviv and I always assume that's the first flight a terrorist would love to blow out of the sky. BOOM!—good-bye to 200 Jews before the peanuts have even been handed out. I always get to the gate and phone my sister. "Ro . . . this thing is going *down*! I can see the bomb strapped to the motherfuckin' wing!" Anyhow, when an editor-in-chief says a column needs some "tweaking," it's like a doctor looking at your brain scan and saying, "We got work to do."

Frankly, I couldn't imagine what work my column needed. All I knew was Downtown was a must-read for a lot of people in the city and there were even times when strangers approached me in *Los Angeles* asking me to autograph copies of my column that they were carrying with them. Now, I know my shit wasn't Hemingway, but let me ask you a question: Have you ever carried an entire newspaper column on you just waiting to bump into the writer? People got on John Hinckley for carrying *Catcher in the Rye* in his back pocket when he shot the president, but I think it's stranger carrying a newspaper column in a manila folder just waiting on the writer to show up. I think those people need "tweaking," not the column.

Anyhow, I've said it a hundred times and I'll say it one more time right now: Pete Hamill was a childhood idol of mine. When I was a kid, I used to grab the *Sunday News Magazine* just to devour his short stories before my father got to the crossword. And the older I got, I couldn't get enough of Pete's writing style—how he balanced honesty and integrity with bravado and machismo. How the big magazines always called him for a huge New York City article. Pete wrote about things your father taught you about if you were lucky: Ebbets Field, the Stork Club, Sinatra at the Paramount, Toots Shor, the joys of drinking until you dropped and loving women until your heart was shot to pieces. Pete came from pain and pain is something we always listen to.

When Pete Hamill was hired to run the *Daily News*, I was okay with it. I was sad to hold the door for Martin Dunn but I was thrilled that I would be working for my idol. It didn't seem like a terrible switch to make. But there was always a tiny voice in the back of my head that whispered something Pete wrote in one of his books many years before.

"Newspapers will break your heart," Pete wrote. And now, with Pete not even at his desk for a month, I was focusing on how that sentence would apply to me. It was creepy.

When your column is running smoothly and it's recognized as a hit, there is always someone at your door. Everyone wants to hang with the columnist, shoot the shit, trade jokes or whatever. Victor the security guard would surprise me with coffee, Drasner saved me a seat at Rao's, reporters tipped me off to hot stories, other columnists asked me my take on things and ran with my opinion as if it were their own. It was some heady shit.

Anyhow, when word gets around that you're a marked man and that your column has been targeted for "tweaking," the people stay away as if that shit were catching. Sometimes it's like you're in prison and other inmates pass you along a message in the yard. I had circulation guys, advertising women and truck drivers coming up on me.

"Hey, man, word is Pete's got a bull's-eye on your back," Eddie Faye told me one day.

"Yeah . . . what the fuck is going on?"

"I don't know but you better get a meeting with him right away."

For the first time in my tenure I was scared. I remember telling Michael, "Let me tell you something; Pete's got a hard-on for the column and he's gonna do something about it and you might get hit in the cross fire."

"How can he hate either one of the columns," Michael would say. "Not to mention you're on TV every day plugging this paper. You're only one of the most visible newspaper columnists in the city, country even."

"Yeah, well, just make sure your resume is ready like mine."

"No fuckin' way."

It took a week or so for Pete to make time for a meeting. And when he did, he looked beat—tie undone, sleeves rolled up and it was only half-past ten A.M. And he had a way of making me feel sorry for him immediately.

"How are you, boss?"

"Oh, you know, can't go one hour without a phone call from Mort. How do you think I'm doing?"

How do you like that? The guy just got there and he was feeling everything Dunn told me about in terms of Zuckerman being a crazy bastard.

He wasn't lying. Zuckerman was famous for riding his editor's ass at every hour—while the paper was being edited, after it was put to bed, when it was being printed, as it was getting delivered and right up until the moment the city was getting their thumbs dirty with their morning cup of coffee. He was George Steinbrenner and every manager was Billy Martin.

"Is it that bad, boss?"

"I've never seen anything like it before. The two of them run around like kings with syphilis." Fuckin' Hamill with his phrasing. I loved it.

Once we got down to speaking about the column, it dawned on me this conversation I was having with Pete was my first one. It only felt like I knew him my whole life because I was always reading his words. But truthfully, we were two complete strangers in an empty room. And suddenly I couldn't look at him like an idol. He was just my boss. Worse, he was the *new* boss. Basically, Pete's lament was that I wasn't focusing in on my beat and pulling out stories that had appeal to a wide variety of readers.

"Sometimes it's too inside baseball, do you follow me? Don't lose sight of the fact that your readers depend on you to put your face up against the glass and allow them to see inside a world they have no access to."

"Well, that's a little bit of the problem, Pete. I'm no longer the guy looking in the fishbowl. I'm in the fishbowl now. I'm one of the fish to an extent."

"You don't have to tell me. I've been there before. But you still have to write for the common reader. Don't tell the story to your buddies. Tell it to the people who don't know you and your buddies. Like Milton Berle used to say, 'Don't tell jokes only the band laughs at.' "

I wanted to tell him he was full of shit and that times have changed and that, frankly, I liked him better when he was drinking and womanizing. But this Pete, the new Pete, was pretty much on target with his assessment of me and my writing style. I wasn't happy leaving his office because, basically, I knew the gig was up. Pete was asking me to do something I didn't want to do. And so I knew it was only a matter of time before we'd clash again.

Michael wanted to know what Pete had to say as soon as I stepped back into the office. He hung up with a friend as I walked in. "What'd he say?"

"It's too inside-inside. Some shit like that. I'm telling you, Mikey, get your resume ready."

"No fuckin' way," he said, like he had said a few times before. Only this time he couldn't look me in the eye when he said it.

And then Larry came in. "Well?"

"Too inside-inside," I said.

And then Larry pressed his palm against his cheek. "Face against the glass?"

"Bingo."

"All right, we'll make it work. Look, try a different approach this week. I'll help you keep your bearings."

That was nice and all, but I didn't want to try a different approach. As far as I was concerned I had the best job in New York and now it was all beginning to come crashing down. I was Humpty-Dumpty with half my ass off the ledge.

Basically, I can't blame Pete for noticing what I had already known— the column was getting away from me. Where there was once a burning desire to punch out a Downtown column in the middle of a busy Friday afternoon, I was now sometimes feeling a bit of dread when nothing came crashing to the front of my skull. There were some days when putting together Downtown was as creatively stimulating to me as building a house of Lego. One fuckin' sentence at a time. The revelations and fits of anger and irony-laced rants—that every loud-mouthed columnist depends upon—weren't turning third as hard as they used to. And worse than that, I was being approached to help people and send messages and cast dispersions and lift spirits almost every time I sat down to write the column. It was mostly secretive shit, but it was weakening the column.

Like the time a powerful acquaintance of mine asked me to help out imprisoned Genovese crime boss Barney Bellomo. It turned out Bellomo was about to go to trial for the murder of a convicted drug dealer even though he had already passed two lie detector tests. Where that fits in a gossip column, I'll never know. But it was almost impossible to turn down the request since the guy making it had done a few favors for me. The way he saw it, it was payback time. And fitting Bellomo's name in a gossip column was my problem to deal with. Those are not the kind of guys who are going to go home and worry how you're going to segue from Barney to Billy Bob Thornton.

"I'm not a writer, you're a writer, you know how to do it," he told me.

"Sure, pal. No problem," I lied.

"You would be doing me a very big favor for a very dear man."

When I look at some of my old columns now, I shudder. I can still taste the bitter coffee and see the black, beady eyes of my friend as he opened up his manila folder and went on with his plea. Meanwhile an old faded head shot of Tony Musante as TV detective Toma stared down at me and no one at the *News* could have possibly known the kind of predicament I was in. I just thank God I had Larry Hackett on my side— an editor who let me slide once in a while. A guy who understood there was a reason—there must have been a really good reason—why I was handing in a gossip column with the unnatural assemblage of names that included a gay fashion icon, a football great-turned-accused-murderer, a TV sidekick, a murdered beauty queen kid, the imprisoned leader of one of New York's crime families and an upstart actor who had a shot at an Oscar. What was I looking for? Free clothes from Calvin Klein?

More TV appearances based on my opinions on O. J. and JonBenét? A favor from Barney once he got out of jail, *if* he ever got out of jail? A movie role from Miramax?

Probably all of the above. It was an abuse of power. Suddenly I cared more about what the column could get me and less about what it was giving the guy in the subway.

I Can't Get No
Satisfaction

f I was changing, then the city was changing along with me. And at the start of 1997 it seemed as if my Ebbets Field of Dreams was slowly being razed. Don't get me wrong—the city is always a thriving place, with a thousand stimuli on every city block and the threat of danger always pushing the euphoria to narcotic levels. But sometimes the magic disappears for bits of time. Sometimes the trip to the zoo ain't such a big deal because the tigers are asleep in the cage.

When JohnnyBoy used to joke that the best part of my job—and most intoxicating thing of our notoriety—was that they moved the cones for us at SpyBar, it gave me the chills, as corny as that sounds. I liked the idea that Spy's doormen, King and Joey Gossett, would hop over the ropes at the first sight of my new Benz or Johnnyboy's classic Benz turning the corner. And we'd laugh as we watched them move the orange cones directly in front of the door so that our cars would have the perfect parking spot. And as JohnnyBoy would stub out the joint on the bottom of his shoe, we'd both laugh until we coughed our high away.

"Buddy, let me tell you something, there's gonna come a day when you're gonna miss them moving the cones for us," JohnnyBoy would say. "Who else they moving the cones for?"

"Nobody, Johnny. Just us."

"That's right."

And then we'd weave our way into Spy and—after squeezing dozens of hands—we'd finally settle upon our reserved perch at the top of the baby grand piano. And from there we could see everything. We were the wise old owls looking through the Forest of Denial that our city, and especially SpyBar, was becoming for me.

It didn't take long before JohnnyBoy and I would turn philosophical.

"If America is the coolest, fastest country," JohnnyBoy would say, "and New York City is the coolest, fastest city . . ."

"Right . . ."

"And Spy is the coolest, fastest bar in the coolest, fastest part of the city—which is SoHo . . ."

"Right . . ."

"And the piano is the best seat in the coolest, fastest bar . . ."

"Right . . ."

"What does that say about us, buddy?"

"I don't know, what does that say, Johnny?"

"It means if you were a Martian on Mars trying to find the coolest, fastest guys on the coolest, fastest planet, you'd aim your high-powered telescope to Earth, on America, in New York City, down on SoHo, on Greene Street, at Spy and there you'd see us—me and you—sitting right here on the fuckin' piano."

"Did you come up with all that from one hit of that joint?" I'd laugh.

"Yeah. Hey, why you laughing? That's the shit that killed Bruce Lee."

Every drug JohnnyBoy had was "the shit that killed Bruce Lee." But I'd be lying if I didn't tell you the high of who I was—or who we were, as JohnnyBoy put it—was beginning to wear on me. And then when the city started to change ever so slightly around me, some of my fizz for the job went flat.

It was incredibly easier reporting on people when they were merely clusters of cool people at different cool tables that I was tragically uncool enough to be seated at. And, it was even easier reaching out to the friends of the incredibly cool people when I really needed to get close to a rumor concerning somebody seated at one of the cool tables. But now that I was getting the cool table—and actually having the cool tables reserved for me and my friends—I was having a hard go of it. And, even worse, my anonymity was long gone thanks to the evil but prosperous advent of cable television and afternoon TV gabfests.

It was one thing suggesting Bono once had an affair with Christy Turlington (as I had in a column), but once you dance with the guy on top of the SpyBar piano (as I had on a drunken night) it becomes impossible to write about those same people objectively. Basically, in the wink of Peter Gatien's good eye, I had become an unmistakable face fishing for news among the unmistakable faces. It was wearing on me. It went like this in the playground of my mind: Whenever the gossip business would wear on me, I'd focus on the perks of being a top player in the industry. But when the perks started to lose their luster or were taken away by Mayor Giuliani, I couldn't focus on anything.

You're gonna laugh, but the truth of the matter is when the "restricted" Night Parking Rules came into effect around SoHo, Greenwich Village and select parts of the Lower East Side, it wasn't as much fun hitting the town. And when the nightly orgy of sex, drugs and rock and roll that was SpyBar started to dry up, there really was no reason to go out at all. And I basically began writing my column without stepping out to one event, and instead relied on sources and publicists and such. I used my time to do the type of things I wanted to do but never made the time to do. All I knew was I had some money and a nice expense account—and virtually every publicist at my beck and call—and I began to take advantage of my city. I went to more ball games. Took in every movie. Went to fancy exhibits. Called in sick. Cashed in on a hundred free dinners and a thousand free drinks I had coming to me from friendly and gracious restaurant owners. I even saw a Broadway play or two, something I was never really fond of in the first place. In essence, I was doing the same thing a disgruntled civil service employee might do when he feels he's through with his job. The only difference is, while they use up all the personal days they have accrued, I was cashing in all the personal favors I had coming to me. And it added up to a lot.

One such night, it felt right to have a good time with Linda Stasi, the woman who gave me my start, the pillar of strength and intelligence and clarity I often clung to when the city winds raged. Since she quit the *News*, Linda had gotten a book deal and was now writing her usual snappy column for the *Village Voice* and its new editor Donald Forst twice a month. I took Linda to see *Rent* and then I had plans to show her *Two Rooms*, the new restaurant Rocco was running at the foot of the 59th Street Bridge. I swear, I'm the only nonfag who lives for *Rent*, and my date with Linda was an unprecedented sixth time I was seated in the Nederlander Theater hanging on every word to every song.

Our date came about after I got a tip from the play's publicist that the publicly grieving Fred and Patti Goldman would be in attendance that night.

"It could make for a great column," the play's publicist chirped, while dangling two free orchestra seat tickets. "And they'd be easy prey."

You see what I'm saying about the way people sell out other people?

"I don't know," I said. "I love the play and could see it a hundred more times . . . but I'm not sure if I want to bug those people."

"A.J., but you're forever riding them every time I read your column or see you on TV."

"Yeah, I know, but who the hell am I?"

"Jesus, what did you have, an epiphany?" he said. "Oh well, suit yourself. I'm sure Cindy [Adams] will grab them in a minute."

When I heard that, I went for the tickets and called Linda.

"Hey, I got two tix for *Rent* waiting for me at the box office tonight. What are you doing tonight?"

"I'd rather die than sit through a play about a bunch of Yuppies who cry about their heat being turned off," Linda said.

"But wait, we both might get a good column out of it. The Goldmans are going to be there. And they're sitting right in front of us."

"I'll see you there at 7:45."

By the time Linda and I found our seats, she was still pointing out the hypocrisy around us. Nothing had changed with her head whatsoever, thank God.

"Don't you love all these rich people coming to the theater in their fur coats to see a play about a bunch of poor drug addicts who have AIDS? So compassionate of them."

The next ten minutes or so were quiet between me and Linda as we both began dreaming up the column angle we'd come away with. The silence was used to conjure up anecdotes, jokes, ironies and truths concerning our doing Broadway with the Goldman family. Every once in a while either Linda or I would let out an emotional burp or a laugh or a snicker. None of which was meant to be mean, but all of it reserved for the next column we would sit down to write. The quiet was nice. It was like old times over on East 42nd Street again.

With about ten seconds to showtime and well after the house lights had gone down, an usher escorted Fred and Patti Goldman—along with their daughter Kim—to their seats directly in front of me and Linda. There wasn't much we could say to one another because the play was on and one of the lead actors was already in song. All we could share were little giggles and knowing glances whenever Fred's giant mustache came into view.

But somewhere in the middle of the play's first act, it hit me that I didn't want to say anything to these people. I didn't want to ask them a question they had answered a million times before and I especially didn't want to raise one they would find offensive. Even though the story of their son's death was part of the biggest story in my time working for newspapers, I couldn't think of one single thing to say that mattered to me. And, when I looked over at Linda—who was hiding her face with the *Playbill*—it was obvious she was feeling the same way.

With the first act over and a number of well-wishers already lining up to pay their respects to the family, Linda and I sat there feeling like fools.

"I can't think of a single thing I want to say to these people," I confessed.

"I'm ready to leave right now," she said.

"But why," I asked Linda. "Why is this happening to me? Every other journalist I know would crawl over the seat for a quote from them. Why am I clamming up?"

"Because you have compassion," she said. "That goes a helluva lot further in life than trying to get a story from a family who is miserable. There's nothing you can write anymore that would help them. Walking away, giving them their space, is the biggest help."

And with that, we did. Linda and I never made the second act. We walked off into the cold, crowded streets of Manhattan's Theater District and hailed a cab.

"Next week, you write a column about how you couldn't work up the nerve to ask the Goldman family a question," Linda said. "Just tell the truth. You're a columnist, you're not a reporter. You can attach your own feelings to a story. And if your editor-in-chief doesn't like it, fuck him."

Well, my editor-in-chief didn't like it. But I was the one who was about to get fucked.

Ventilator Blues

I know I told you I never wanted to be a "reporter." But I did basically become one in the final weeks of my tenure at the *News*. In essence, that's what Hamill was asking me to be when he sat me down in his office and rolled up his sleeves and laid down the law.

"There are stories out there," he said. "Go find them."

And so I went. Begrudgingly. But I didn't have to go far. When you're a high-powered columnist, all you simply do is ring up a few friends and ask them, "Whattya hear? Whattya know?" And since I was lucky enough to run with the "in" crowd—and fast enough to run where the "in" crowd ran—I was almost always having stories dumped in my lap at the right time. I tell ya, so much of being a good columnist is having all sorts of friends with their eyes and ears always peeled for you. It has less to do with the questions you ask and more to do with the people you listen to. There's a big difference. I have said this before and I'll say it again: A columnist is only as good as the people he relies on to help him shape the column. He is actually a processor of all the thoughts, ironies, hypocrisies and truths that are fed to him. The words he chooses are merely the final mechanisms that drive the point home. What's missing at the end of every column are the credits—the names of the dozens of other voices who spoke in the columnist's ear.

So, when Hamill essentially told me that Downtown was my *beat*—and not merely the name of a column to advertise my adventures and musings—he was driving the point home that I needed to hit the streets. And if I didn't hit the streets, I'd be pounding the streets—for a new job. At this point in my career, saving my career took on the same flavor as saving face. Meanwhile, the whole newsroom was watching. Half of them wanted to see me swim. The other half took bets on how fast I'd sink.

Normally, I wouldn't touch a story about where a bunch of drug deals were going down. First of all, I think the scope of that story affects too few people to matter and, second, I didn't have any desire to disrupt the highs of many of the city's big, boldfaced names with the scoop. But with Hamill breathing down my neck, I was forced to deliver a big story. And that was dangerous since I was privy to a lot of big stories— many of which would shatter illusions, knock down walls and virtually threaten the careers of way too many people I didn't want to hurt—and printing them would make life decidedly more difficult for me and my lifestyle. And, frankly, I didn't need that. But when one of my friends came through with the story of the druggie bodega, I went for it. If Hamill was jonesing for a good column, I'd give him something to feel comfortably numb about.

I'd always known about the Alphabet City bodega and how everyone from fashion photographers to supermodels to designers to movie stars to rock stars would wander in and ask the front clerk if he had any "Gerber baby food." And, presto!, the man would then alert them to the back of a specific aisle where they'd lay their money in a hole in the wall. Within a few seconds a hand would appear, take the dough and replace it with its equivalent in dope. To some of them—and I'm talking big, *big* names here—it was not at all different than the way you *have* to make a stop at Starbucks. What can I say? Coffee, jogging, yoga, cigarettes, Sportscenter, heroin—whatever gets you through the night. I also knew about the seedy guys who used to deal outside the Laundromat near Avenue B and 7th Street. One guy stood at the top of the block and another guy, usually a kid, stood at the bottom of the block ready to whistle at the first sight of a cop. All junkies had to do was walk to the stoop outside the Laundromat and make their drug deal with a knowing glance and a visible flash of some green. The whole thing took about twenty seconds, as long as you made sure the dealer didn't have to make change. Hell, I even knew about Tasty Treats or We Deliver—two different phone businesses wherein junkies would call in their account numbers and their locations, and within a half-hour a driver would appear with a cornucopia of drugs.

I knew about all of these things. I had even used some of their services. But this was one of those times when I had to burn a bridge to save a village. I ran with the story and, of course, was met with the usual rounds of concerned editors who wouldn't know a bag of dope if it bit them in the ass.

"What are we saying about the bodega?"

"That it's a drug den," I'd say.

"Can we say that about the bodega?"

"Why the hell not, it's true."

"I'm going to have to call Legal on this one."

"Well, they're gonna want me to confirm it."

"Well, can anyone in the bodega confirm it?"

"No."

"Why not?"

"Because it's a fuckin' drug den!"

Long story short. The story ran. And when I tagged the death of young fashion photographer Davide Sorrenti to it, it really hit a nerve among many downtown denizens. Sorrenti was a twenty-one-year-old kid with a big future in photography, before he ODed on heroin at a buddy's house. He learned the trade from his mom, Francesca, and big brother, Mario—both great photographers in their own right. And, at the time of his death, Davide was dating supermodel James King, a beauty who had been on the needle since her early teens. Of course, Sorrenti's mom, Francesca—who allowed me to interview her a week after her son's death—was ecstatic with my column and so were a host of modeling agency heads, most of whom were oblivious to the fact that their own young moneymakers knew the bodega's secret password all too well. I'm telling you, heroin was making a major comeback in New York City in early 1997. And when I coupled Sorrenti's death with a female mannequin in the window at the Antique Boutique—with hypodermic needles sticking out of her body—I took the topic to task. And when I was done with the column, several people in the newsroom—people I never dreamed even read my column—sent me all sorts of congratulatory notes. The first line of opposition I came across was some downtown folk who made it known they didn't like where my story was treading. I came across one such guy, a lounge owner, at Bowery Bar a few days after the piece ran.

"Not cool, man," he said to me. "Definitely not cool."

"What's not cool?"

"That story. Why'd you have to go and print that shit? Aren't there other things to write about?"

Obviously the guy was sore that his convenient little drugstore was a memory and from that point on he'd have to cop somewhere else. Maybe even take a subway to get it. *Boo-hoo!*

"Sorry to pee on your parade," I told him. "But a kid died, man. And there's a mannequin in a window on Broadway glorifying the shit. If you want to live your life that way, go ahead. I didn't kick the needle out of your hands. Don't kick the typewriter out of mine."

Christ, you'd think I'd killed the fuckin' Good Humor man.

But much to my surprise the biggest opposition I got came from Hamill. About five days after my piece ran, a note was tacked on my computer that detailed Pete's negative feelings about the column. I do recall Pete thinking it contained "good reporting" and whatnot, but his final take on the column was that it wasn't enough of a broad topic. Of course, I vehemently disagreed and relayed my feelings to Hackett.

"Larry, this guy's got no idea," I said. "This is a huge problem out there. That wasn't just me going off on something that bugs me. This is a big topic and it affects a billion-dollar industry."

"I know. I know."

"Well, what am I supposed to do for God's sake?"

"I think you'll be fine. I'll talk to him."

"I mean, I know he wants to write for the new wave of immigrants in the city and all . . . but ain't this still the paper for all the people who've been reading it forever?"

"You're right."

And then Larry did that thing he always did, placing his palm against the side of his face.

"Yeah, yeah, I know. Face against the glass."

It didn't matter. Hackett was handcuffed. And, the truth is, once Martin Dunn left the building, Hackett lost his hierarchical ear to whisper into. So really, I was speaking to a guy who could do nothing in the way of saving my ass. So, I did the logical thing by turning to Drasner for some assistance. His door had always been open for me in the past.

"Fred, this Pete's on my ass like crazy."

"What's the matter?"

"I don't know. He's unsatisfied with the column, didn't like last week's story on heroin. He's just got my number."

"You want me to talk to him?"

"Would you? I mean, just find out exactly what he's looking for."

"Yeah, I could do that."

"I mean, the column's been successful for so long and all of a sudden he doesn't like it. Hey, man, if it ain't broke . . ."

"Don't fix it."

"Right."

"So . . . don't fix it."

"Yeah, then I'm out a job. You haven't heard he wants to fire me, have you?"

"No. I haven't heard anything like that at all."

"All right, boss, just keep your ears peeled and see what you can do."

"Will do."

And then Fred Drasner went out and did absolutely nothing. And that was the last conversation I had with the man.

Just for kicks I sent a call upstairs to Mort Zuckerman, too. But the closest I got to actually airing my concern with Mort was his secretary telling me he'd call me back. I'm still waiting. It's been four years.

So, I got the picture. I felt like the guy who's sticking up a bank teller and everyone in the bank begins to slowly shift away from the guy because they see a sniper cop setting up a clear shot to take him out. Hamill had me in his sights and they were all clearing a path for him. No one wanted to be hit by a ricochet.

The small dose of consolation I got from my heroin abuse sentiments came three months after I ran my column. On May 22, all the city's newspapers ran up-front stories of President Clinton ripping the fashion industry for peddling heroin-chic ads that make druggies seem glamorous, sexy and cool.

"The glorification of heroin is not creative, it's destructive. It's not beautiful, it is ugly. And this is not about art, it is about life and death.

And glorifying death is not good for our society," Clinton told a conference of mayors.

I sat home and got a kick out of knowing that what Pete thought
wasn't a broad enough topic for a column was enough of a topic for the
President of the United States to address.

19th Nervous Breakdown

To say Scores was a haven for me is like saying Radar knew his way around the *M*⋆*A*⋆*S*⋆*H* unit a little bit. Let me put it to you this way: There was a time when the relationship I had with the strip club, as well as many of the peelers inside it, was as beautifully symbiotic as a shark and a pilot fish. And by that I mean we each prospered because of the other's presence. I was forever giving the club splashes in the column and on television and the club was forever keeping me stacked in good times.

Many of my mob pals were secretly running the joint, the club's gracious publicist Lonnie Hanover was there for anything I ever needed, Chico was managing the place and many of the girls were close friends of mine. No matter when I showed up, no matter how many people I dragged in behind me, no matter how much money I had in my pocket, I never paid for a dinner, never laid down dough for a drink and very rarely squeezed a twenty-dollar bill into a lovely's garter belt. The club's waiters would deliver giant lobsters and steaks to my table, hostesses would bring snifter upon snifter of fine cognac and cigarette girls would drop off a Cuban now and then and Lonnie would sign for everything. Just like that. Didn't matter if the damage was $10 or $500—I never saw a bill. And somewhere along the night, Lonnie would amble by with his usual well-rehearsed speech.

"Now, as you know, A.J., we have taken care of the food and drinks for this evening for you and your friends but the lap dances are on you." *Ba-dum-bum.*

I used to laugh as we were leaving the place. "I'm like crime," I'd say. "I don't pay."

I've said this sort of thing a million times but still all of my ex-girlfriends don't understand why I spent so many nights there. It ain't all about the girls, I tell them. After a while a girl at your table has you feeling just as uncomfortable as the violinist at an Italian restaurant playing "Come Back to Sorrento." It truly was all the extra perks that attracted me.

And it wasn't just me who was getting preferential treatment at Scores. There were always dozens of VIPs in the place on any given night and another dozen you heard were going to show up. The reason I was plugged in to the place like crazy was because of the lengths I'd go to to help publicize the joint's popularity. Lonnie knew he could call me at any hour of the night to tip me off as to who just arrived. It could be three A.M. and my phone—which was always on my bed with me—would ring.

"Lonnie Hanover calling."

"Yeah, pal."

"Well, Rodman is in the President's Club and Madonna just walked in. Do you want to be here to see the sparks fly, brother? Does the *Daily News* want the exclusive?"

"Be there in fifteen minutes."

Or Lonnie would call because Al Cowlings just wandered in, or Dwight Gooden was there drinking on the same day he was suspended from baseball for drug use or John Wayne Bobbitt was flashing his new scar in the Champagne Room or Demi Moore was buying lap dances like tomorrow was the end of the world. Whatever late-breaking news there was, Lonnie called and I showed up. And the next day's paper reflected that.

The excitement the club generated in my life reached a crescendo when I walked into my Madison Avenue duplex one night around four A.M. and there were two Scores girls rolling around my living room carpet on an Ecstasy high and Chico was sitting on the couch watching them, smiling wider than the Cheshire Cat with a canary in his belly.

"Pope, say hello to Ebony and Ivory," Chico said. "Fresh from Texas."

"Well, I'll be. Has Ebony seen the view from our roof yet?"

"No, I was waiting for you to show her."

"Wanna see the Empire State Building, Ebony?" I asked. "It's so close you can almost touch it."

"Okay."

I stayed in touch with Ebony for a few years. One day she told me she thought Mount Rushmore was a natural rock formation. And then about a week later, upon seeing *Titanic* she said, "It's a good thing that was just a movie or else nobody would ever book a cruise again."

Strippers, God bless 'em.

Anyhow, by the time early 1997 rolled along, Scores was a different sort of place for me. The girls were still gorgeous, the food and drink were still on the arm, Lonnie was as affable as ever but the club was in a little bit of trouble with the law. After two of the club's doormen were gunned down on a summer night in 1996 and rumors spread that Junior Gotti was extorting money from the club, Mayor Giuliani grew a huge hard-on for the joint not seen since the first time a Cleveland insurance salesman stumbled in on a business trip. Giuliani was hell-bent on shutting it down because it was affecting the quality of life in the city. He should only know how much shutting it down would affect the quality of *my* life. At any rate, I found that a good excuse as any to pen a column about the place and the fact that a new zoning law was threatening to close it down. In my opinion it was a big enough topic that it wouldn't upset Hamill. At this point, I didn't care if he called me to the carpet again. But something worse happened—Hamill didn't say a word. He also didn't respond to my requests for a meeting. He also didn't return my e-mails. It was worse than him disliking my column. It was him not caring about my column enough to talk about it. It was benign neglect. And how do you combat that? Approach the guy and say, "How come you aren't telling me how much you don't like the column?" It was weird and disheartening and the silence even had Michael phoning friends around town—publicists, editors, reporters and just people with their ears to the ground, in general. And suddenly outsiders were hearing what I had predicted weeks before—the axe was coming down.

"I fuckin' can't believe this," Michael said. "Is Hamill *insane?*"

When I couldn't take the rumors any longer, and no word was coming down from Hamill or any other *News* upper-ups, I took to my phone, too. And suddenly, the Hot Copy boys—the guys who always got a glove on a rumor no matter how deep in the hole they had to go—were trying to field the hot rumor of our own demise. It was a play we didn't want to make, but it was a wicked line drive we didn't trust anybody else closing their glove on. And let's face it, judging from the prowess of our gossip reporting, there was no doubt we were going to nail the story. Like everything else we attacked, it was just a matter of time.

The next several days were almost impossible to bear. I didn't rush out to many parties that week for fear of facing the vultures who, by now, were all circling for my job. And they all would've taken it at half the pay and twice the hours. I stayed home. When I wasn't rolling over in my bed and grabbing a handful of Vicodins from the giant dish of pills on my night table, I was hitting the "replay" button on my CD player, crying to Dionne Warwick as she sang "Valley of the Dolls." You know the song.

It sounds like real pussy shit and it was. I'm not gonna lie to you. If you hate the way it sounds, imagine how I felt. It was only a few months earlier that I was opening my checks on Fridays and turning to Michael to say, "Fooled 'em again, pal." Then I'd go home and listen to John Lennon sing "Baby, You're a Rich Man."

The Academy Awards were approaching and it wasn't going to be easy traveling to California to cover the three days of festivities, but I knew a change of scenery would do me good. And besides, I didn't think Hamill would lower the boom while I was 3,000 miles away. But he did. So, don't ever let me apply for a job on the Psychic Friends Network, is all I'll say.

I took my twenty-six-year-old nephew Jack along for the trip. It was good to have family with me, plus I knew he loved being near the stars as much as I did. Shit, to us nothing's bigger than the Oscars. We booked two rooms at the Mondrian Hotel on Sunset and I tried not to think about all the bullshit back in New York City. My first order of business was covering the Independent Spirit Awards, which were held under a tent on the beach over in Santa Monica. I always loved covering this event because of the caliber of non-Hollywood actors it attracted. Meaning that the quotient of phonies is always low. And, truth be told, I'm most comfortable around those kind of guys and girls. I like the Billy Bob Thorntons, Laura Derns, Lili Taylors and Sean Penns of the world. I like anybody who sits a little bit outside the row. Anyway, that went well as usual. And later that day, all I had planned was an interview at the Beverly Hills Hotel with a young Australian actress named Radha Mitchell, who—at the time—was working with Ally Sheedy on the film *High Art* for October. The interview was set up by a longtime pal of mine, October publicist Donna Daniels, who prefaced it by saying, "She's young, she's cute, she's funny and she's gonna be a star. You should meet her."

And so I did. But before I went, I was preparing to file a story through my laptop to the *News* desk when Hackett called.

"Hey, buddy."

"Hey, what's up, Larry? I was just sending you my stuff on the Spirit Awards."

"Listen, my friend, I think Pete's gonna do this when you get back."

"Fire me?"

"Yeah."

"Jesus Christ. What a dick. All right."

All that waiting, and that's really all it came down to—"Jesus Christ. What a dick," and "All right." Shock, anger, acceptance.

"You all right?"

"What am I gonna do?"

"I know. I know."

"Well, what do I do, buddy? Do I stick around and cover the awards or do I come home?"

"Finish the job. Show them you're a company guy to the end. This way, when a severance package comes up, you can show them you didn't leave them in a lurch."

So, in a matter of two minutes, I went from filing a story to talking about a severance package. I was brain boggled. I immediately called Michael.

"Hey, buddy," I said.

"Hey, what's up?"

"Our time at the *News*."

"What?"

"Time's up. Pete says so."

"Jesus Christ. What a dick."

"That's pretty much what I said."

Unlike me, Michael would have a hard time with the acceptance part of the equation. It had nothing to do with his mettle but more to do with the fact that he didn't have as many options as I had once we'd walk out the *News* building. That would change in time, but Michael stayed bitter for a long while. To this day, as far as I know, he's never bought the *Daily News* again. Shit, he even went and got a job at the *Post*.

Despite the bad news, I hung up the phone and prepared for the interview with Radha. I didn't want to bother my nephew Jackie, who was downstairs in the pool talking to a few girls. So I split, left him a note on the phone and headed off to the big pink building that would thereafter forever be the Heartbreak Hotel for me.

Radha was young and sweet and seemed to be having an easy time of it here in the States. She spoke so long and enthusiastically that the sorbet on her plate melted into a passion fruit puddle. The only time she stopped was when a stranger came by and politely interrupted us for an autograph.

"I read you all the time, Mr. Benza," he told me. "Would you mind autographing something for me?"

"Sure, no problem."

And with that, the guy whipped out one of my old Downtown columns. "I can't believe I'm finally running into you. This is great." The guy wasn't gay or nothing, just damn happy to see me.

I signed it,

> *Today is the first day of the rest of my life.*
> *Peace and Love,*
> *A.J.*

The guy didn't even read what I wrote. He just put it back in his folder and split.

Radha had no idea what was going on. "Why did he just ask you for an autograph?"

"Long story," I told her. "But I guess I have a bit of a cult following.

Gossip is pretty big back in New York City. And I do it differently than a lot of other people do."

Radha was content with that answer, if not a little confused, and she went back to her enthusiastic stories—how she started, where she studied, how she got to America, her lesbian scenes with Ally Sheedy, etc. Meanwhile my head was about to explode. I stopped her in midsentence.

"Listen, Radha," I said. "I'm sorry I have to tell you this. You're probably not even going to understand, but anyhow . . ."

"What is it?"

"I'm getting fired from my job when I go back home. It's a long story, a stupid story and you won't understand any of it. But the bottom line is, none of what you're telling me is going to make it in the paper. And it's not your fault."

"Oh . . . I'm so sorry."

"Thanks."

We sat there in an awkward silence for a moment.

"I'd ask if you want to get a cup of coffee," she said. "But we're already having one."

"I have a better idea," I said. "My mother always told me to go shopping when I'm depressed. So I'm gonna go to Barney's for a little while. You wanna help me shop?"

"Okay . . . cool."

We got up to go, but there was only one problem. Actually, two problems. Both of us had absolutely no money on us. In her haste to get to the interview, Radha forgot to grab her cash. And in my haze of just finding out what was awaiting me in New York, I didn't grab any cash either. All I had on me was my American Express corporate card. That meant I could pay for lunch, but I couldn't pay the valet for my car. When I told the maître d' my problem, he calmly and coolly slipped me a fiver and away we went. We drove to Barney's and I told Radha, "We can't ever forget this day when we're big stars. The day we didn't have enough dough to get our cars from the valet at the Beverly Hills Hotel."

I blasted "Get Off of My Cloud" the whole way to Barney's as Radha bounced in the shotgun seat of my rented Benz. And seeing the young blonde cutie with the Southern California sun bouncing off her silver

bangle bracelets and the reflection of palm trees in her sunglasses, I remember thinking everything was going to work out just fine. If things
were this good out here with a complete stranger, how bad could they
turn out back at home with the guys I worked with for four years? I
also remember silently thanking JohnnyBoy who'd always told me to
travel with a Stones tape in my car. "If not for nothing else," he said,
"other than Mick's been through everything you're going through and
more and, you know what else, I never met a girl who didn't like the
Stones."

When we emerged from the store, I was $2,700 poorer having pur-
chased a $1,000 brown suede jacket, a $500 pair of Gucci slacks, two
pair of Jennifer Fennestrier patent leather shoes at $500 apiece and a
giant sun hat for Radha. I kissed her on the cheek as I dropped her back
at the hotel.

"You like your hat?"

"I love my hat."

"Good. I'm glad."

"Would you have bought me one if you hadn't been fired?"

"I would've bought you a bigger one."

And that was the last I saw of Radha Mitchell. I didn't like her film,
High Art, when I finally saw it many months later, but I did enjoy her
performance quite a bit. Especially her lesbian scenes.

Oscar weekend is an incredibly busy weekend, but I made sure I saved
time to squeeze in phone calls to my family and pals back home. As a
group they all had conflicted philosophies on dealing with the blow.

"Well, if it's any consolation, pal, the whole city is gonna be in
shock," Rocco said.

"The whole thing sucks but you know what, buddy?" JohnnyBoy
told me. "When one door closes another window opens. You know
what I'm saying."

"Hey, listen," my lawyer and great friend Frankie Giantomasi told
me, "it's gonna be a blessing. You were too big for the job. Too big."

"The fuckin' Irish," my sister Rosalie said of Hamill. "If they can
screw an Italian, they will."

And finally Chico was most direct. "You want I should whack him?"

I wanted to send them all bouquets of flowers, but I had a private
Miramax bash to get ready for over at the fancy Beverly Wilshire Hotel

and, to tell you the truth, I was sort of looking forward to telling a select few of my sudden situation. Most of the publicists I spoke to were all compassionate, if not in shock. Even my gossip colleagues George Rush and Joanna Molloy were a little taken aback.

"You getting anything good?" Joanna asked me during the cocktail reception.

You getting anything good? I always got something good and she knew it.

"Yeah, you know. My story on Brando asking for $100,000 to attend the special screening for *The Godfather*'s 25th anniversary party was picked up all over the wire."

"Oh, great."

"But it really doesn't matter, Jo," I said with a tight, embarrassed smile. "Pete's gonna fire me when I get back."

Joanna acted incredulous, but—who was she kidding?—me and Michael had been her and George's nemesis as soon as they got to the paper. They didn't like the attention our column generated, hated the fact that E! wouldn't hire them and practically threw a party every time me or the column was met with a slap on the wrist. This is what Nancy Jo Sales meant when she said gossip columnists are the most catty, jealous bunch of people she'd ever met.

"Come on, A.J., you can't be serious," she said.

"Yep. Yeah, it's over. Me and Pete just don't see eye to eye. Anyhow, I just wanted to say it was cool working opposite each other. And also I meant everything I said to you when you were home and in bed recovering from ovarian cancer. The paper wasn't the same without your byline."

"Ah, thanks, A.J. I appreciate that so much."

"It's true."

"Hey, you were getting a little tired of this anyhow, weren't you? I mean, isn't this kind of what you wanted?"

"Yeah, I guess. I just wanted to make the call myself," I said.

"Hey, you know what . . . I bet we'll be writing about you someday soon."

And they sure did. It came after I had left the *News* and it was over a story that no doubt had them doubled over in euphoria: Kara had succumbed to the pompous advances of Donald Trump and George and

Joanna dove on the story like it was a live grenade under their baby son's swing set. Their front-page headline, "For Trump—Love Is Not Blonde"—replete with a story and a picture of the new couple, signaled the beginning of the end for me and Kara. Almost instantly other stories and sightings followed, including nauseating TV appearances and dozens of colorful magazine pix. But the crusher came one evening when I was home flipping the remote and *Dateline* came on. And before I could change the channel, I see Stone Phillips chatting to Trump about the "new woman" in his life. And as old pictures of Kara in her *Sports Illustrated* swimsuit issue appeared, Phillips went for the kill.

"Are there marriage plans in the future?" the smug tape head asked.

"It's too complex to say," Trump quipped.

I sat up in bed all crazy. "Complex how? Maybe because I read her son to sleep last night?"

My compulsion even got to the point where I couldn't start my day without scanning the gossip columns for the mention of his name. And I remember how I couldn't even see the words *Triumph* or *Trumpet* because they bore too close a resemblance to his name. I finally just phoned the guy one day and put him on the spot.

"Trump, it's Benza."

"A.J., how are you, my friend?"

"Never mind that. Close your door. We gotta talk."

And we did. And we got to the bottom of things—or as close as you can come to the bottom of things when you're dealing with a guy like Trump. But none of what we said is for a book. The sad truth is, I understand a woman's needs—especially when she's in the middle of divorcing her millionaire husband, the modeling jobs aren't coming in as much as they used to and your boyfriend has just moved three time zones away. Though we were still very much in love, it was impossible to see each other more than once every four or five weeks. I still loved her to a fault, but I was tired of her dating so *publicly*, exhausted with checking up on her and disgusted with her latest choice in men.

"Why that guy?" I used to ask her. "Why that old guy?"

In my mind, she had given up the black leather Elvis and taken up with the sequined Elvis. Anyhow, we parted for good about sixteen months after I was fired. But many times since our relationship ended—even in terrific fits of rage and sadness—it's been hard to think of anything except the feel of her skin against mine. I never really tried to keep Kara out of my mind. And, in any event, it would have been impossible to do so.

Anyhow, back at the party . . .

I slinked around the room and I remember taking it all in—almost sniffing it up like a junkie would the last line on the mirror—and motioned for Jack to put down the jack and Coke and head out.

"You ready?" he said.

"Yeah, what the fuck. I think I got enough. What are they gonna do if I don't—fire me?"

As we turned to walk up the stairs, I leaned in to say good-bye to Miramax boss Harvey Weinstein.

"Hey, Harv, good luck tomorrow night."

"Thank you, thank you. Treat us right, A.J."

"Hey, I always do. I remember when Miramax had twelve employees and [head of development] Meryl Poster was answering phones."

"Did you get everything you needed? Is there anyone you want to speak with?"

"Nah, thanks. But listen, I just got word when I get back to town Hamill is gonna fire me?"

"What? What the hell for?"

"A million reasons and no good reason," I said.

"What are you gonna do? You gonna go somewhere else?"

"Nah. I'm done with gossip. I'm not sure yet."

And then Harvey did something that allowed me to keep my apartment when the *Daily News* severance money ran dry. He offered me a deal to write this book.

"Listen, fuck 'em. Write a book for me, you'll be fine. I'll get you an advance and we'll go to work."

"All right, don't forget."

"A.J., I don't want you to worry about a thing. When I get back in town we'll work it out."

Say what you want about Harvey Weinstein, just don't say anything bad to me about him. We shook hands and I bopped up the steps, saddened with bidding farewell to my days as a columnist but anxious with the prospect of becoming an author.

On the plane back home, Jackie and I downed three drinks apiece in our First Class seats before we even began taxiing. While the plane rumbled down the runway, I turned to Jackie and managed to get out a few sentences before my two Vallies and two Drammies kicked in.

"Hey, the fuckin' *News* is gettin' rid of me. Can you believe it?"

"No, I really can't," he said.

"I'm leaving the *News*, for Pete's sake."

"Christ. I know. I can't even talk about it."

"No, listen, you didn't hear me. I said, 'I'm leaving the *News* for Pete's sake.' "

"I know, I heard you."

"Get it?" I said. "I'm leaving the *News*, for *Pete's* sake."

We laughed like crazy. We laughed until the drinks came out of our noses and then we laughed some more. In fact, we laughed until I turned my face toward the window and found a comfortable spot to rest my head. And it was then, with the lights of LA twinkling beneath me like diamonds on a jeweler's pad, that I first cried. And the tears were big and they rolled hard down my cheeks like ballbearings.

The Last Time

On the day the nickel dropped, Michael and I were in our offices phoning friends and sources, peeling pictures off the wall and packing golden memories into cardboard boxes when Pete poked his head in our door.

"Hey, guys, you got a minute?"

Do we have a minute? Was that how long it was going to take him to considerably alter our lives? Wouldn't it have been better if we were given a time to show up and we could've walked there with a lot less fanfare than what looked like the two delinquents following the school principal into his office? Why'd we have to be summoned like that? It was like Mike Tyson giving you a ride to the ring before he beats your ass.

"Guys," Pete began, "I'm gonna have to make changes around here and some things aren't gonna be easy. But the fact is, this paper has to change to reflect the city we work in."

Blah, blah, blah. He went on for another minute but I'll give you the abridged version.

". . . It ain't you guys. It ain't the column. It's just the economics of the situation. I need to trim some fat and, to be honest, I can hire three or four more reporters with the money you guys are making."

"Let me ask you a question," I said. "You've had a load of jobs in your career. Is this the first time you've ever fired someone?"

Pete pondered that for some time. "Actually, yes, it is. I've never fired anyone before. How can you tell?"

"Because you're bad at it," I said. "I knew you were gonna fire us when I was in LA covering the Oscars."

"Well, that's nonsense," he said. "Because I just made up my mind today."

"Well, that's neither here nor there," Michael said.

"Right," I continued, "because either way we're fired."

"I'm sorry," Pete said. "There'll be severance packages that Eddie Fay will deal with in the next week or so. But other than that, that's about all I can say."

"I remember once you wrote in a book, 'Newspapers will break your heart,' " I said. "Is this what you were talking about?"

"This is just one of the things."

We shook hands with the guy and walked out, skirting the newsroom and feeling the darting eyes of everyone in the room upon us. When we got back to our office, we began the tiresome and—what seemed like—useless task of compiling a column for a city that knew we were history. We kept our door open to make it easier for all the well-wishers who came by for hugs and best wishes. And, it's funny how you sometimes have to console other people when the grief is all your own.

Hackett came by. "Hey, how you guys doing? You gonna be all right?"

"I'll tell you what," Michael said with indignation, "after what he said to me, I could never work for that man again."

"What did he say?"

"You're fired!"

We did a lot of shit like that over the next several days. Rolled out the dog and pony show so that our coworkers knew they weren't coming to speak to a couple of sappy guys in a suddenly maudlin room. But still, it hurt. Especially when some people walked in with tears of their own. That's some heavy shit to deal with and, to be honest, I'd just as soon tell them to e-mail me.

"Come on, come on. No tears," I told them. "You're gonna get us all emotional."

"Yeah and then my glass eye will fog up," Michael said. "And I hate when that happens."

Just to be cute, I put Tupac Shakur's "Check Out Time" on my outgoing message at work. And I swear I should've saved the phone messages I received from some of the city's most influential people—all expressing their anger, sorrow or confusion over Hamill's decision. To Pete's credit, he let me write a farewell column, which is, more or less, a no-no in journalistic circles. And to his credit again, he didn't change a single word. He let me say good-bye the way I wanted to. The only change the column suffered came at the hands of Hackett, who didn't think it was cute or funny for me to compare myself to Jesus Christ at the very end of my final column.

"But, Larry," I half-heartedly argued, "we were both thirty-three and we both had a resurrection on Easter Sunday. What are the chances of that?"

"A.J.," Hackett calmly assured me, "you did some good work. But you're no Jesus Christ."

It's actually a good thing Hackett stuck to his guns on my way out the door. Because the more I look back on the time that has passed since I filed my last column, I'd have to disagree with my assessment of the word *resurrection*. What has transpired since that time is not truly a resurrection anyhow. It's not quite a reawakening or a renaissance either. I like to think of it as a spiritual rebirth without the epidural.

Anyhow, here's the way my final Downtown column went, word for word. I titled it, "Don't Cry for Me, Wilhelmina."

By the time you read this, I'll be gone. I always wanted to say that. Maybe you didn't hear, but me and the *Daily News* ain't married anymore. The divorce is amicable, mind you: I get to build on the successes this column generated for me, and they get to fill the space I leave behind. It's okay, I'll be fine. It's a lot like the end of my marriage went—I still loved my wife, but I was always turning my head.

For a good four years, I didn't write the conventional sort of gossip column. I always aimed to report the truth, but tried to spice it up with a little humor and attitude. It was about stone-cold honesty in the rubbery face of hypocrisy. Some of you got behind it, some of you didn't. In time, I kinda liked reporting on my fun more than anything else. I was living a life and compiling memories that competed with the people I was reporting on. Do you know how many nights me and my boys—Rocco, Chico, JohnnyBoy and Frankie Giant—would turn to each other and say, "How we gonna top tonight? How we gonna top it?" And then we'd go out the next night and top it.

I'd be a liar if I said this approach won me the respect of all my colleagues. But I'm a guy who'd rather change his address than his style.

The thing is, one day it just didn't seem right to eavesdrop on Jack Nicholson; I wanted to make him laugh in his limousine. It didn't seem right to corner Warren Beatty; I wanted to talk girls with him. It didn't seem right to get dirt on Bob Evans; I wanted to sleep in his famous bed. It didn't seem right to degrade Hugh Hefner's marriage; I wanted to swim in his grotto. It didn't seem right to knock Sly Stallone; I liked shooting at his gun range. It didn't seem right inquiring on Frank Sinatra's health; I liked running around with Nancy. I didn't like snooping on John Kennedy, Jr.; I'd rather toss a Frisbee with him. And, finally, it didn't seem right spying on Mel Gibson's personal life; I liked sharing screen time with that guy.

In the end, I grew tired of walking into a room and having to decide which half of the room liked me and which half was only pretending to like me because of my job. And, believe me, I've figured it out, so you can all stop frontin'. What's more, I resented sitting across from Robert De Niro and having him think of me as someone he should fear. I hate that Sean Penn won't look me in the eye; that Christy Turlington thinks I don't like her and that Cindy Crawford once referred to me on television as "that evil person." Me, evil? Hey, if Sean, Christy and Cindy knocked on my door tomorrow, I'd put up a pot of macaroni just like my mother taught me.

Frankly, the gossip industry has been diluted with too many people who think they have a hook into every rumor out there. And they don't. And it makes those of us who do—those of us who've worked hard at making contacts and honing our intuitions—seem like vicious hacks. And really, who's kidding who? You guys know I have Hollywood on my mind, and my gossip credentials don't get me past the gates at Paramount Pictures any easier.

The bottom line is, I wished too hard for something and I got it. I had penetrated a group most gossip columnists cannot. I got beyond the velvet ropes, didn't need the special ticket and always had a table waiting for me. I did the things. *I* became the item.

On the way out, I want some of you to know a few things about me: I kept more secrets than I revealed, I protected more of you than I could've hurt and I threw a lot more left jabs than right hooks. And, yes, my conscience did keep me up at nights. And thanks to your phone calls, letters, death threats and backroom beatings, I learned a lot about myself along the way. You helped shape me and that helped me shape the column.

And here's a little irony for you on the way out. It was my editor-in-chief Pete Hamill's short stories—published in the *Sunday Daily News* some twenty years ago—that motivated me to become a writer in the first place. Our parting is just another form of him motivating me to move on with my dreams. In a sense— and pardon the pun—I'm leaving the *News*, for Pete's sake.

So Downtown dies and my own resurrection begins on Easter Sunday.

Time Is on My Side

A few weeks after my last column, on a lonely walk back to the Village, my cellphone rang heavy with the number of that peeler who used to pencil me in on Wednesday nights.

"Whatcha doin," she said.

"Just walking home from Spy, kid. What are you up to?"

"Passing your apartment in a cab and I thought of you so I thought I'd call. It's Wednesday, you know."

"Yeah, I know. But I'm beat tonight, baby."

"Yeah, me too."

"How's your hair—straight or natural?"

"Neither," she said. "Extensions."

"Damn. Sorry I'm gonna miss that. Next time."

A little interference played with our connection before she told me what she was really calling about.

"I miss your column, baby," she said.

"I do, too, kid," I told her. "But, you know, everything has a run and then it comes to an end. It doesn't matter if you're talking about a racehorse, a Broadway play or a centerfielder or a hurricane. It's all about the run."

"Even with strippers," she asked.

"Even with strippers," I said.

And we shared a laugh.

But then I grew curious. It had been weeks since my columns were ripped from the *Daily News* and the condolence calls I was getting were mostly from people more closely associated with my field: writers, actors, club owners, models, etc. And, now, here was a college-educated, Jamaican-born stripper with a two-year-old son who was supporting her mom and sisters back in Brooklyn and I had to know why and how my words were able to reach them.

"It comes down to this," she said. "You sold Jack the jacket and kept the coat."

The sentence struck me hard. I had never heard that before and it sounded especially cool with her West Indian lilt.

"What does that mean, baby?"

"Oh my God, I'm telling you something you don't know?"

"Yeah. I've never heard that before. What's it mean?"

"To me, it means that you were able to do the job at hand and, yet, keep your dignity and cool in the process. You were honest and true for your whole run."

"Wow, that's so cool of you," I said. "Now, I ain't so tired anymore. Tell that cabbie to turn around."

"I'm already at the tunnel," she said. "And I'm seeing somebody now, anyhow."

"Oh yeah? What's he do?"

"He's a trader."

"What can I trade him for Wednesdays with you?"

"No, that wouldn't work. He's a very jealous man," she said.

"Ah shit," I said. "Is our run over, too?"

"For now, I guess," she said. "Anyhow, I just wanted to tell you how much I miss your column."

I was standing in my doorway now, beneath a streetlight on Horatio, trying to remember the words she used that sized me up so sweetly.

"What's that you said about me, kid? What are the words again?"

"You sold Jack the jacket and kept the coat."

"Fuck . . . I love you for that," I said.

And then her voice crackled and disappeared somewhere beneath the East River as I leaned hard against the elevator wall, another night's useless energy spent.

A lot of crazy things happened after the fire. For starters, Hamill got the axe no less than six months after he whacked me and Michael. A lot of people will tell you that Hamill was caught in a power play with Mort and Fred who wanted him to take the paper "down market." But I don't think you need to look any further than the fact that *News* sales were plummeting with Hamill at the helm. Circulation changed dramatically with Hamill's changes to the tune of 30,000 fewer papers per day and 155,000 less on Sundays. And since I was undoubtedly Hamill's most dramatic change, I'd like to think the *News* took a beating on the street because I was no longer there. Just let me think it, even if I'm wrong.

Anyhow, it ain't like Hamill and I stayed at odds with each other. About a year or so later I literally called him by accident when I took out my little black book and attempted to reach Larry Hackett. Hamill's number was written right beneath Hackett's and hearing the unmistakable rumble in his voice startled me.

"Pete?"

"Yeah."

"I'm sorry," I said, "I dialed the wrong number. This is Benza."

And then a genuine laugh broke free from Pete's throat and we just started bullshitting like crazy from "How the hell are you" to "Let's stay in touch."

At one point, Hamill said, "Listen, I did you a favor. Guys like you are guys like me. We don't change. I was asking you to do something you didn't want to do. But obviously you landed on your feet nicely and I knew you would."

About a week later Hamill's latest book *Why Sinatra Matters* arrived in my mail and inside it my former editor-in-chief wrote:

To A.J. Benza . . . who understands that we never know about a fighter until he gets knocked down. All the best, Pete Hamill.

The sentiment went bulls-eye to my heart and my eyes filled up again like a big sissy. Because once again I had Hamill's words to take me through a hard chapter in my own life. Just like when I was a kid and I would run out to the driveway and rip the *Daily News* magazine from the rest of the paper so I could devour one of Hamill's short stories before my father got his hands on the crossword.

And again, years later, when Hamill's *Loving Women* got me through the messy and unfortunate divorce I suffered with Jennifer and the subsequent dating life I whipped up once the little house on Long Island echoed with our fits of pain and displeasure.

And finally with his memoir, *A Drinking Life*, which I read—oddly enough—as my own life and career were spinning out of control along parallel lines with the beautiful pages of his vivid portrait.

And here was Hamill and his words again as I prepared myself for the most bittersweet chapter of my life. The year when Uncle Sam said, "Fuck you, pay me." The year I lost the Benz and the beautiful girl went bad. The year everyone stopped taking my calls and every columnist and tabloid producer took clean shots at me when I couldn't answer back with my own crisp combinations. The year all the shit fermented and distilled in my gut until the day it manifested itself with my brutal beating of a cab driver at 40th Street and Fifth Avenue. And when my last punch knocked him out cold and bloody on the pavement, I calmly sat down next to him and waited for the cops to take me away.

"Come on," the cop told me as he slapped the cuffs on and the paparazzi popped off a few rounds. "The loser goes to the hospital. The winner goes to jail."

But I hardly felt like a winner in the cell when I realized that all of this had turned into the year when I had to look the city I once ruled directly in the eye and accept the fact that it had no more room for me.

The next phone call I received, from E! producer Michael Danahy, was a job offer to come to LA and host a TV show called *Mysteries & Scandals*.

"How do you feel about that?" he asked.

"Well, pal, I got the scandal part down pretty well."

About a thousand tears later—all shed on the shoulders of my family and my best friends—there was the surreal sight of Chico packing up the U-Haul and starting the drive cross-country two days before my flight would land me in Hollywood for a new start. In a matter of months I got myself a '64 Caddy and a cute little bungalow that Marilyn Monroe once lived in—so I hear. And within a relatively short period of time, the TV show became a hit and everyone became convinced that the bad boy was, in fact, a good hire. So good, there just might be another TV show in him. Even a few movies. A screenplay or two. And, hey, maybe another book.

And then there's my social life. It's no secret Los Angeles is filled with a lot of beautiful women and I suppose I've had my share. But after a while they all seem to blend into the same girl: She is the ex-wife of the starmaker. She is the belly in the *American Beauty* poster. The Soul Train dancer. The girlfriend of the platinum rap star. The former veejay. She is the hostess at the hotspot. The *Playboy* Playmate. The Penthouse Pet. The girl behind the glass at the Standard. She is the middleweight's girlfriend. The Cinemax sexpot. Drive-time radio's hottest voice. She is the greenlight girl at a major studio.

She is achingly beautiful but she always seems to come equipped with a story that precedes her. And in time that story swirls around us before it eventually smothers us and makes it impossible to maintain any type of relationship of merit. But I suppose if LA is a town always in search of a good story, then those girls have come to the right place. It's me who's in the wrong spot.

And then there are the girls with absolutely no story whatsoever. Her name is usually Stacy or Julie. And she lives in Studio City and she drives a convertible Jetta and she can only see me between her three P.M. callback for the Herbal Essence campaign and her six P.M. extreme yoga class because *Buffy the Vampire Slayer* is on tonight and she never misses it. When I ask her what she likes best about me, she says she's never dated a guy who wore a gold chain before and she's "totally stoked about it."

I can't win either way.

I miss Rocco and Frankie terribly, but I'm comforted by the fact that I'm slowly building my team out here. A few weeks ago my nephew Jack found a place in the Valley, my cousin Mario is staying on my couch until an acting gig comes in and JohnnyBoy is supposedly headed out here for good soon. We all go to Vinny's house on Sunday for meatballs. I still see Kara from time to time, too. That never fades away. Just the other day, I was back in New York and I spotted her walking on West 4th Street and it stopped me cold. She was about 100 yards away, but I could identify her gait from a mile away if I had to. I dialed her cell and watched her answer my call.

"Hey, I'm watching you walk up the block. Slow down, I want to see you."

There was silence from Kara's end. "I don't know if I'm ready for this yet."

"Just stay there," I said. "Just stay there. What's the worst that could happen?"

"Oh . . . God . . . I don't know if I'm ready for this yet." She was choked up a little.

Truth is, I didn't know if I was ready for it either. We had just spent the better part of one year dealing with each other's indiscretions with raised fists and clenched teeth and that was followed by another hellish year of not touching each other at all. But it all faded away when I reached her at the corner of West 4th Street and Seventh Avenue and hugged her from behind. We stayed there a long time in that embrace until we ducked into our favorite coffee shop, The Bagel, and had some eggs. It was a sweet morning. And there have been some unforgettable nights since then. It feels like another beginning. But until I move back to New York City, it will just have to serve as hope. Kara and I are wild horses in a sense. And wild horses are always more beautiful when they are left to run on their own, making mad dashes at the sun. It hurts to see them in a stable.

I'll tell you, there was a time when the thought of even visiting LA— let alone living here—would send chills up my spine. My big battle cry those days was, "I could visit LA or I could piss down my leg. Same thing." But I was wrong. The calm of this place coupled with Hollywood's laid-back mentality has been soothing for me. I have a bunch of red and yellow bougainvillea vines in front of my apartment and a little garden patch outside my bedroom window where pineapple sage, lavender and night jasmine grow wild. And sometimes me and my puppy, Chezzie, sit out there in a sun spot as I furiously tap on my laptop while butterflies dart and dodge around his little head. He growls to try and scatter them, but I'm sure butterflies can't hear little doggies like him. And it's in peaceful moments like that when I think back to how lucky I was to have had a shot at being one of the tireless engines that make the great city of New York run like a locomotive. I think back to my beautiful run and I remember it as the end of an era at the close of a century inside a powerful city to which I owned a set of keys. And I smile.

And whenever people ask me what I'm daydreaming about, I tell them, "You don't know the half of it."